FROM THE BALTIC TO THE CAPE

The Journey of Three Families

Ivan Kapelus

FROM THE BALTIC TO THE CAPE

ISBN 978-0-620-56659-9

Other titles by this author:

REFLECTIONS ON A VISIT TO LITHUANIA

ISBN 978-0-620-56286-7

First edition 2013

Set in Warnock Pro 11/15
Cover design by Liezel Meintjes
Text design and layout by Liezel Meintjes, SUN MeDIA Stellenbosch, South Africa
www.africansunmedia.co.za
Printed by Kadimah Print, South Africa

The Three Families

Sarah and Leib Kapelus

Louis and Rachel Dorfman

Leah and David Hotz

The Journey

North Sea
Baltic Sea
White Sea
NORWAY
SWEDEN
FINLAND
UNITED KINGDOM
IRELAND
Celtic Sea
GERMANY
POLAND
BELARUS
UKRAINE
FRANCE
Bay of Biscay
AUSTRIA
ROMANIA
Black Sea
Caspian Sea
PORTUGAL
SPAIN
ITALY
TURKEY
SYRIA
Mediterranean Sea
MOROCCO
ALGERIA
LIBYA
EGYPT
SAUDI ARABIA
Persian Gulf
WESTERN SAHARA
MAURITANIA
MALI
NIGER
CHAD
SUDAN
YEMEN
Red Sea
Gulf of Aden
SENEGAL
GAMBIA
GUINEA BISSAU
GUINEA
BURKINA FASO
CÔTE D'IVOIRE
GHANA
TOGO
BENIN
NIGERIA
CAMEROON
EQUATORIAL GUINEA
CENTRAL AFRICAN REPUBLIC
ETHIOPIA
SOMALIA
KENYA
GABON
DEMOCRATIC REPUBLIC OF THE CONGO
TANZANIA
ANGOLA
ZAMBIA
MALAWI
MOZAMBIQUE
ZIMBABWE
NAMIBIA
BOTSWANA
SOUTH AFRICA
MADAGASCAR
Mozambique channel
South Atlantic Ocean

Contents

Preface

The Jewish population of South Africa has often been referred to as a 'colony of Lithuanian Jewry'. Between 1880 and 1930, some 70,000 Jews from Lithuania (in the broadest sense, meaning Jews from the North West Provinces of the Russian Empire (the 'Pale of Settlement'), entered South Africa. This wave of migration was halted by the Quota Act of 1930.[1] The Kapelus and Hotz families were part of this migration. The Dorfman family, also from Lithuania, first settled in Scotland before migrating to South Africa in 1936.

To appreciate fully what made our grandparents' generation leave their families, their friends and support groups, in the knowledge that they would probably never see them again, it is necessary to know something about the history of Lithuania and particularly the history of the Jews in Lithuania as part of the Pale of Settlement. Lithuania had ceased to be an independent country in 1795, when it was annexed to the Russian Empire by Catherine the Great.

These people left for a distant land of which they knew little if anything at all, where they would not be able to speak the language and where they would encounter a mix of cultures alien to them. Most of them arrived in Africa with meagre resources. Yet they and their descendants, within a short time of settling in their new home, were contributing to every sphere of endeavour.

Their success, and the impact they had on the Jewish community of their new home, cannot be completely comprehended unless one also understands that their process of acculturation was hard, often lonely and inevitably influenced by the racial, language, political and economic tensions and issues that were part of their new homeland. To do this we need to explore some of the history of South Africa.

The lives and experiences of the three families that feature in this book will seem familiar to many readers, as they mirror in many ways the history of all 'Russian immigrants', as they were called when they arrived in South Africa. Every effort has been made to intertwine the personal with contemporary political events and issues that had an impact on their lives.

The only primary research I have undertaken has been in relation to the genealogy of the Kapelus, Dorfman and Hotz families, as well as searching the archives in South Africa for relevant material relating to Lithuanian immigrants. Otherwise I have relied almost entirely on the large body of work available on Lithuanian, Jewish and South African history and I have tried diligently to acknowledge my sources. I apologise if in any instance I have failed to do so.

How This Book Came to Be

This project started because I wanted to write an intensely personal biographical note on my dear late wife Esther, so that her descendants would know as much about her as I was able to pass on. Esther had a fascination for, and a deep interest in, the history and background of her family. She was keen on stories about her family and avidly collected and kept photographs of her ancestors. However, often she did not have any or sufficient information about the subjects of the pictures. I did not want that to happen when future generations of our family saw pictures of her.

Sadly, she died after a long illness at the age of 56, a young grandmother, or Bobba as she preferred to be called. She was hoping to enjoy many more grandchildren. I hope that her wish will be fulfilled and her children will oblige, even if Esther will not know those future lives.

Writing a biographical note on Esther would also give me the opportunity to express my love for her and tell our descendants about our life together, in the hope that it might be of value to them. As this project progressed, however, because Esther and I had known each other for so long, the story became *our* story rather than simply Esther's, even if the emphasis was on her.

This inspired me to broaden my tale to include the lives of our grandparents. In looking for material on them, I became fascinated with their journey to South Africa from Lithuania, where they had lived under a tyrannical regime and suffered appalling anti-Semitism. In stark contrast to that experience, both our parents and we had lived in a society substantially free from prejudice against Jews, which enabled us to prosper in every way: economically, culturally and spiritually.

Yet there was another migration: my generation of the family left South Africa for Canada, Australia and the United Kingdom from the 1970s onwards. As we shall see, the reasons and circumstances of our migration in the late twentieth century were very different to those of our grandparents in the late nineteenth and early twentieth centuries.

I commenced my research in the archives in Cape Town by concentrating on finding material on my paternal grandfather Louis (Lewius) Kapelus (Mordukh Leib Kapelyush), as he was the person about whom I had the most information. Scouring the computerised list of names in the Archives in Cape Town, I found several files listed under the name of Kapelus. At first my interest was lukewarm, but I decided to look at them anyway. Having done so, I became fascinated and inspired to know much more about my grandfather's generation.

This is how I found out about my grandfather Leib's brother Abel, his sister Eva and her husband Wolf Brickman, as well as Rachel Kapelus, who became Mrs Feldman and was the mother of my father's cousins: Lilly, Molly, Natie, Morris and Harry (Cocky) Feldman. I vaguely remembered that my father had referred to Jack and Natie Brickman as his cousins, but he had never explained the relationship in any detail. Now I know that their mother was my grandfather's sister. I discovered that Oupa was not alone in South Africa, as he had a brother and two sisters there.

My father and his generation had a host of cousins, the Feldmans and the Brickmans on their paternal side.

Why had I been so ignorant about my family? Surely, my father, uncles and aunt could have or should have told us more about their own background? What is more, my paternal grandmother lived in our house in Van Rhynsdorp from December 1946, when I was 4 years old, until her death in 1960. Yet I knew very little about her or about her relationship with my father and her other children. Why were they so secretive, almost furtive?

My mother spoke only a little about her life in Scotland, but she also never explained the relationships in the family. As this story unfolds, it will become apparent why.

Esther was fortunate to have her maternal grandparents, Leah and David Hotz, living with her in the family home from 1960, when she was 15 or 16 years old, until their death. Nevertheless, she too knew only sketchy details about their past lives in Shavl and Ponevezh.

What was the reason for all this reticence? When I met Granny (Leah) and Zeida (David) they were of sound mind, but I never heard them speak about Lithuania with any nostalgia or fondness. They told no stories about their childhood, the towns from which they had hailed or their early experiences.

Esther and I, with our children Leora and Ilan, also left our homeland of South Africa to settle in England. We consider ourselves to be South African and delight in talking about our lives in the Cape. My father, mother, Jessie and Mike Broude all thought of themselves as South Africans. Yet their parents never seemed to have considered themselves Lithuanian; Jews, of course, but never Lithuanian.

I did not appreciate or focus on the difference between the South African generations of the family and those who had migrated from Lithuania until I read *Yiddish Civilisation* by Paul Kriwaczek, who wrote:

> *It wasn't that the Yiddish-speakers seemed to live one part of their lives perfectly normally in modern Britain – actively and successfully involved in business or the professions – and the other part in some unfathomable eternal world of their own. But that, unlike German, Austrian, French, Italian, or even Sephardic Jews, they seemed to have no history. Or, to be more exact, no interest in or recollection of people and places outside their own very recent family traditions.*
>
> *Moreover, many did not know the names of the east European towns from which their families had emigrated, and some had even forgotten what their family names had been before being anglicised to something that the blunt English tongue could more easily negotiate – and, what is more, they didn't seem to care. Twice dislocated, first from the European 'heym' to London's East End – where they had originally settled close to their point of arrival in the docks – and in the next generation out to the suburbs, most of the Yiddish families I knew seemed to have abandoned their past altogether...*
>
> *So awful had been the memory of what they had left, so painful their struggle to put it forever behind them, that they had no interest in – indeed strong antipathy to – bringing the old country back to mind.*[2]

Even some of my generation still feel this last sentiment strongly. Recently, when I asked close friends whether they were interested in visiting Poland and Lithuania with my wife Cynthia and me, Maureen Fisher was adamant that she could not bring herself to visit Lithuania, a place about which her late father had spoken with much hatred and anger because of the treatment he had suffered in his youth. The strength and depth of her feelings were such that Lithuania was a place he, and thus she, wanted to forget.

The more I learnt about the history of our ancestors, the more important it became for me to tell Esther and my descendants the story of their lives in Lithuania. More specifically, I needed to relate our grandparents' and their generation's remarkable journey in the late nineteenth and first years of the twentieth century to a country whose local languages they could not speak and of which they had little knowledge. Yet within a very short time, they and their children had made a hugely significant contribution to every sphere of life in South Africa; a contribution out of all proportion to their numbers.

Acknowledgements

During the writing of this book, a journey that started in Upington and Van Rhynsdorp during the 1940s metamorphosed into a journey back in time and to places about which I knew nothing.

From the twentieth century I moved back to the fourteenth, not in South Africa but in Lithuania, to trace the history of my ancestors and to look at the life and times of the Jews there and at the journey from the Baltic to the Cape so many of them made.

When I set out on my journey I had no knowledge of Lithuania, the Jews who lived there and the suffering they endured from olden times to the present age, culminating in the Holocaust from 1941 to 1945.

For help I turned to Saul Issroff, a veritable expert on the Jews of Lithuania. He not only lent me a sizeable part of his extensive library, but also guided me through the learning process until I had established a sound base from which I could progress to do some independent study and build a library of my own. His quiet, calm and encouraging voice is in much of the book, as he kindly undertook a final edit of what I had written. Without Saul this book would not have become a reality!

During my visits to South Africa while I continued my research, I was fortunate to have the very early pages edited by Gwynne Schrire. Her patience and gentle prodding made the initial draft into a story.

As I neared completion, I asked my dear friend Sam Aaron if he would be willing to read the manuscript in its 'raw' state. He very kindly agreed. His editing made what was a long, cumbersome story into a book.

My very basic computer knowledge was augmented by the skills of my ever-willing daughter-in-law Marcelle Kapelus, whose formatting and design created a rounded book. Maps were the bane of my life! Thanks to my nephew Leon Whine for coming to my rescue.

Luckily, my cousin George Arbuz came from Paris to a family function in London, during which time he gave me the sage advice to write a Preface and an Epilogue, thereby bringing the whole to completion.

My dear wife Cynthia has over a period of nine years been a constant adviser, editor, proofreader and consultant, often being taken from her own labours to help me solve a problem, bolster my flagging resolve or simply keep my nose to the grindstone.

I also owe grateful thanks to my children and friends, who over this long time have been plagued by me nagging them for an opinion on whether facts were interesting or relevant, who have encouraged me when my spirits were low and who have kept me enthusiastic.

Introduction

Part of the reason for our ancestors' phenomenal success was their emphasis on giving their children the education they had been denied in Lithuania. Thus, when I finished school, my father sent me to study law at the University of Stellenbosch, a town in the centre of the wine-producing region of the Western Cape, some 50 kilometres from Cape Town.

By February 1964, I was 21 years old and felt the need to meet Jewish girls. I had left home at the age of 9 to go to boarding school in Cape Town and had not lived with my parents since, except during school or university holidays. I wanted a home of my own as soon as I was able, and meeting my life's companion was high on my list of priorities.

After graduating in December 1963 with a BA in Law, my friend Simon van den Bosch and I worked in the Kleinzee diamond mine in Namaqualand for three months. Then, in the first of two postgraduate years studying for the LLB, Simon, Solly Epstein and I rented a primitive cottage in Jonkershoek Road on the outskirts of Stellenbosch, once the home of the gatekeeper of the famous Lanzerac Estate. I spent all the money I had saved in Kleinzee on a car, a box-like Ford Anglia, reasoning that this would enable me to date Jewish girls in Cape Town. (There were only 27 Jewish students at the university, and only three of them were female.)

Stellenbosch is a town named after the second Governor of the Cape, Simon van der Stel, which nestles under three blue granite mountains known as Simonsberg, Hells Hoogte and twin peaks known as Die Pieke. Stellenbosch has retained its historical character by restricting the height of new buildings and jealously guarding and maintaining old buildings in and around the town. Lanzerac was one of the original farms in the nearby Jonkershoek valley, with a stately Dutch-gabled farmhouse, magnificent outhouses and the original slave bell used to call the staff to work. It also produced a range of popular wines. By 1964 Lanzerac had become a luxury hotel owned by the Rawdon family, with a student-friendly pub that we loved to frequent.

In 1964 the Easter weekend coincided with Pesach. I wanted to enjoy the holiday with my parents, who lived in Van Rhynsdorp, some 210 miles northwest of

Cape Town. The village lies on a huge semi-desert plain punctuated by mountain ranges of rare and stately beauty, the nearest being Maskam to the south, the largest mountain of which is known as Gif Berg (Poison Mountain), and the Bokkeveld range to the northeast. Van Rhynsdorp is at the very south of a vast area known as Namaqualand, famed for diamonds and the Namaqua daisies that flower in profusion for a short time in early spring each year – if the area has been blessed with three to four inches of rain, that is.

A profusion of Namaqua daisies with Maskam mountain in the background

At that time it was a dusty village, with only five tarred roads, the rest being constructed of gravel. There were only two Jewish families in Van Rhynsdorp, us Kapeluses and the Rosenthals: Uncle Percy, Aunt Lottie and their two children, Shirley, 18 months younger than me, and David, a contemporary of my sister Yvonne, who is five years my junior. The total population of the village and district then numbered about 11,000.

Van Rhynsdorp in the shadow of Maskam mountain

Our home was the second last house in the village on Van Riebeeck Street, situated on a five-acre smallholding on the western side, in the direction of Vredendal. From the veranda we had a similar view of Maskam to that shown in the photograph above. The smallholding featured a vegetable garden and a chicken coop. Planted along the perimeter was a variety of guava and fig trees. Sultana grapes, from which my father made raisins, covered most of the garden. In addition, my mother was very proud of her orange, lemon, peach and apricot trees. She made jam and canned the fruit every year, labelling each jar meticulously with the date.

I had agreed to travel home in my car with my classmate Klaus von Lieres (later to become the Attorney General of Transvaal), a strapping six-footer who also lived in Van Rhynsdorp. Both of us had shopping lists from our mothers. The car was thus going to be loaded with the shopping and our gear, particularly my golf clubs.

About three weeks before the Easter weekend, Shirley Rosenthal, who was working at the Trust Bank in Cape Town, telephoned me for a lift home. Knowing that she was not particularly punctual, I agreed on condition that she was ready to leave by no later than 3 pm on the Thursday afternoon.

On the preceding Monday, Shirley telephoned me again, this time to ask whether there would be room for another passenger. She wanted to take a friend home for company. I told her that there were already four people (a housemate was travelling with us as well) and the luggage, so the car could not accommodate any more. Shirley was insistent and said they would only bring vanity cases. I gave in and agreed to meet them at the Trust Bank in good time to leave on schedule.

I arrived at the bank at ten to three. Shirley was ready, but her friend was nowhere in sight.

'Shirley, where is your friend? If she's not here on time we'll leave without her!' I said.

'She's gone to Millys to buy some food for the road,' replied Shirley.

'Millys? How did she go?' I asked.

'By bus,' said Shirley.

'You're not serious, Shirley!' was my anguished response. 'She'll never be back in time. We have over three and half hours of travelling to do!'

Shirley started doing some work and it was obvious she was going to delay finishing it to ensure that I waited for her friend, which of course I would have done anyway.

So there I was, at the bottom of the stairs that led from the entrance to the banking hall, waiting impatiently for a young woman whose name I did not even know. The clock on the Groote Kerk opposite started chiming three o'clock. I looked up and saw a dark, slim, attractive girl with Millys carrier bags walking slowly down the steps towards me. I realised this was Shirley's friend – and that is when it all started to happen.

'You are not top of the hit parade,' I said to her.

'And you, Ivan Kapelus, are not getting any food!' she retorted.

These were the first words Esther and I exchanged. I was smitten! The banter did not stop for 36 years. We dated for two years, were engaged for a year and finally we married on 18 December 1966.

A few weeks after Esther and I started dating I told Simon I was going to marry her. I was then 21 and she was 19. I remember his exact words, using my middle name: 'Percy, there is many a slip 'twixt cup and lip.' Simon attended our wedding and we are still very close friends. These days he says that meeting Esther is the best thing that ever happened to me. I agree.

Why were we so comfortable with each other? In a word, roots. We were both second-generation South Africans of Lithuanian origin, whose grandparents and parents lived (in my case) or had lived (in Esther's case) in 'the country', as the rural areas of South Africa were called. The Kapelus family had lived in Ceres, Calvinia and later Van Rhynsdorp, and the Broude family had lived in Upington before moving to Cape Town.

Both Esther and I grew up speaking English at home and primarily Afrikaans outside the home. Yet we were both very aware of and close to our Jewish roots. We, like our grandparents, were integrated into the Jewish, Afrikaans and English-speaking white groups of South Africa.

Esther and Ivan Kapelus, photographed outside the Tifreth Israel (Schoonder Street) synagogue on our wedding day, 18 December 1966

And as I discovered more about the lives of each of the families, I was inspired to try to write their story within the context of the political, historical and cultural events that they experienced and that inevitably influenced their lives. That is what you can read in these pages.

PART I

Jewish Life in Lithuania

Early History: 1388-1764

Present-day Lithuania is the largest of the three Baltic States on the east coast of the Baltic Sea, with Latvia to its north and Estonia further north; to its east is Belarus (formerly White Russia and later Byelorussia), to its south is Poland and to its west Germany and the Baltic Sea.

Lithuania is the largest of the three Baltic States on the east coast of the Baltic Sea

It is in this small country that the origins of both my (the Kapelus and Dorfman) and Esther's (Broude and Hotz) families are to be found. The Lithuania in which our grandparents and their families lived was part of the Russian Empire.

In earlier times, it had been part of the Grand Duchy of Lithuania (GDL), a very much bigger country that from 1569 to 1795 was joined with Poland in a federation. In a series of three partitions between 1772 and 1795, the territory of the federation was divided between the powers of Austria, Prussia and Russia, the last of which annexed Lithuania.

The map gives us a valuable view of two Lithuanias: the boundaries of the Grand Duchy of Lithuania in the mid-fifteenth century marked in green and the other, Jewish Lithuania (Lite) marked in blue [Map by courtesy of Dovid Katz[3]]

The area inhabited by Litvaks includes Riga, which is not part of the Grand Duchy, but does not include any of Ukraine south of Chernobyl.

Jewish Life in the Grand Duchy of Lithuania

In the years before Russian annexation, life for Jews in the Polish-Lithuanian Federation had been relatively comfortable. Unlike many of the surrounding countries, during the Middle Ages the GDL welcomed Jews into its midst. Lithuania was an under-developed agrarian feudal society and Grand Duke Gedimimas (1316-41), the builder of the Lithuanian Empire, was keen to enhance its economy. In 1323, he made Vilnius his capital and extended an open invitation to people to settle in his land, promising privileges such as tax exemptions, freedom of worship and religious tolerance. The Lithuanians were still pagans and did not share the prejudices, doctrines and policy of the Catholic Church, which held sway in the neighbouring lands. Gedimimas wrote to Pope John XXII saying that he believed in religious tolerance and freedom of worship.[4]

As a result, Germans, Russians, Tartars, Jews and Karaites (a sect of Judaism) migrated to the GDL and its territories to ply their trades and do business. It is known that by 1388-9 there were substantial, influential and valued Jewish communities in the towns of Troki (Trakai), Brisk and Grodno.[5]

In 1388, Prince Vytautas (from 1392-1430 Grand Duke of Lithuania, also known as Witold) granted the Jews of Troki and Brisk a Charter of Rights, which he extended to Grodno the following year.[6] Its preamble stated:

> *All deeds of men, when they are not made known by the testimony of witnesses or in writing, pass away and vanish and are forgotten. Therefore, we, Alexander, also called Witold, by the grace of God Grand Duke of Lithuania and ruler of Brest, Dorogicz, Lutsk, Vladimir, and other places, make known by this charter, to the present and future generations, or to whoever it may concern, to know or hear of it, that, after due deliberation with our nobles we have decided to grant to all Jews living in our domains the rights and liberties mentioned in the following charter.*

The Charter set out the legal rights of Jews, under which they formed a class of freemen subject in all criminal cases directly to the jurisdiction of the Grand Duke and his official representatives; in petty suits they were treated on the same footing as lesser nobles. In addition, synagogues and Jewish cemeteries were exempt from taxation and the Charter made provision for the Jews' personal and religious security.

In most Catholic countries at that time Jews were forbidden to own land, but the Charter allowed them to be granted property rights by means of licences purchased from the Grand Ducal Council.[7] Jews were free to trade in the same way as Christian citizens by owning shops, selling merchandise at markets and peddling goods in the streets. They were able to work as artisans and craftsmen and could live wherever they wished. By order of the Pope, the Charter prohibited blood libel and the Jews enjoyed the protection of the Grand Duke of Lithuania and, later, that of the nobles.[8]

The Charter was the foundation of the political, legal, economic and social structure under which the Jews lived in the GDL from the late fourteenth to the eighteenth century.

The Jewish population swelled during the reign of Vytautas to about 6,000, with co-religionists arriving from Bohemia, Germany, France, Spain and Crimea.[9] The economy flourished and, despite the objections of the Church, Vytautas's successor Casimir (1444-92) reconfirmed the Jewish Charter in 1453, stating, 'We take the Jews under our protection, in our own interest and in the interest of the State, so they may feel safe.'[10]

The sympathetic and tolerant treatment of the Jewish population in the GDL during this period was in stark contrast to the virulent anti-Semitic attitude of Catholic Western Europe. The cities of Vienna and Linz expelled Jews in 1421. Other expulsions of Jews from European cities, states and countries continued throughout the fifteenth century: from Cologne in 1424, from Augsburg in 1439 and Bavaria in 1442, from Spain in 1492 and from Portugal in 1495.[11] By this time, the usefulness of Jews to the rulers of European city-states was in sharp decline and the guilds, which protected Christian citizens, viewed Jews as an economic threat.

Fear of competition and religious intolerance reinforced Christian anti-Semitism and the expulsions followed one after another as the power of the Catholic Church grew ever stronger.[12] The entire Jewish population of Venice was confined to a segregated area of the city (*ghetto nuovo*, hence the term ghetto) during 1515-16. This enabled the city to obtain the maximum economic advantage from the Jews by imposing special taxes on them, in addition to their normal tax burden, and to subject them to the most difficult circumstances both socially and economically.[13]

The situation was no better in Germany. As Paul Johnson writes:

> *Luther had the Jews expelled from Saxony in 1537 and had them driven from many German towns in the 1540s. In his 1543 pamphlet, 'Von den Juden und ihren Lugen' (On the Jews and their Lies), he urged that synagogues should be set on fire and whatever was left should be buried in dirt so that no-one might ever see a stone or cinder of it. He also urged the destruction of Jewish prayer books; their rabbis to be forbidden to preach; their homes smashed and destroyed and their property seized. Furthermore, he recommended the banning of Jews from roads and markets and the drafting of Jews into forced labour. In 1572, his followers sacked and burned the synagogue of Berlin and the following year Jews were banned from the entire country.*[14]

The Counter-Reformation brought no respite for the Jews of Europe. In May 1555, Cardinal Caraffa, Grand Inquisitor and scourge of the Jews, became Pope Paul IV. Two months after his election he applied the Venetian solution to the Jews of Rome. The Papal States extended the ghetto to all cities and in 1562 'ghetto' became the official term used in anti-Jewish legislation. Monarchies that had previously been accommodating to the Jews living in their realm took up this anti-Jewish philosophy.[15]

The GDL's position as a haven of religious tolerance could not last. When Casimir died, his son Alexander Yagiallo (1492-1506) became Grand Duke of Lithuania and later King of Poland. In 1494, Alexander concluded a peace treaty with Ivan III of Muscovy, who had annexed strips of the GDL. Finally, in the late fourteenth and early fifteenth century, the GDL embraced Christianity, becoming the last European country to do so.

Alexander came under increased pressure from the nobles and the Church to take action against the Jews, who were seen to have a privileged position, particularly in commerce. In 1495, he expelled the Jews and Karaites from the GDL and confiscated their property.[16] By then the Jewish community had become the backbone of the economy. They were the financiers, traders and merchants of the GDL's commercial life and without them, the country's economy could not survive.[17] After eight years Alexander had to invite them back, restoring their property as well as the right to recover the debts owed to them. He also reinstated and reinforced the rights and privileges granted to the Lithuanian Jewish community by his father Casimir.

After their return in 1503, the Jewish residents of the GDL continued to flourish.[18] The Union of Lublin of 1569, which harmonised and merged the Polish and GDL administrations, recognised the importance of the economic role of the Jews in their capacity as tax collectors and estate managers. In 1573, the Jewish community of Vilnius built the first official synagogue in the city.[19]

Jews were granted an even greater measure of self-government by the creation of the Synod of the Four Lands in 1581 by King Stephen Istvan Bathory (1575-86). This elected body would collect the taxes and other charges due from the Jewish Community and regulate Jews' internal affairs. The Jewish Regional Council, which had represented the Jews of the GDL since 1520, as well as the community councils (Kahal/Kehillot) continued to play a role.[20]

The Jewish Community of the GDL thus enjoyed unheard-of autonomy over their affairs. The Council operated on four levels: dealing with government authorities; handling relations between and with other Jewish communities; managing internal community affairs; and regulating and monitoring religious, moral and ethical behaviour in all areas of life.

After nine years, it was clear that the Synod would be more effective if it were split into two. In 1590, the new Council of Lithuania (in Hebrew, *Va'ad Lita*), an independent body, gained official status in GDL law.[21] The Council operated until 1764, when the government discovered that the Jewish Councils had been collecting larger sums than the tax assessments required and using the surplus for communal needs. This led to the abolition of the Council of Lithuania and the ending of nearly 200 years of self-rule.

A new system for taxing Jews was then instituted – a 'poll tax', initially two zlotys and later increased to three zlotys per head. Every Jew over the age of 1 year was required to pay the tax and each community was responsible for collecting the poll tax from its members and paying it to the government.[22] To be able to enforce and collect the poll tax, it was necessary to hold what was to be the first census of all Jews over that age. This was completed in 1765, showing a Jewish population of 587,658 in Crown Poland and 157,649 in Lithuania.

The Council of Lithuania

The Council of Four Lands (purple) and Council of Lithuania (green) [Map by courtesy of Dovid Katz[23]]

- ● Plunge/Plungyan – Kapelus
- ● Skuodas/Shkud – Dorfman
- ● Siauliai/Shavl – Hotz
- ● Panevezys/Ponevezh – Abramson
- ● Kaunas/Kovno
- ● Vilnius/Vilna
- ● Klaipeda/Memel (which was in Prussia and from 1871 in Germany)

An outline map of Lithuania: The coloured dots on the map highlight the towns from which the families we are discussing hailed, as well as the principal cities of Lithuania

The Kapelus Family of Plungyan: 1765-1888

Kapelus Family Tree

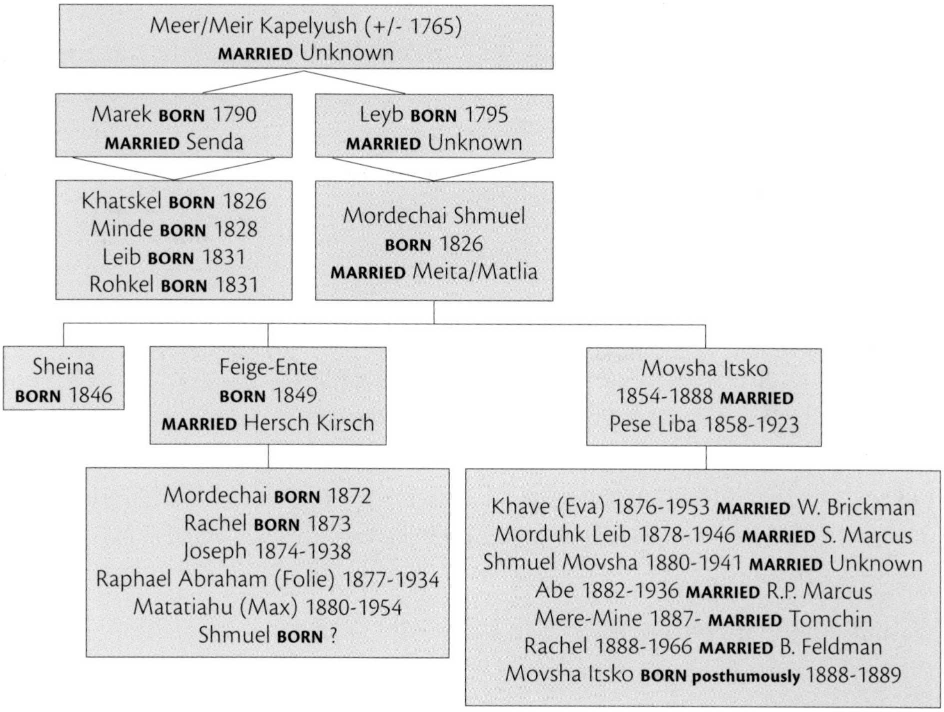

Plunge/Plungyan

Plungyan, the Yiddish for Plunge, is a thriving market town in the northwest of Lithuania in the Zhamot region, some 17 miles from the city of Telz. The Jews have lived there for centuries, earning it the reputation of being among the first towns in Lithuania to have a Jewish community. The Jewish cemetery attests to that, with headstones dating back some 300 years. The first synagogue built on church land in Plungyan in 1719 was a wooden structure. In 1769, the Bishop of Zhamot agreed to the rebuilding of the synagogue as long as it was not higher than the Catholic Church. In the event it was, so the Church imposed a heavy fine on the Jewish community.

The Kapelus family was part of the history of the town. The first member of the family for whom we have a record, Meier Kapelus (Kapelyush), was born there in about 1765, the year the poll tax was introduced and the census recorded the Jewish population of Plungyan at 816.[24]

Meier grew up at a time of continuing change, uncertainty and increasing hardship. In 1772, when he was 7 years old, Russia, Austria and Prussia partitioned the commonwealth of Poland-GDL for the first time. By the time Meier was married with a 5-year-old son Marek (b.1790), Lithuania was no longer an independent state. It was part of the Russian Empire's Northwest Provinces. Then Catherine II (the Great) annexed it in the final partition of the Poland-Lithuania Federation, and the Jewish community of Plungyan became part of Czarist Russia.

Partition Brings a Russian Regime

The Romanovs and their governments were hostile to every minority within their territory and subjected all of them to intensive Russification. Minorities had to give up their language for Russian, change their religion to Russian Orthodoxy and amend their names to the Russian equivalent. No minority was as hated and despised as the Jews; so much so that, in 1727, Russia expelled all Jews from its territory.[25]

Ironically, after the land grabs of 1772, 1793 and 1795, the Russian Empire found that along with the land it had also acquired a substantial, unwanted Jewish population that finally reached between 800,000 and 1,000,000. The Russian government recognised this as the 'Jewish Problem'.[26]

Having banned Jews from living within its traditional boundaries, it now decided that the solution would be to confine the Jews to an area called the Pale of Settlement, the territory that Russia had taken from Poland-GDL during the period 1772-95. Pale is a noun, meaning a stake or pointed piece of wood used for fencing in areas. The 'Pale' was thus the area within which Jews were confined. Other Pales were used for similar reasons, such as in Dublin and Calais.

The area marked between the blue lines in the green area on the map shows the North West Province or Pale of Settlement [Map by courtesy of Dovid Kotz[27]]

At the outset, the Russian authorities simply continued to apply the existing policy to its newly acquired Jewish population. This did not last long, however. During the short reign of Catherine II's successor, her son Pavel Petrovich, known as Paul I (1796-1801), the Russian Senate began to consider how best to deal with the country's burgeoning Jewish population. The solution preferred by the Russian administration, central and local, was to be brutal, harsh and systematic.

The virulent hostility and hatred of the Tsars for the Jews were such that during successive reigns, a progression of edicts, laws and proclamations made life for the Jews intolerable. The noose was drawn ever tighter during the reign of Alexander 1 (1801-25). In a series of statutes starting in 1804, the law defined where in the Pale Jews could live and what work they could do.

The most damaging aspect of the 1804 statute related to Jews who lived in the villages, *shtetlach* (sing. *schtetl*), forbidding them from selling liquor or holding the leaseholds of village inns and hostelries. In many instances, they were ordered to move out of these rural areas completely. This destroyed the livelihood of a third of the Jewish population and further impoverished them, resulting in a migration of the poor from the rural areas to the already overcrowded and poverty-stricken towns.[28]

This legislation did not directly affect the Kapelus family, who were traders living in a town where most of the Jews were engaged in agriculture, trade and crafts such as tailoring, shoemaking, carpentry and butchery. Plungyan was only 12 kilometres from the Prussian border, so there was plenty of cross-border trade in livestock and other goods. And Plungyan, like many other towns in Lithuania, in fact accommodated refugees forced out of their villages in the heart of the Pale of Settlement by these new laws.

In 1795, Meier Kapelus was blessed with a second son, Leyb, my great-great-great-grandfather. Meier's eldest son, Marek, married Senda in 1824 and it was not long before Meier became a Zeida (grandfather), as the first of Marek and Senda's children, Khatskel (Ezekiel), was born in 1826. In the same year, Leyb provided him with another grandson, Mordhke (Mordechai) Shmuel Kapelus, my great-great-grandfather.

Along with every Jewish household in the Pale of Settlement, the Kapelus family was about to feel the crass cruelty of the new Tsar, Nicholas I (1825-55), who succeeded his father Alexander l. Nicholas was a savage autocrat whose reign is remembered for its cruelty and oppression. In 1827, he issued the Cantonist Decree. This conscripted all male Jews aged between 12 and 25 into the army for a period of 25 years. The object was to convert these child conscripts to Russian Orthodoxy. The 'cantonists' were the soldiers, the 'cantonment' the barracks in which the conscripted children lived.

Every Jewish community in the Pale of Settlement, through its *Kahal* (council), was given a quota of cantonists that it had to provide. The leaders of the community were obliged to fill their quota by law. The sons of the rich, of scholars and of prominent members of the community were less likely to be conscripted. The rich could sometimes bribe officials, Jewish and non-Jewish alike. Inevitably, the burden fell on the poorest of the community, even though they needed their sons most to help provide their basic sustenance.

The punishment for not providing the quota was harsh and was visited on the whole community. Communal leaders were loath to send married men to the cantonment, particularly those with children; it was easier to send younger boys. The *Kahal* started to employ *Khapers*, as the professional kidnappers were called, to snatch boys as young as 8 or 9 to help fill their quotas. Tragically, in all about 50,000 boys were torn from their families.[29] Fortunately neither, Khatskel, Leyb nor their cousin Mordechai was conscripted.

A Glimmer of Hope

In 1855, the hated Nicholas I died. At the coronation of his successor, Alexander II, in 1856, the new Tsar declared that Jews would be conscripted into the army on the same basis as non-Jews, 'except for those who lack a permanent domicile or are not engaged in productive work'. At the same time, he reduced the term of military service from 25 to 16 years for all citizens. Thankfully, this ended the nightmare of young children being taken from their parents by the *Khapers*. Times seemed to be changing for the better for the Jewish community of Plungyan and throughout the Pale.

Two years later, Jews were allowed to move anywhere within the Pale and to leave the area temporarily for educational or occupational purposes. The university educated, artisans, merchants and certain others benefited from this relaxation of movement.

In 1861, serfdom was abolished, creating a new labour force to compete with the Jews, but it also opened up new opportunities for the Jews themselves, who were better educated and more economically astute than the liberated serfs. They took advantage of the business opportunities afforded by this liberalisation. By 1865, some 100,000 Jews had left the Pale. Many now moved from their traditional role of middlemen to participating in the industrialisation of Russia. Some became manufacturers and many more became factory workers. For the great majority, however, all this made little difference, as they remained very poor.[30]

Secular study was unknown in the Jewish communities of the Pale and nowhere more so than in Lithuania. Children learnt only a religious curriculum of Torah and Talmud. The Russian authorities started to encourage the teaching of secular subjects in Russian, thus attempting to aid the process of Russification.

The religious establishment opposed the introduction of secular learning, as they saw it as a road to assimilation as well as a diversion from religious study. However, the power of the rabbis had been weakened, as they could no longer invoke the fear of *herem*, excommunication.

By now, the winds of *Haskala* or Jewish Enlightenment were blowing into the towns and *shtetlach,* and its champions, the *maskilim,* encouraged secular studies, arguing that the Gaon of Vilna himself had favoured the study of secular subjects if it enhanced the study of Torah. By 1820, there were many *Haskala* associations in the Pale and they were particularly active in Lithuania.

The *maskilim* did not wear the traditional garb but dressed in the German fashion, causing them to be called *Deychn* or *Berliner.* Unlike their German counterparts, they did not write solely in German but used Hebrew and Yiddish, although some preferred Russian as a 'purer' language. The *maskilim* developed a secular literary form in Hebrew and Yiddish, not only in literature and polemics but also in reporting on everyday matters, local and international news.

For the first time, Yiddish was used to encourage a new way of life and reform. Books in Yiddish educated the Jews in the ways of the wider world, in the hope that they might be emancipated and ultimately integrate into society in general. The modern Hebrew novel was developed by Abraham Mapu (1808-67) and writers such as Shalom Jacob Abromovitch (1835-1917), also known as Mendele Mocher Seforim; Sholem Rabinowitz (1859-1916), better known as Shalom Aleichem; and Isaac Leib Peretz (1852-1915) all found a ready audience.

Modern Hebrew poetry also flourished. In his poem '*Haqitsa 'ami*' (Arise my people), Yehuda Leib Gordon (1831-92) made a plea for his people to 'be a Jew in your home and a man in the street'. He called for them to abandon their self-segregation, their Yiddish and their rigid customs and to integrate into their surroundings, in so doing improve relations with their non-Jewish neighbours. Others were more radical and called for assimilation. Although retaining a great respect for the Jewish traditions in which they were steeped, the *maskilim* were severely critical of the rigid conservatism and isolationism of rabbis and community leaders.[31]

Thus, the children of Mordechai, and of his cousins, Khatskel, Minde, Leib and Rachel, were the first generation of the Kapelus family to benefit from the more enlightened regime, as well from the considerable influence of the Lithuanian *maskilim.*

The Kapelus Family Takes Shape

Soon the Kapelus family was growing: Marek and Senda had a daughter, Minde, born in 1828, a sister for Khatskel, and three years later twins, Leyb and Rachel. Meanwhile, Leyb's son Mordechai turned 18 and married Meita; their first child, a daughter, Sheina, was born in 1846, whose sister, Feige-Ente, followed on 29 May 1849.

My paternal great-grandfather Moshe Yitzchak ben Mordechai – Movsha Itsko (Morris Isaac) – was born in 1854. (The birth records for this period are no longer extant, but we are able to place the year of his birth by reference to the official record of his death.) By now the Jewish population of Plungyan had grown to 2,917, according to the 1847 census.

Movsha Itsko married Pese Liba (Polly) shortly after his 21st birthday in 1875. Their first child, Chavah (Khave) bat Moshe Yitzchak (Eva), was born on 20 May 1876.

Her brother, my paternal grandfather Mordukh Leib ben Moshe Yitzchak (known to the family as Leib and to us as Oupa), followed on 23 November 1878. The registration of his birth records the names of his parents and paternal grandfather. The *mohel*, Leib Shafer, with Rabbi Zundel Blokh in attendance, conducted his *bris* on 30 November 1878. We have not found any record of Mordechai's death, but we must assume that he died between the birth of Eva and the birth of Movsha, as the boy was named after him.

In the next 10 years, Movsha and Pese were blessed with four more children: two brothers for Leib, Shmuel (b. 10 October 1880) and Abel (b. 2 November 1882), and two younger sisters, Mere-Mine (b. 13 February 1887) and Rachel (b. August or September 1888).

New Horizons

The *Haskala* movement made more and more ordinary Jews aware of what was happening outside of the Pale and awakened their desire to move to where they could enjoy a better life. Dr Ruth Leiserowitz has examined the factors that influenced this migratory process.[32] During the Crimean War (1853-56), Russia suffered a trade boycott by European states other than Prussia. To break this blockade and ensure the flow of goods to the Russian Empire, the Russians used the border posts of Memel and Tilsit as transit points. This inevitably led to a liberalisation of border controls between the Lithuanian border (western Russia) and Prussia (later Germany), which in turn created commercial opportunities for Jews living in these border areas.

Gaining residence status or even citizenship in Prussia at this time was relatively easy (although that was to change by the late nineteenth century), and also created a route to other ports from which the later migrants could leave Europe.

Another advance was the spread of the railway network during the 1860s, which made neighbouring towns more accessible and movement easier. The decision to migrate was facilitated by the changed perception of space as well as new knowledge about the world brought about by *Haskala*. In addition, anti-Jewish propaganda from the government and the virulent anti-Semitism of the Russian Orthodox Church, which continued unabated, made the decision to leave more compelling.

The vast majority of Russian and GDL Jews lived under appalling circumstances in this period. Unemployment was widespread. Wages for those who could obtain work were meagre and insufficient to provide for their very basic needs. A large percentage of the Jewish population of the Pale were receiving charity from the community or from the Jewish Diaspora, particularly during the famine in the GDL in 1867, followed by a cholera outbreak the following year. Luckily, the generosity of their brethren who had migrated to the east Prussian port of Memel helped the Jews of the GDL to survive. It was not enough, though, as many did perish.

In 1881, Tsar Alexander II was assassinated by revolutionaries, triggering devastating pogroms throughout most of the Pale, except for Lithuania. The pattern of the pogroms was such that it soon became clear that the attacks were being planned and carried out to a specific model. The behaviour of the police was evidence of government involvement. The world was shocked by the savagery of the pogroms. Accounts of murder, maiming and ferocious attacks on the Jews in Russia were published in the press in Britain, France, the USA and South Africa.

Under the leadership of Reverend Rabinowitz, Cape Town raised the massive sum of £4,000 for the pogrom victims, with support from nearly all members of both Houses of Parliament in Cape Town, many of whom sat on the Relief Committee. The Stellenbosch newspaper *Het Volkblat* wrote:

> *When, however, we remember how very liberally our Jewish fellow citizens, headed by their Pastor, always come to the front, when anything is to be*

done to relieve sufferers by such dire calamities as, some years ago, the fire at Stellenbosch, we cannot help reminding our Western country friends that it is now in their power to show that they are neither forgetful nor deficient in sympathy with those who are victims of the prejudice and the spirit of persecution.[33]

However, in Russia, Jews who had been embracing the liberalism and Russification under Alexander II were very disillusioned at the lack of assistance given by their non-Jewish fellow citizens.

The GDL was spared from these state-sponsored pogroms, but it was not long before its towns and villages experienced horrific arson attacks on Jewish homes and businesses. Both the pogroms and the arson attacks continued sporadically for the next 25 years.[34]

Alexander's successor, Alexander III (1881-94), was a reactionary determined to stamp out the winds of liberalism. He also implemented harsh anti-Jewish measures. Jews were forbidden to trade on Sundays and Christian holidays, forbidden to own land outside the towns, forbidden to settle in the villages and forbidden to vote in municipal elections, and a 10% quota for Jewish students was imposed in high schools and institutes of higher education. Furthermore, a 300-rouble fine was imposed on the family of every Jew who evaded conscription, a general draft having been instituted in 1874, conscripting all males aged 20. With their experience of the Cantonist Decree, many Jews now tried to avoid the draft by any means possible.

Anti-Semitism, pogroms and savagely restrictive laws made it extremely difficult for the Jewish population of the GDL and the Pale to earn a living and support a family. Fortunately, from 1881 Russia opened its borders, enabling them to leave the country. They rushed to take advantage of this opportunity and poured out in their hundreds of thousands.

The government's callous attitude to the plight of the Jewish community was underlined by the response of the Tsar's principal minister, the former Procurator General of the Holy Synod, Pobyedonotzev, to a delegation from Paris in 1898. When asked what would happen to the Jews under a regime of constant persecution, he remarked, 'One third will die out, one third will leave the country, and one third will assimilate without trace!'[35]

For the Jewish community of Plungyan, 1888 was a difficult year. In the summer a fire broke out, destroying 25 Jewish houses and leaving 48 families homeless and penniless. The Plunge Estate had passed into the ownership of the Oginsky family in 1873 and it was largely due to the Count's immediate response to the tragedy, rushing to the scene with his workers and horses and commanding the firefighting himself, that the blaze was prevented from spreading. In the aftermath of the fire, he led the efforts to help its victims.[36]

A Family Tragedy

For the Kapelus family in Plungyan there was to be an even heavier blow that year. After the devastation of the fire in the summer, Movsha Itsko died on 21 November 1888 at the age of 34, leaving Pese Liba a young widow, six months pregnant, with six children to feed. The oldest, Eva, was only 12 and the youngest, Rachel, just eight months.

My grandfather's 10th birthday was two days after the death of his father. It was not a celebration. Sadness, not joy, pervaded the family home. How does a young family come to terms with the sudden death of a 34-year-old husband and father? How does a mother who needs comforting herself look after six young children?

The Jewish tradition of sitting *shiv'ah*, remaining at home, refraining from going to work or school and being consoled and attended to by family and friends, is a great help psychologically. The daily ritual of morning, afternoon and evening prayers gives some focus. Having the time simply to be together and to talk, to mourn, to remember and to cry helps assuage the loss and heal the terrible hurt. However, what happens after the seven days of intense mourning is over?

Pese Liba's thoughts had to turn to matters that were more practical. How would she manage financially, with her young family of six, soon to be seven, children? Khave (Eva), her eldest, would be turning 13 in May. She could already sew. If she became a seamstress, she could work at home, bring in some money to help the family and perhaps manage to attend some classes to learn to read and write.

The family and the community would help to keep 10-year-old Leib at *cheder* (Jewish elementary school) until his *barmitzvah*, and the same would go for Shmuel, 8, and Abe, 6, but after that it would be very difficult indeed. Even if Pese Liba, as a widow, could have afforded – or wanted – to send one or more of her children to a secular school or to university, there would have been the quota system to overcome. Mine and Rachel were still babies, so Pese would have her hands full, especially after her last child, a boy named Movsha Itsko after his deceased father, was born on 5 February 1889. Sadly, the little boy died aged six months on 20 July 1889.

What future was there for the Kapelus children? Would they be able to make a basic living? Would they be able to support their families? Would they be able to look forward to a better life? The answer seemed to be a resounding *no*.

The Great Fire of 1894

Plungyan served as a trade centre for the surrounding rural area. Mondays and Fridays were regular market days, and large fairs were held twice a year. On these occasions, the town was crowded with traders, artisans and shoppers from the outlying villages. Getting about the narrow streets with the wooden buildings and houses all close together was difficult on market days when the streets were crowded with shoppers, horses and laden carts and animals brought in for sale. On the days of the biannual trade fairs it was well-nigh impossible. The trade fair of July 1894 was no exception. It was hot and crowded as usual – and then a fire broke out.

Soon most of the town seemed to be ablaze. Firefighters were sent from the Oginsky estate, but the crowds fleeing from the flames blocked the already crowded roads, preventing them from reaching the source of the fire. The narrow streets and closely built wooden houses were a tinderbox. Many buildings were destroyed, including 400 houses, of which 323 belonged to Jews, who lived mainly in the centre of town close to the synagogue and their businesses. This fire devastated the magnificent synagogue, erected in 1814 and known throughout the region, as well as many other important public buildings. It left a large number of Jews homeless and penniless, although fortunately not the Kapelus family.[37]

A relief council was set up, headed by Count Michael Oginsky and with Rabbi Zevulun Leib Barrit as a member. The latter's appeal for help was published in the 20 July 1894 issue of *Melitz*. It was directed at all the Jewish communities of Lithuania as well as the émigrés of Plungyan. All donations were to be sent to Oginsky, who in the aftermath of the fire most generously sheltered hundreds of homeless townsfolk in buildings on his estate, as well as providing them with sustenance.

Near the market where many Jewish traders' shops were destroyed, Oginsky erected 36 shops that were sold to those who had lost theirs in the blaze at a low price and on easy terms: payment over 12 years for most buyers, the poorest being given 24 years to pay. Furthermore, at his own expense the Count built a large bath-house for the Jewish community and in addition made them a loan enabling rebuilding of the fine synagogue; half was repayable during construction and the balance over two years. The synagogue was reinstated by 1896, two years after the fire. Nevertheless, although the Oginsky family was hugely supportive, hospitable and exceedingly generous to the Jewish community, the reality of the situation in Lithuania for young Jews remained the same.[38]

The Dorfman Family of Skuodas: 1851-1898

Dorfman Family Tree

Moshe (Morris) Dorfman **BORN** +/- 1830
MARRIED Rachel Mokit

Joseph Dorfman 1851-1915
MARRIED Eva Reiff 1856-1926 (**BORN** in Zidikai)

Louis Samuel (1879-1953)
Israel (1884/1885-?)
Sarah (1889-1965)
Kate (1896-1986)
Polly (1899-?)

The Reiffs of Tzidikai

Abraham Reiff **BORN** ?
MARRIED Krayna (Annie)

Chava (Eva) (1856-1926)
Simkus (Simon) (1883-1950)
Leah Rachel (1884-1951)

Skuodas (Shkud)

Shkud was the home of Morris (Moshe/Movsha) and Rachel Dorfman (née Mokit), my maternal great-great-grandparents. Morris ran a drapery business in the Old Town. In 1851, Rachel gave birth to a boy, named Yosef ben Moshe at his *brit mila*. Yosef (Joseph) Dorfman was my maternal great-grandfather.

An old but certainly not ancient town, Skuodas, known in Yiddish as Shkud, received its municipal powers in 1572, when it was permitted to build a city hall and a court of law and to have a coat of arms. The town is in the Zhamut region of northwest Lithuania, a stone's throw from the Latvian border, 2 kilometres away. Shkud is cut in half by the Bartuva River, creating an 'Old Town' on the left bank and a 'New Town' on the right bank, with a bridge connecting the two.

At the start of the eighteenth century, the Jewish community built a synagogue in the Old Town, regarded as one of the three oldest in Lithuania. It was constructed of wood and was 15 metres high. The Holy Ark was elaborately embellished with wooden carvings, including the tablets of the Ten Commandments, and it is said to have reached up to the ceiling. The synagogue was so large that it could not be properly heated in winter, so that it was only used from Pesach to Succot. In winter, the services were held in a nearby Beit Midrash. The New Town also had a synagogue and two *Kloisim* (prayer rooms), one of which was also used as a *cheder*.[39]

Crimean Refugees

The first settlement of Jews in Shkud is inextricably linked to the expansion of the Poland-Lithuanian commonwealth and the subsequent massacre of Jews in Ukraine and Poland during the Cossack uprising, which culminated in an invasion of Poland between 1648 and 1649.

The territory ruled by Poland and Lithuania was greatly expanded to include Ukraine and Byelorussia during the reign of Sigismund III (1587-1632). The Jews participated in the development of these new regions. Their reward for this was to be allowed to own some of the lands they developed.[40]

Many Jews were still engaged in money lending, tax collection, peddling and brokerage, as other professions had been closed to them. However, many others now took the opportunity to become involved in agriculture and trades such as forestry, dyeing, trading in livestock and particularly import-export. Jews, being considered experts at economic administration, were appointed to manage many of the estates of the absent Polish nobles. They became the lessees of mills and taverns. Many were granted brewing and distilling rights and were allowed to purchase dairy concessions from manors and villages.

Jewish communities were spreading across the countryside. On their estates, noblemen were creating private towns, *shtetlach*, and in many of these, Jews formed the majority of the population, conducting every trade and activity the law and their privilege allowed.

Often they were the intermediaries for the magnates and nobility and were obliged to enforce the decisions of the Polish nobles against the Ukrainian peasants; this led to the Jews being seen as the oppressors of the peasants. Despite possessing the right to participate in the economy and the prevailing religious tolerance, the Jewish communities of the *shtetlach* did not engage with their neighbours socially or politically, clung to their dress code, and strictly adhered to their religious customs, thus always remaining outsiders.

During the reign of Wadislaw IV (1632-48), the peasants of Ukraine, then controlled by the Polish-Lithuanian commonwealth, started to show their resentment. Poland and its farmlands in Ukraine had been the breadbasket for the troops of the Thirty Years' war. The Polish nobles whose estates in Ukraine were managed by Jewish lessees and sub-lessees benefited hugely from the war by supplying both sides with food and fodder, through mainly Jewish traders.

When taxes were increased, the Jewish tax collectors were the ones who were obliged to enforce the new harsh measures on behalf of the absent Polish nobility. The Ukrainian peasants, who had been impoverished by high taxation and artificially low crop prices enforced by Polish magnates, started to display their social and economic discontent. As the Polish nobility pressed their Jewish lessees for increased rents on the renewal of leases, so the Jewish landlords in turn pressed the Ukrainian peasants for increased returns so that they could pay the rent.

The hatred shown by the peasants (Cossacks) was exacerbated by religious differences. The Ukrainian peasants were Eastern Orthodox; the Polish nobles were Catholics; and the lessees of the land and most of the fixed assets such as mills, breweries, distilleries, inns and tolls were Jews. It was against the Jews that the rising hatred of the Cossacks was directed. From 1637-40, Cossack raids developed into ongoing revolts and insurrections. Led by a petty aristocrat, Bogdan Chmielnicki, the raids by Ukrainian peasants, aided by the Dnieper Cossacks and Tartars from the Crimea, developed into a fierce uprising in 1648, which targeted the Catholics (Jesuits), the Polish magnates and particularly the Jews.

Whole villages were torched, over 400 Jewish localities were destroyed and tens of thousands of Jews, men, women and children, were murdered, raped or maimed. Thousands of Jews fled Ukraine to settle in Lithuania. The Synod of the Four Lands and the Council of Lithuania assumed responsibility for the victims.

A number of these refugees from Ukraine were the first Jewish inhabitants of Shkud. We do not know the exact number, but by the first official census in 1766, the number of Jews in Shkud was recorded to be 576. By 1847, the Jewish community had grown to 1,872; by 1897 it had swollen to 2,292, fully 60% of the total population of the town (3,814).[41]

The Dorfmans

Like all Jewish families in Lithuania and indeed in the Pale of Settlement, Rachel and Morris Dorfman feared that Joseph would be drafted into the Tsar's army for 16 years. Luckily, this did not happen. Joseph attended and was educated in the *cheder* in the Old Town. It was here that he met Eva Reiff and it was not long before they were married.

In the summer of 1879, Joseph and Eva (Chava) Dorfman's first child, a son, Samuel Leib (Louis), was born. Louis, or Zeida as he was known to me, was my maternal grandfather.

Unusually for those days, Louis had to wait five years for a sibling. His brother Israel was born in 1884. They had time to get to know each other, as it was just the two of them until 1889, when Sarah, the first of their three sisters, was born.

By the time Eva gave birth to his two younger sisters, Kate in 1896 and Polly in 1899, Louis was very much a young man. He had by then completed his apprenticeship and was a cabinetmaker. Israel, his younger brother, was beginning to learn the art of tailoring.

By that time, Louis was madly in love. We are not aware of exactly when he met his beloved Rachel, but we do know that Rachel Leah Reiff was related to his mother. Family rumour has it that Eva and Rachel were sisters, which would make her Louis's aunt. Jewish law forbade such a union and if the rumours were true, the couple could not legally get married in Shkud. However, if they left Shkud for foreign parts, where no one knew their background, they might overcome this problem.

Louis and Rachel wanted to get married. There was little future for them in Lithuania and they also wanted a better life. Louis was a skilled artisan, a master cabinetmaker, and Rachel was a very resourceful woman. To achieve their dual aims, they, like many around them, would have to leave Shkud and Lithuania for pastures new. The pull of Great Britain or South Africa was compelling; all they needed was the means.

The Hotz and Abramson Families

My wife Esther's maternal grandparents, David and Leah Hotz, made their separate journeys from Lithuania to South Africa, where they met and married. David hailed from Siauliai (Shavl) and Leah from Panevezys (Ponevezh), both large towns with substantial and important Jewish communities.

I met David and Leah Hotz, who lived with the Broude family, on the day after my very first date with Esther in April 1964. I was soon asked whether I played *klawerjas*, a card game much enjoyed by many of the Jews of South Africa. When they found that I was a keen player, my welcome was assured.

Every time I arrived to see Esther, Zeida (David) would invite me to *nem ein hand* – take a hand. He was by then some 84 years old and Granny (Leah) a few years younger. The format was always the same: four handed, with Zeida and I as partners and Granny and Esther as the other pairing. Granny would always sit very close to Zeida in a show of affection. It would not take long for him to notice that she was staring at his cards before playing hers. This would inevitably lead to him asking me if I knew what a sledge was. 'Yes,' I would answer. Quick as a flash, he would say, 'If a sledge enters Ponevezh and stops, the head of the horse would be on one side of the town and the back of the sledge on the other side.'

> *Granny would not stand for such an insult to her schtetl and she would counter, 'Ivan, do you know what Shavl is known for?'*
>
> *'No, Granny,' I would reply.*
>
> *'Well, for horse thieves, all horse thieves, I tell you,' was her response.*

It was through this little contretemps that I learnt that David hailed from Shavl and Leah (née Abramson) from Ponevezh. I was aware that Shavl and Ponevezh were the names of *shtetlach* in Lithuania, but that was the sum total of my knowledge. I could pinpoint more or less where Lithuania was on the map, but at that time I knew nothing of its history or about the times and lives of the Jews there, other than that they had suffered anti-Semitism.

Furthermore, both Zeida and Granny were reluctant to talk about their previous lives, so we left the topic well alone. Their only surviving son, Ellie Hotz, now in his 90s, is in good health and of sound mind, but has no information about his parents that can assist me in tracing their family in Shavl or Ponevezh. He too cannot remember his parents talking about Lithuania in any detail or with any enthusiasm.

While playing *klawerjas* and during our evenings at home, Esther and I asked Zeida and Granny about their lives in South Africa. From these chats, we learnt that they had met in South Africa, and it was evident that each of them had made the journey from Lithuania on their own. We also knew that they had been married in Paarl in 1910. Zeida had told us he had lived in Pniel, a village between Stellenbosch and Franchoek.

A search of the records at the archives in Cape Town resulted in me finding two applications made by a David Hotz for naturalisation as a citizen of the Cape of Good Hope. One was dated 1904 and the other 1905, both signed in Paarl and giving the applicant's place of residence as Pniel in the district of Paarl. On 13 March 1905, the Colonial Secretary approved the application signed by David on 28 January 1905.

A quick glance at its contents showed that it was indeed Zeida's application. He states that his place of birth was Saville (Shavl), Russia and his age next birthday as 25 years. By this time he had been in the Cape of Good Hope for four years and his occupation was general dealer.

Shavl (Siauliai)

So now I knew that Zeida had been born in Shavl, probably in 1879/80, and that he had arrived in the Cape in 1901. In our conversations he always referred to his birthplace by its Yiddish name. The city is some 210 kilometres northwest of Vilnius/Vilna and 142 kilometres from Kaunas/Kovno.

The first indication we have of a Jewish community in Shavl appears in the tax records of 1776, where 687 Jews were recorded as paying 'head tax'. However, there is a legend suggesting that the first settlement of Jews there was in 1681. Reb Zev Nurok Ka'tz, a Jew, and his household are said to have been given special permission by King John III Sobiesky (1674-96) to live there. One day while on his way home, Reb Zev is supposed to have come across some Christian residents of Shavl attempting to cross a river with a huge bell destined for the newly constructed (1634) cathedral. The current dislodged the bell and it fell into the river. Reb Zev, risking his life, went into the river and salvaged the bell. The Christians were so grateful that they offered to pay him whatever sum he demanded.

Reb Zev Nurok responded by saying that he did not want anything for himself; what he desired was for his brother Jews to be allowed to live in the city. His wish was granted and soon a small Jewish community formed in Shavl. His son, Reb Israel Nurok, who died in 1791, was famous throughout the region. He is credited with the creation of the first Jewish cemetery in Shavl in 1748, a year before the first wooden synagogue was built in the city.

This was considered a fine building, with coloured windows set high in the walls. On the south side was a large brass menorah with a cup-shaped base, made by a local artist. The wooden synagogue served the Jews of Shavl until 1881. By then the structure was in need of repair and the government shut it so that restoration could be undertaken. The synagogue reopened in 1889 and remained a place of worship until it burned down during the First World War, along with the city centre and 65% of the buildings in Shavl.[42]

The Jewish population grew slowly at first. By 1847 it had reached 2,565, a number that had increased to 3,787 by 1864. Between 1836 and 1871, the infrastructure throughout the Pale of Settlement and into Russia developed rapidly and completion of a road between Tilsi and Riga improved access to Shavl. During the Crimean War, when the European nations except Prussia boycotted Russia, the priority was to develop rail transport from Prussia to Russia. Shavl benefited particularly when the rail link between Libau and Romania was completed in 1871, as well as a road link between St Petersburg and Berlin.

Being at the crossroads of important trade routes, Shavl began to develop as an industrial town. With industrialization came jobs, particularly in the leather industry. This led to a growth in the Jewish community from 6,990 in 1897 to 9,848 by 1902, out of a total population for the city of 16,968. Shavl's Jews became a well-respected, influential and important part of the community.[43]

Chaim Freinkel established a leather goods factory in 1877, which by the early 1900s was one of the largest producers of leather goods in Russia. The family expanded into weaving, knitting and shoe manufacturing. His wealth in 1914 was estimated to be 25 million roubles! The Freinkels had a substantially Jewish workforce and built a synagogue near their factory in Shavl for their employees.

The Nurok brothers were equally well known. They owned a leather manufacturing enterprise of some note, expanded into banking and established a private bank in the city, as did two other Jewish families, Benzion Kagan and Choronzhitzki. In addition, there were Jewish-owned tobacco factories, ironworks, soap manufacturers, flax and grain producers as well as merchants.

Once it had a substantial Jewish community, Shavl became a centre for Jewish learning and study, with a long line of distinguished Rabbis. The rich could send their children to the private school that opened in 1851. The masses were initially suspicious of the government Hebrew School for Beginners, opened in 1879, and the Hebrew School for Girls that started with one class in 1894. Gradually the community was more accepting of this government school, however, so that by 1900 there were 138 children there.

For ordinary Jews, the Talmud Torah and *cheder* were the front line of their education. The Freinkel family fed and clothed 250 children in the Talmud Torah and, through the generosity of Reb Chaim Freinkel, the old rundown facility was abandoned for a two-storey brick building that employed qualified and enlightened teachers paid by Freinkel, teaching both religious and secular subjects.

Like every Jewish community in Lithuania, charity and the establishment of communal institutions were priorities. The women formed a society to provide clothes for the poor (Malbish Arumim) and another group offered lunch to some 70 pupils a day. By 1891, the city had a 12-bedded Jewish hospital housed in a wooden building. The Efrati family generously funded the building of a two-storey stone building for the Jewish hospital in 1898, with 24 beds for general patients and a 10-bed section for the isolation of contagious patients. The old wooden hospital became a home for the elderly, housing some 16 people, and was in use until it burned down during the First World War.[44]

Hotz Antecedents

With the little information available about the Hotz family in Shavl, it is not easy to create a genealogical picture. All one has to go on is the fact that David's father was Dov Ber (according to the inscription on his gravestone), in English perhaps Beryl. Matters are further complicated by the Russian alphabet not having an *h*, so Hotz is spelt 'Gots.' In addition to the dearth of personal information, there is a lacuna in the vital records for Shavl for the period 1878-81.

Like most of his contemporaries, David would not have seen a future for himself in Lithuania. It is safe to assume that like many before and after him, he crossed the border into Germany without papers and made his way to either Hamburg or Bremen, from where he would have sailed to Cape Town via either London or Southampton.

I have not found any record of him having used the Poor Jews Temporary Shelter in London, nor could I find a match for him in *Jewish Migration to South Africa*.[45] However, his application for naturalisation clearly states that he arrived in the Cape in 1901, without giving an exact date.

Ponevezh (Panevezys)

So where and what was the village of Ponevezh of which Zeida was so dismissive? It was where Granny hailed from and, as we shall see, it was a significant town in Jewish life in the GDL and later independent Lithuania.

Panevezys, as its Lithuanian name tells us (meaning 'along the Nevezys'), is a town built on both banks of the Nevezys River. It is some 82 miles from Vilnius and 60 miles from Kaunas. The first official mention of the town seems to be in a document signed by the Grand Duke of Lithuania, Alexander I, in 1503, granting it the right to build a church and other buildings. The first settlement was on the right bank of the river, where the Old City developed.

During the period from the mid-sixteenth century to the beginning of the eighteenth century, the Nevezys played an important role in the commerce of the area, since ships could sail up the river to Ponevezh. By the seventeenth century the left bank began to be populated, the New City developed and expanded, and it is here that the first Jews seemed to have settled very soon after its establishment.

This is a town that has had a Jewish community since the days of the Poll Tax, as in 1766 it is recorded that 254 Jews paid the 'head tax'. As the town grew, so did the Jewish community. By 1847, the community totalled 1,447; by 1857, it had more than doubled to 3,566, 60% of the population. The Jews chose to live around the market square, since many were shopkeepers and merchants. As in most of the larger towns, the Jews were skilled artisans and were involved in small industries, usually family owned.

A rail line from Daugavpils (Dvinsk) through Ponevezh to Radviliskis (Ravilishok), completed in 1873, connected to the main rail line to Prussia. In addition, the building of a narrow-gauge rail link from Ponevezh to Utena (Utyan) and Svencionys (Shventzian) gave the town the economic impetus needed for the establishment of factories and more expansive trading in agricultural as well as manufactured goods.

The Russian census of 1897 recorded a total population for Ponevezh of 13,044, of whom 6,627 were Jews, 51% of the total. By now there was a growing artisan class as well as an emerging professional class of doctors, pharmacists, lawyers and teachers. During the late nineteenth century and the early years of the twentieth century, Ponevezh developed into a leading economic and cultural centre, and it was during this period that the town's famous *yeshivot* or Jewish secondary schools came to prominence.

The more famous of the two *yeshivot* was the Ponevezh Yeshiva, whose head, *Rosh Yeshiva*, was Rabbi Yosef Shlomo Kahaneman, known as the 'Ponevezher Rov'. He moved the *yeshiva* from Ponevezh to Bnei Brak in Israel.

The other famous *yeshiva*, established in 1912, was known universally as the Ponivezh Kibbutz. It was founded by Rabbi Yitshak Ya'akov Rabinowitz (Itsele Ponivezher). The *yeshiva* accepted only 20 of the most talented students. Although it existed for no more than seven years, some of the best-known rabbis in the Jewish world were its alumni.[46]

Leah Abramson

According to the death notice filed at the Master of the Supreme Court on her death (16 April 1966), Granny, as the family called Leah Abramson, was born on 7 May 1887 in Lithuania. The notice does not mention the town of her birth or the names of her parents, marking them 'Not Known'; it also wrongly states that she was married in Lithuania. Granny died some three weeks before her 79th birthday. Why the death notice states that the names of her parents are not known is a mystery, as on her headstone she is described as the daughter of Abraham Abramson.

According to family folklore, Granny was no more than one or two years younger than her husband David, but this is clearly not so. In fact, she was some seven or eight years his junior. No naturalisation records for Leah Abramson have been found. Having in 1910 married David Hotz, a naturalised citizen of the Cape of Good Hope, there would not have been any need or urgency for her to seek naturalisation in South Africa herself. (She would have had to do so if she wanted a South African passport, but we know she never travelled abroad.)

We are not aware of exactly when Leah left Lithuania. A Miss Abrahamson, tailor by trade, aged 22 years, sailed steerage on the vessel *Scot* from the UK bound for Cape Town on 7 February 1903.[47] Could this be Granny? The age is wrong but the timing is right. We will never know!

Emigration

After the assassination of Tsar Alexander II in 1881, the migration of Jews from Russia accelerated in response to the vicious pogroms and anti-Jewish legislation. It is estimated that between 1881 and 1938, approximately 5 million Jews fled from Eastern Europe, mainly to the United States of America but also to Canada, South America, South Africa and Palestine. Of the 755,000 Jews living in Lithuania in 1897, only 260,000 were living in independent Lithuania in 1923, so this was a mass exodus by any standards.[48]

The migration to South Africa of some 70,000 Jews between 1881 and 1930 was overwhelmingly from the Kovno gubernia (province) and the two adjoining gubernias, including Suwalki and Courland. Why would they choose South Africa, an unknown country, at the tip of such a vast continent?

The 'push factors' were obvious: poverty, anti-Semitism resulting in a lack of opportunity, vicious arson attacks in the wake of the pogroms in the rest of the Pale of Settlement, the threat of conscription and the seeming hopelessness of their situation.

The obvious 'pull factor' of South Africa was the rapid industrial development that followed the discovery of diamonds in 1867 and that of gold in 1886, as is more fully dealt with later. Furthermore, until the passing of the Immigration Quota Act in 1930, one did not have to satisfy any official requirements to gain entry to the Cape of Good Hope.

A number of other circumstances made South Africa attractive to young men from Lithuania, Latvia and Suwalki. The letters home of the sizeable number of Plungyaners who had chosen to migrate there spoke of the freedom they had to trade, live and practise their faith without interference from the law.[49]

Articles about the success in South Africa of Lithuanian Jews from other towns were appearing in the local Jewish press. Two weekly newspapers, in particular, featured articles that were widely read in the Kovno region: *Hamelitz* and

Hatzfira. Nehemia Dov Ber Hoffmann, who emigrated to South Africa in 1889, wrote a series of 23 reports on the country between 1890 and 1892 for *Hatzfira*. Meir David Hersch wrote a sequence of letters for the same paper published in 1895, aimed, like Hoffman's, to serve as information and a guide for intending emigrants. These and other articles told of communal developments in the country, making it clear that Jews were free to practise their faith and that Jewish institutions and facilities were being established. The success of these pioneers was as real as the money they sent home. The articles and letters from emigrants to their loved ones also told of a warmer way of life, not unlike in the *shtetlach* of Lithuania.

Invariably, the young menfolk left first and once they had settled they would bring out their families: married men their wives, children and even in-laws; single men their parents and siblings. The Lithuanian Jewish community was a close-knit society where families had very strong ties. Thus, the successful migration of one part of a family often led to the later migration of those who had been left behind.

The majority of Jewish migrants to South Africa were traders, artisans and workers, a class of people who worked for themselves rather than being industrial wage earners. Unlike those who migrated to the USA or UK, who worked in the sweatshops of the Lower East Side of New York or the East End of London, Lithuanian migrants in South Africa worked mainly for themselves as soon as they were able. They were not used to factory life. The situation was different for Poles, as Poland was an industrialised country. Perhaps that is the reason so few Poles migrated to South Africa but chose the USA and UK instead.[50]

The Role of the Union and Castle Shipping Lines

However, even with the positive information they were receiving, there had to be other circumstances to explain the sudden explosion of migration to far-off South Africa from such a small area of Eastern Europe. These circumstances were totally unrelated to the plight of these intended Jewish migrants.

History professor Aubrey Newman, looking for a project to provide his students with computer skills, came across the records of the Poor Jews Temporary Shelter in Leman Street, Whitechapel. The work done by his students enabled analysis of where the emigrants came from, where they were going, their ages and professions. As he delved deeper into the information, Newman became involved in studying the circumstances surrounding their emigration.

From these records, he has shown that from about the 1860s there was considerable promotional activity by locally based shipping agents and representatives, which penetrated right to the villages of central and northern Europe. The ships plying the Baltic needed cargo. The agents had direct links to the shipping companies, such as the Cunard, White Star, Allan and Wilson lines. Just like any other commodity, the traffic in Russian Jews was carved up between the shipping magnates who dominated the Baltic trade. Once in England, this human cargo was handed over to the transatlantic lines, which transported this easily garnered revenue to its final destination.[51]

The Union Shipping Company and Castle Lines between them had been granted the Royal Mail contracts between the UK and the Cape. They needed substantial additional cargo and found it by providing cheap third-class and steerage fares to the Cape, which they advertised in London and Cape Town. For a time, their cheap berths were filled by Cornish tin miners going to South Africa to work in the newly discovered gold mines; this source evaporated as more miners returned to the UK than travelled to South Africa, and these passengers had to be replaced.

Indeed they were: by the burgeoning traffic of Jews wishing to migrate from Lithuania, who were attracted to the ships by aggressive advertising in the local Yiddish newspapers and the appointment of local agents offering cheap and subsidised fares. They provided a means of escaping a life with few prospects at a cost people could just about manage.

The Poor Jews Temporary Shelter in London

An interesting aspect of this route was the role played by the Poor Jews Temporary Shelter in London. The Shelter was not unique; a number of organisations existed both in the UK and the rest of Europe for the specific purpose of helping migrating Jews from Russia and Eastern Europe. The Poor Jews Temporary Shelter was different, however, because of the scale of its operations and the particular role it developed and played in the migration of Lithuanian Jews to South Africa.

The records show that virtually all movement to South Africa through the Shelter was from Lithuania, overwhelmingly from the Kovno area. This surprising feature has also been pointed out by the Jewish Colonial Association when discussing population movements in the Pale of Settlement. Only two provinces in the northwest showed this desire to go to South Africa.

Another fascinating aspect is the Shelter's relationship with the Union Shipping Company and the Castle Lines, which continued when these amalgamated into the Union Castle Lines. It seems that most of the Lithuanian Jews who left for South Africa would buy their tickets from local agents and travel from their port of embarkation via London. The shipping lines had an agreement with the Shelter that they would meet the migrants at the docks in London, accommodate and chaperone them and then see them off on their onward journey to Cape Town, Port Elizabeth or Durban. The Shelter charged the shipping lines for this service and even arranged for those who left from Southampton to be similarly looked after. The records show that the charges were 5s (25 pence) for meeting and seeing off a migrant, and 1s 6d (7.5 pence) per night.

Not all Lithuanian migrants travelling to South Africa went through the Shelter, as many had friends or *landsleit* (people from the same town or village) in London with whom they could stay. Nonetheless, it played an important role in the migration process and the Shelter records are a rich source of information about this period, particularly as they list the dates of arrival and departure and the name of the passenger ship.

The Hamburg-American Shipping Line (HAPAG)

At that time, passports were not required to enter Western European countries, the USA, the British Colonies or the Independent States of Southern Africa, but official documents were required to leave Lithuania legally. The Russians maintained that the western border was open to Jews, but in practice it placed many restrictions on their departure. Officials used every excuse to delay issuing the passports applied for, continually requiring additional information that resulted in further and new charges being levied. It became so difficult to satisfy officialdom, which the Jewish migrants did not trust in any case, that many, even those who could get their papers, preferred to be smuggled over the border, particularly if they were evading military service.

From January 1892, the border controls between Russia and Prussia had been tightened up by the Prussian authorities to prevent the spread of contagious diseases. The border was completely closed after a cholera epidemic in Hamburg in August 1892, because the Russian émigrés were suspected (wrongly) of carrying the disease. Emigrants were only allowed to cross into Prussia if they had a clean bill of health. In addition, they had to be in possession of a rail ticket to either Bremen or Hamburg, as well as a ticket from a European port to their ultimate destination. The Germans wanted proof that the Russian Jews would not take up residence in Germany nor be reliant on handouts from the government.

The border closure was a disaster for the shipping lines, particularly the large German concern Hamburg-Amerikanische Packetfahrt-Actien Gesellschaft (HAPAG), which had thrived since the appointment of Albert Ballin, a practising German Jew, to its board. That success was in large measure due to Ballin's concerted expansion of the HAPAG network of travel agents, which targeted emigrants from eastern and southeastern Europe.

When the 17-year-old Albert's father died, in order to support the family Albert entered the family business, an agency that arranged passages for emigrants seeking to travel to the USA. There had been a surge in migration to America, in particular by people disgruntled over the failed uprisings of 1848 and the severe downturn in the economies of Germany and Eastern Europe. By the time Albert joined the firm in 1874, it was no longer only the conditions in Eastern Europe pushing people out – there was now a strong pull factor, the economic boom in the USA.

On the back of this demand, Ballin and a business partner established a new shipping line plying the route between Hamburg and the USA. Their ships were custom built to ensure their full use in both the outward and inward journeys by dispensing with creature comforts for outgoing passengers who sailed steerage, so that the passenger space could be converted to cargo holds for the journey back to Europe. Through a combination of low fares for emigrants, a network of agencies in Eastern Europe to service passengers and carrying cargo on the inward journey, the business grew at the expense of the larger shipping lines, particularly HAPAG.

In 1886, HAPAG agreed with Ballin and his partner to take over their business. Ballin was appointed to the board of directors as well as becoming head of the passenger division. Thirteen years later, in 1899, he became managing director of HAPAG. Under his management, it grew to become one of the largest shipping companies in the world.

It was of paramount importance to his business interests that the border was reopened. In the circumstances, Ballin negotiated a deal with the German authorities to reopen the border in exchange for HAPAG and another shipping company, Norddeutsche Lloyd, bearing the costs of examining and disinfecting emigrants at border checkpoints. This agreement effectively gave the two shipping companies control of the emigrant business. So effective was the new system that in 1901, HAPAG opened the *Auswandererhallen* or Emigrants Halls, purpose-built premises with their own rail link, to process the wave of emigrants from Eastern European countries.

The Russian Empire in 1888 includes the territories taken from the Polish Lithuanian Federation, including Poland and Lithuania. The border of Russia runs along that of Germany and the Austrian Empire, so that Lithuania and Germany have a common border

Leib Kapelus Migrates

By 1894, when Nicholas II became Tsar, Leib Kapelus was 16 years old and the possibility of conscription was becoming a reality. Every few years new discriminatory laws were introduced, adding to the existing discriminatory legislation to which the Jews and thus the Kapelus family were already subject. The accession of Nicholas II did not bring any relief. He rejected the proposal of the gubernator (governor) of Vilna region to ease the Jews' deteriorating economic situation by allowing them to settle outside the Pale of Settlement.

The Russian authorities continued to blame the Jews for exploiting the peasants. In this atmosphere, there was a significant rise in hostility on the part of the Catholic Lithuanian peasants towards the Jewish population. It was becoming more difficult for Jews to improve their lot at home and emigration was now a solution adopted by many. In these circumstances, the push to leave Plungyan was strong. The number of Jews in the town plummeted from its height of 2,917 in 1847 to 2,502 out of 4,498 (56%) in 1897, and then to 1,861 out of 4,236 in 1923, now only 44% of the population.[52]

Leib was lucky that family members his own age had already migrated to South Africa. His first cousin, Raphael Abraham Kirsch (known as Folie), the son of Movsha Itsko's sister Feige-Ente, had left for South Africa in 1893 and in 1896 had helped his brothers, Joseph and Matatiahu (Max), to join him there. They were all living in a town named Ceres, in the Cape Colony, some 150 kilometres northeast of Cape Town. Leib and his siblings had grown up with their cousins in Plungyan and were close friends.

Before Leib, by then 18, could plan his journey, he needed instructions from Raphael and Max on how he was going to get from Cape Town to Ceres and how much it would cost. His cousin's advice would make this daunting undertaking that much easier.

The planning of this enterprise required time. Correspondence between the Cape and Plungyan was not easy and took months. If the correspondent in Africa was not in Cape Town the letter would first have to reach the port, either by mail coach or train, which could take up to a week or longer; then it would travel by boat to the UK, a journey of 23-30 days. From the UK the mail entered the European system, moving by boat to Hamburg, by train to Memel and then by road to Plungyan.

There were sub-agents for shipping companies operating in Plungyan, which was only 12 kilometres from the Lithuanian/Prussian border and 58 kilometres from Memel (Klaipeda). These agents were offering cheap passages by boat from either Bremen or Hamburg via Southampton to Cape Town. Minors got an even better deal.

Leib's problem was how to get from Plungyan to Memel, where he could board a train to Bremen or Hamburg. As he had not done his military service, he needed to cross the border illegally. He planned to do this with traders on their way back from Plungyan to Memel after a Monday fair. There was a regular flow of business back and forth across the border, so as long as he looked like one of the traders and seemed to be part of their group he should be safe, even without papers. He would have to pay the traders for helping him, but this would be cheaper and more efficient than trying to get papers.

Pese Liba, 1858-1923

Leib could not take the chance of crossing the border without both rail and boat tickets for his entire journey. Once he reached the border, he had to ensure that the agents of the shipping line cleared him. This was quite an undertaking for a teenager who had always lived in a village surrounded by family and close neighbours who were all Jewish. Luckily for him he would not be alone, as thousands of Jews from the Pale were now voting with their feet.

By Pesach 1897, Pese and the family knew that Leib was going to leave in the summer. As Pese prepared for Seder, she inevitably mused that this might be the last time she would have her eldest son at the Seder table. These thoughts added poignancy to the holiday that celebrated the Jews attaining freedom from slavery. Perhaps in South Africa Leib would taste true freedom and be able to raise his family as Jews without fear and without being subject to special laws. Perhaps Leib's children would have the right to be educated, to trade, to follow any profession and to live like everyone else in the country he was going to make his home.

For some time now, with the assistance of his family, he had been saving money for his travelling expenses. This would include money to pay the traders who helped him cross the border, to pay for the train ticket from Memel to his port of embarkation, for the boat ticket from Europe to England, from England to Cape Town and from Cape Town to Ceres, as well as funds for his sustenance on the journey.

By the middle of April 1897, Leib was ready. His first priority was to get on a boat. Although 18 years old, he looked much younger, as he was only 5 feet tall, slim, with a mop of black hair and dark brown eyes. He obtained a berth in steerage as a minor aged 14 out of Hamburg via Southampton to Cape Town. The vessel was sailing from Hamburg to Southampton on 5 June 1897. At the same time, he purchased his rail ticket from Memel to Hamburg. Before he could board the train, he had to submit to a medical examination by the doctors for the Union Line, who were the agents of the boat on which he was to travel. But first, he had to make his own way across the border.

From the moment Leib crossed the border into Germany, until he reached his point of embarkation, the German Jewish Associations, controlled and mobilised from Berlin, would probably have assisted him. The city of Hamburg provided a site on America Quay on which eight sheds were erected that could house 1,400 people. Migrants paid one mark a day for accommodation and food. Trains were directed straight to the sheds and steerage passengers were not allowed to leave the train until they reached the Quay. On arrival, all the migrants were subject to a medical examination and they had their clothes disinfected.

We do not know whether Leib took a photograph of his mother with him on his journey. My cousin, David Kapelus, son of Morris Isaac (Mokey to us), Leib's eldest, found a photograph of her, in a family album kept by his father. We think it dates from about 1911, when Mere-Mine left for New York. Pese Liba lived to the ripe old age of 75, dying of pneumonia in Plungyan on 5 April 1923.

The Sea Voyage

Leib reached Hamburg in time to board the Union Line ship *Greek*, sailing under a British flag, which departed from Hamburg to Southampton on 5 June 1897. A copy of the original *Verzeichnis* or manifest shows passenger no. 17 as Kapolus, Leib, aged 14 from Plungyan and an *Arbeiter*, labourer or worker. The master of the vessel was a Captain G.W. Armstrong.

When the *Greek* reached Southampton we do not know, but the records show that the boat sailed for South Africa under the same master on 12 June 1897, with L. Kapolus sailing steerage. The passenger list known as Schedule B states the 'Total number of Statute Adults exclusive of Master, Crew and Cabin Passengers which the Ship can legally carry' to be 238, but there were only 192 such passengers on the voyage. Most were bound for the Cape, although after the boat had docked in Cape Town it was also calling at Algoa Bay (Port Elizabeth), East London and Durban. The vessel carried food for 200 'statute adults' for a journey of 49 days.

The *Greek*, launched on 17 May 1893, was part of a fleet known as 'The Gs', as all her sister ships' names began with *G*. These were new and steerage was more comfortable than on the older ships, steerage passengers being allowed onto the deck. Specially commissioned for immigrants, the *Greek*, like her sister ships the *Gaul* and the *Goth*, could carry 52 first-class, 66 second-class, 60 third-class and a large number of 'open-berth' passengers. These boats were built for intermediate service between Southampton, Cape Town and Port Elizabeth and Durban, with a shallow draft for the ports beyond Cape Town. Other sister ships the *Guelph*, the *Gascon*, the *Gaika*, the *Goorkha*, the *German*, the *Galeka* and the *Galicia* were successful cargo/passenger carriers on the UK to Africa route. (On the merger of the Union and Castle Lines in 1900, the *Greek* continued to sail under the flag of the combined enterprise, Union Castle Lines, undertook some troop-carrying duties in the Boer War, then resumed intermediate sailings.)

The journey to Cape Town took over three weeks, leaving Southampton in summer, travelling through the tropics and crossing the equator. The only direct information about Leib's journey is the information contained in Schedule B. From this passenger list we can see that there were 151 passengers who travelled steerage, of whom 93 are described as 'Foreign'; that is, not English, Scots or Irish. In fact, these passengers form a roll call of very familiar South African Jewish names. Leib was among Yiddish speakers from Lithuania and Latvia, some of whom had also boarded the *Greek* in Hamburg (according to the manifest). By and large they would have been observant Jews who ate only kosher food and they would have wanted to maintain the daily ritual of saying the morning (*shachrit*), afternoon (*mincha*) and evening (*ma'ariv*) prayers. The women would have wanted to light the Friday night candles (Shabbat) and say the traditional blessing.

Observing these rituals was not easy, as we discover from an article by Gwynne Schrire.[53] As she makes clear from the outset, little literature and few records exist about this epic journey. Using anecdotal evidence taken by the Kaplan Centre History Collection, published reminiscences and other sources, she gives one a sense of what it was like travelling steerage on one of these vessels.

The overwhelming and universal memory of the steerage passengers was the lack of space or privacy. One passenger described the experience as follows:

> *... my head against somebody's feet, my feet against somebody's head and my mother and her cousin could not take down there – they slept on the decks. That smell! All humanity crowded together.*

Lighting candles on a Friday night was forbidden because of the danger of fire, although some women ignored the rule.

The food was monotonous and poor quality, consisting in the main of salt herring, boiled potatoes, black bread and occasionally cabbage. The other memory that seemed still to rankle was of the lack of table manners and the almost depraved and despicable behaviour at meal times. One passenger remembered:

> *... the food was not so bad, but the people! We were sitting down at the table to eat – herring, potatoes – and a man took a herring, tore it in half and started eating it. I was ashamed to be Jewish the way they behaved at table. If you did not grab quickly, you did not get."*

All of this must have been a difficult and frightening time for an 18-year-old who had never been out of his home town. My grandfather Leib Kapelus finally arrived in Cape Town in July 1897, in the middle of the Cape winter.

The Migration of the Dorfman Family

The migration of Louis Dorfman and Rachel Reiff was very different from that of Leib Kapelus.

They knew that they could not get married in Lithuania and it seems they decided that the UK offered them the best chance of tying the knot, as well as having a better future than if they remained in Shkud. Louis was a master cabinetmaker, a skilled artisan, who could ply his trade in London. However, he also did not serve in the Tsar's army, so he too would have had to leave Lithuania by crossing the border illegally. Rachel would have been able to leave the country through official channels provided that she satisfied Russian exit requirements.

How Louis and Rachel got to the UK we do not know. To date no record has been found of where they boarded a ship, nor any recording their arrival. All we do know is that they left Shkud some time between 1899 and 1900 bound for London, where they married at the East London Synagogue in Mile End on 4 March 1900.

Why had Louis and Rachel decided to stay in London, when many of their generation were making for South Africa? The reason is probably that the Anglo-Boer War started in 1899 and migration to South Africa dropped to a trickle.

What's in a name?

The date and place of the Dorfmans' wedding are confirmed by the birth certificate of their daughter, my mother Mary Kapelus (née Dorfman).

However, this birth certificate shows my Bobba's maiden surname as Hudskin. I had always thought that her maiden name was Reiff. How could she have been a Miss Hudskin?

Her brother was Simon Reiff, who had owned the Railway Hotel at Kalabaskraal, a railway siding between Cape Town and Malmesbury, from some time in the 1930s to the early 1950s. As a child, I went with my parents to visit my mother's Uncle Simon at the hotel, as it was on our route from Cape Town to Van Rhynsdorp. Later, Simon moved to a flat in Marais Road, Sea Point and then to a house in Green Point, a suburb of Cape Town. Our family frequently visited Uncle Simon and Aunty Malie at both these addresses. Simon's daughter also lived in Cape Town and her maiden name had been Reiff.

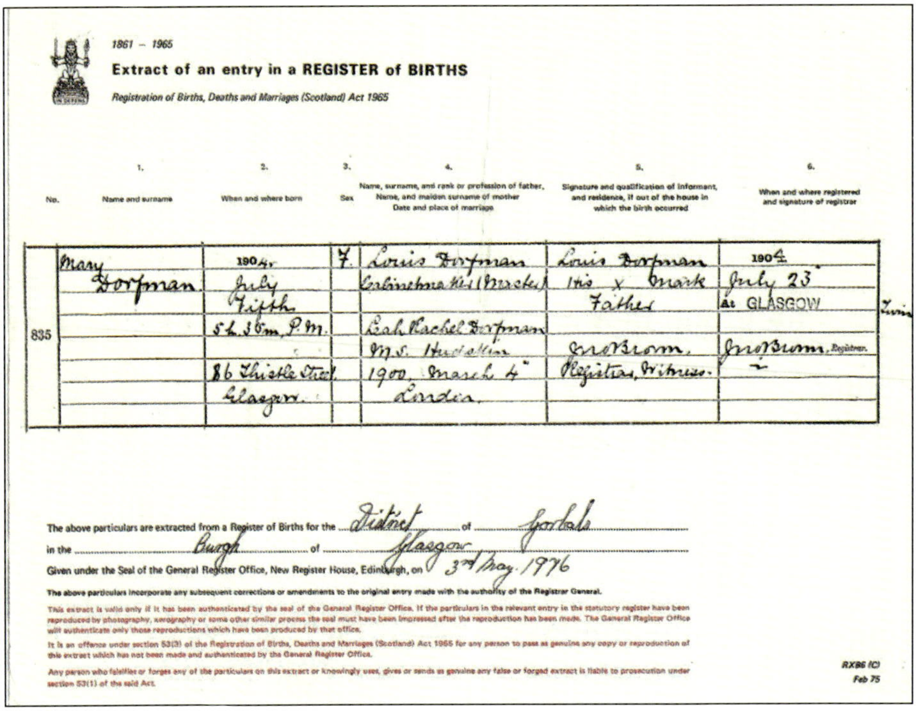

1861 – 1965

Extract of an entry in a REGISTER of BIRTHS

Registration of Births, Deaths and Marriages (Scotland) Act 1965

No.	1. Name and surname	2. When and where born	3. Sex	4. Name, surname, and rank or profession of father, Name, and maiden surname of mother, Date and place of marriage	5. Signature and qualification of informant, and residence, if out of the house in which the birth occurred	6. When and where registered and signature of registrar
835	Mary Dorfman	1904. July Fifth 5h. 30m. P.M. 86 Thistle Street, Glasgow.	F.	Louis Dorfman Cabinetmaker (Master) Leah Rachel Dorfman M.S. Hudskin 1900, March 4th London	Louis Dorfman his x mark Father Jno Brown, Registrar, Witness.	1904. July 23rd At GLASGOW Jno Brown, Registrar.

The above particulars are extracted from a Register of Births for the District of Gorbals in the Burgh of Glasgow

Given under the Seal of the General Register Office, New Register House, Edinburgh, on 3rd May. 1976

The above particulars incorporate any subsequent corrections or amendments to the original entry made with the authority of the Registrar General.

This extract is valid only if it has been authenticated by the seal of the General Register Office. If the particulars in the relevant entry in the statutory register have been reproduced by photography, xerography or some other similar process the seal must have been impressed after the reproduction has been made. The General Register Office will authenticate only those reproductions which have been produced by that office.

It is an offence under section 53(3) of the Registration of Births, Deaths and Marriages (Scotland) Act 1965 for any person to pass as genuine any copy or reproduction of this extract which has not been made and authenticated by the General Register Office.

Any person who falsifies or forges any of the particulars on this extract or knowingly uses, gives or sends as genuine any false or forged extract is liable to prosecution under section 53(1) of the said Act.

RXB6 (C)
Feb 75

Birth certificate of my mother Mary Kapelus (née Dorfman)

Who was the Leah Rachel Hudskin who had married my Zeida? I was confused as well as bemused.

With all the changes of name, I decided to search the archives in Cape Town for information on Simon Reiff. Most interestingly, I found the Passenger Registration Form for the *Garke*, from which it appears that Simkus Reef travelled third class from Tilbury (UK) to Cape Town with his wife Johanna and his two daughters Chaika (8 years old) and Roche (aged 7). Simkus gives his age next birthday as 45 and that of his wife as 38. He was born in Zedok (Zidikai), Lithuania, and travelled on a Lithuanian passport issued in Kaunas on 25 May 1925. His occupation was dealer and he had £105 in his possession. The *Garke* arrived in Cape Town on 29 June 1925 and the remarks of the immigration officer noted that Simkus Reef had an affidavit confirming that he was 'coming to his brother in law, Michael Balkin, in King Williams Town.'

How do we know this Simon Reiff is the brother of Leah Rachel Dorfman? In a file headed 'Immigration Papers Mr and Mrs Reiff', I found an application for a passport of the Union of South Africa dated 19 August 1946, made by a Mr Simon Reiff of 5 Marais Mansions, Marais Road, Sea Point. This was the very address at which we visited him. He gives his place of birth as Zidikai, Lithuania and his date of birth as 16 June 1883. He provides no information about his parents. The photograph with the application indeed shows the man I knew as my mother's Uncle Simon. A photograph of him, together with a note addressed to my parents is shown below.

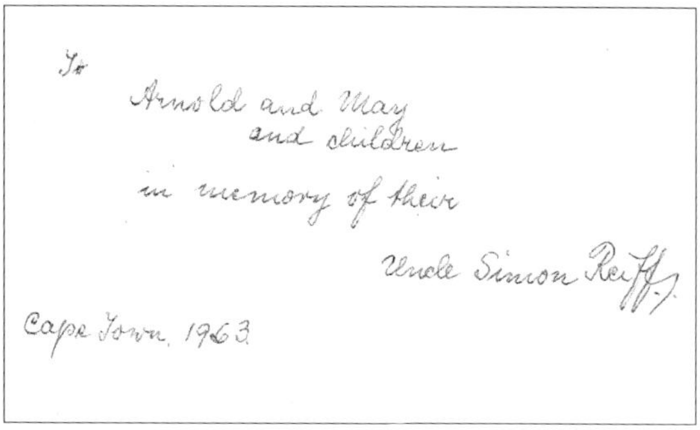

To
Arnold and May
and children
in memory of their
Uncle Simon Reiff.
Cape Town, 1963

Simon Reiff, who I knew as my mother's Uncle Simon

Mrs Amalie Reiff, formally Joseph born Flecker, made a similar application. The photograph accompanying the application is that of Aunt Malie, whom Uncle Simon married after the death of his first wife Johanna.

The identity of my Zeida's wife was not the only mystery I had uncovered in the records. My mother had always celebrated her birthday on 21 June and gave her date of birth as 21 June 1914, so my sister and I grew up believing that our mother was some six months older than our father. What a shock to discover from her birth certificate that she was in fact born on 5 July 1904, ten years earlier. As she was always so active and vital in all she did, it was difficult to believe that she was not six months but actually ten and a half years older than my father. I knew that her twin sister Crayna had died on 21 June 1905, so had she chosen to use that date in Crayna's memory?

To return to Rachel, could the marriage registration officer have made a mistake? I decided to compare the details given in column 4 of my mother's birth certificate with those for her siblings, to make sure. I obtained the birth certificates of my uncles Abraham (known to us as Alex), born in London on

23 February 1901, Morris, born in Glasgow, Scotland on 17 April 1902, and Isaac Israel (who changed his name by deed poll to George Graham), born in Glasgow on 7 May 1903. On each of them the date of marriage was identical, 4 March 1900, London, and the mother's name was Leah Rachel Dorfman, maiden surname Hudskin.

So there had been no mistake. What I now needed was a copy of my grandparents' marriage certificate, which I duly obtained this from the National Archives in Kew. It showed that the marriage was solemnised at the East End Synagogue in the parish of Mile End Town in the County of London on 4 March 1900 between Sam Dorfman, aged 21 years, a cabinet maker, and Leah Hudskin, aged 21 years, a teller hand. The father of the bridegroom is given as Hyman Dorfman, a dealer, and that of the bride as Abraham Hudskin (deceased), a bookmaker.

What now appeared to be certain was that Sam Dorfman and Leah Hudskin, the couple who were married on 4 March 1900 at the Mile End Synagogue, were my grandparents Louis Dorfman and Leah Rachel Reiff. What was also becoming clear was that the personal information they gave to the marriage officer was not correct and did not match their actual identities.

We also know from the records that Samuel Leib (Louis) Dorfman was born in Shkud in 1879 to Joseph and Eva (Chava) Dorfman. This is further supported by a number of official documents. Joseph Dorfman died in Glasgow on 19 January 1915. His son, Samuel Dorfman, reported his death. Joseph Dorfman was 64 when he died, putting his birth date at 1851. The death notice filed on the death of my Zeida, Samuel Louis Dorfman, in Cape Town in a motor accident on 2 April 1953 clearly confirms the names of his parents as well as his date of birth.

So why would he give his father's name on his marriage certificate as Hyman Dorfman and not Joseph? Was there such a person and if so, was he at the marriage ceremony and under the *chupa* with the bride and groom? All this confusion will remain, as there is no person alive today who can give us any explanation.

Where did Rachel get the name Hudskin? We do not have her birth records, but we do have the death notice filed on her demise in Cape Town on 11 August 1951. It shows that she was born in Zadek (Zidikai), Lithuania in September 1884 to Abraham and Annie Reiff. It further states that she was married to Louis Dorfman in London in 1900. So her father was Abraham Reiff, not Abraham Hudskin. Why did she tell the marriage officer she was Leah Hudskin? We know her father (Hudskin) was not at the marriage ceremony, as he is recorded on the marriage certificate as being deceased. From her death certificate we can also see that at the time of her marriage she was 16 years old, not the 21 stated on her marriage certificate.

Why all the subterfuge? Perhaps there was some truth to the family rumour that Leah Rachel Reiff was too closely related by blood to Samuel Louis Dorfman for them to be legally married.

To try to answer this question, I searched for as much information as I could obtain on Chava (Eva) Dorfman, mother of Louis and wife of Joseph. The only official document available is the notice of death filed in Glasgow. According to this, Eva died on 29 December 1926 at the age of 62, which would put her date of birth in 1864. Her parents were Abraham and Kranie Reiff. Abraham was a general dealer.

There is a question mark over her stated age of 62 years, however. We know that she gave birth to a son, Samuel Louis, in August 1879. Louis died in April 1953 at the age of 73 years and 9 months. His age was given as 57 on the passenger list of the *Kenilworth Castle*, the ship on which he sailed to South Africa in 1936. This also confirms his date of birth as 1879.

If Eva was born in 1864, she would have been 15 in 1879. Say that she got married the year before, in 1878. It is unlikely, even at that time, that she would have been married at the age of 14. It seems that she made out she was three years younger than she was, because a search of other records puts her date of birth at 1861, which is more likely.

Eva was born in Zadek; her father was Abraham Reiff, her mother was Kranie. Rachel was born in Zadek; her father was Abraham Reiff, her mother was Annie (perhaps an Anglicised version of the Yiddish name Kranie?). Rachel was 23 years younger than Eva. Both Reiff girls having Abraham as their father would seem to be too much of a coincidence for it to be a different man, particularly in a small village. So were Eva and Rachel sisters? Was Eva's son Louis marrying his mother's sister, his aunt? Is this the reason they chose to marry in London, not in Shkud, and to give false information?

The love affair between Louis and Rachel was no secret. Joseph and Eva would have known of their relationship and probably were aware of their plans to leave Shkud for England. What we do not know and will never be able to find out is how Joseph and Eva reacted to this incestuous relationship. Their son was in love with and running away with his aunt, his mother's sister. It is highly unlikely that they would have approved of the relationship or their plans to marry. The Jews in Shkud in 1897 numbered 2,292: a small, tightly knit community where almost everybody would have known the Dorfman family. Joseph and Eva were probably mortified by the relationship. Perhaps they thought that the further away from Shkud the better!

There was a custom in the *shtetlach* that if one had a near-death experience one would change one's name, in order to fool the angel of death into thinking one was someone different. The name usually chosen was Chaim, which meant life – Hyman in Yiddish. Is this why Louis named his father Hyman not Joseph? Was he seeking reconciliation?

I can only conjecture as, sadly, I can no longer ask any of them why they acted as they did. With the deliberately inaccurate names provided to the marriage officer, it would have been impossible for anyone in London to cross-check the information and discover the subterfuge.

The Move to Glasgow

The Dorfmans in Glasgow

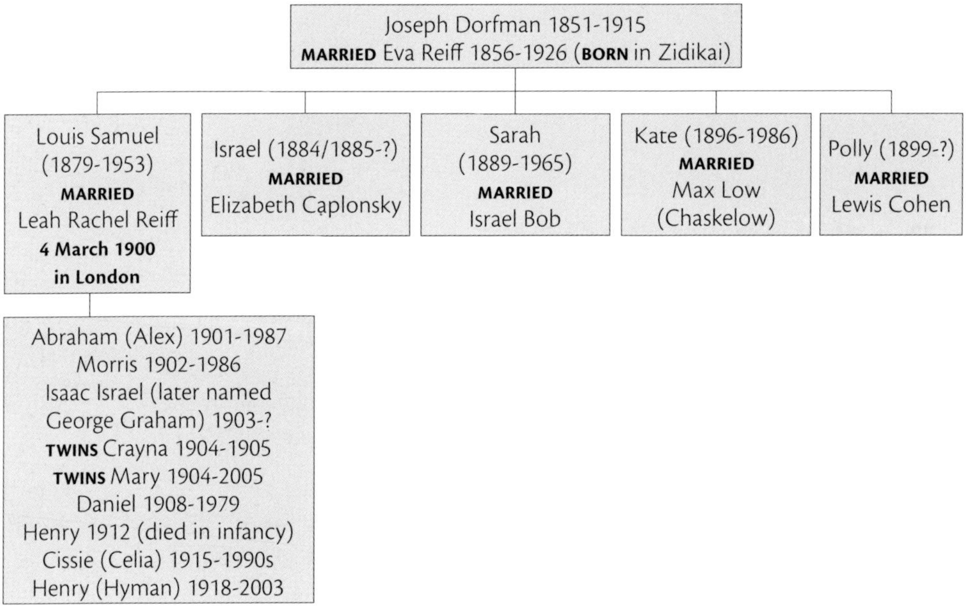

After their wedding, the couple lived in the East End of London like many of their compatriots, where on 23 February 1901 Rachel gave birth to a boy, Abraham, known to the family as Alex. The pair and their newly born son did not remain in London for long. By 1902 they were living in Glasgow, Scotland, where their second child, Morris, was born on 17 April 1902. A third boy, Isaac Israel, later known as George Graham Dorfman (he changed his forenames by deed poll), was born in Glasgow on 7 May 1903.

So within three years of their marriage, Louis and Rachel had three boys. It was quite a shock when on 5 July 1904 they were blessed with twin girls, Crayna and Mary; Mary Dorfman became my mother. Sadly, Crayna died on 21 June 1905, a few weeks before her first birthday. Perhaps she was named after Rachel's mother Kranie.

My mother, Mary Dorfman, aged 1 year

By the time of the twins' birth, Louis and Rachel, now the proud parents of five children, had established themselves and settled well in Glasgow.

It seems that time and distance had helped Louis to make peace with his own parents, as he arranged for Joseph and Eva, as well as his siblings, Israel, Sarah, Kate and Polly, to join him and Rachel in Glasgow. Joseph was by now 54 and Eva some years younger at 43. Israel was 19, Sarah 15 and Kate 8, with Polly the baby at 5 years old. They all made their homes in Glasgow. How did Eva react when she was reunited with her sister who was also her daughter-in-law and the mother of her grandchildren? Time has made these questions unanswerable.

It was not long before Sarah and her brother Israel were both married. Sarah, aged 18, married Israel Bob in Glasgow in 1907; a year later Israel, aged 23, married Elizabeth Caplonsky in Edinburgh. The younger sisters both married in 1919, Kate to Max Chaskelow (who changed their name to Low) in Belfast and Polly to Lewis Cohen in Glasgow.

Louis and Rachel had moved to Edinburgh and were living at 22 Salisbury Street some time before Danny was born in 1908. Henry Dorfman was born on 27 March 1912 (sadly, he died as an infant in the year of his birth). Cissie (known to us as Celia) was born while they were still living at this address on 12 May 1915.

By this time, Louis had established himself as an antique restorer of some note and was building his business as an antique and furniture dealer. They had also moved house, and by the time their youngest and last child, Hyman Henry, was born on 16 May 1918, the family's address was 20 Marchmont Crescent, Edinburgh, a home often referred to by my mother. Henry, although mentally handicapped, had inherited some of his father's skill as a cabinetmaker. He lived much of his life in a government facility for mentally handicapped persons, where he worked in a workshop employing his skills.

My mother, Mary (Mae), was by now a young teenager of 14. She grew up in Edinburgh, attending a local school. Her first work experience was as a shop assistant in the town. However, the family seemed to have been split between Glasgow and Edinburgh. Louis' parents, Joseph and Eva, continued to live in Glasgow, as did Louis' siblings. Morris and the other children also moved

Eva and Joseph Dorfman, a photograph probably taken shortly after they arrived in Scotland in 1904/05

to Edinburgh, but Alex seems to have remained in Glasgow until he migrated to Canada.

To continue the story of Mae I have to jump forward, first to 1949 and then to 1978, so that readers can appreciate the intrigue woven by Rachel Leah Dorfman, Mae's mother, and the influence she had on the family.

Introducing Cecil (Carl)

When I was growing up I obviously knew that my mother was Scottish, but she did not tell us a great deal about herself. In 1949 when I was 7, a young man from Scotland called Cecil (I did not know his surname then) arrived to visit us in Van Rhynsdorp. I was told that he was my cousin, and I accepted this without giving the matter another thought.

Cecil settled in Cape Town and I vaguely remember attending his wedding. In January 1952, I started my schooling in Cape Town as a boarder at South African College School (SACS), which was then in the Gardens, a suburb in the city bowl, so called because it was near the Public Gardens and a short walk down the Avenue to the Houses of Parliament. The Gardens Synagogue was nearby, as were the National Art Gallery and the Museum. On the odd occasion my mother came to Cape Town, she would fetch me for the afternoon and Cecil would take us for a drive. A special treat was stopping for a milkshake at the Doll's House, a drive-in eatery. Cecil and my mother were adults so I, as a 10-year-old boy, paid little attention to how they related to each other or their conversation. I cannot recall seeing Cecil again during my youth.

Many years later, in 1978, when I was married with two children and living in Constantia, Cape Town, my cousin Brenda Madeisky (née Dorfman), eldest daughter of my Uncle Alex, often visited us in the evening for a chat. On one such evening, we were having tea and discussing the television programme *Dallas*. South Africa only entered the world of television in 1976, so everyone watched such an American soap with fascination. In the episode screened days before her visit, there was a revelation that a farmhand was the son of one of the main protagonists. I questioned how it was possible that all the characters lived cheek by jowl and did not know his parentage.

I had been in Johannesburg about two weeks earlier and my mother had asked me to contact Cecil, who then lived there. I had not had time to do so, but he was in the back of my mind. It suddenly dawned on me that I did not quite understand our relationship and I asked Brenda how Cecil was our cousin. Whose child was he?

Brenda looked at me as though I was mad. Incredulous, she asked:

> *'Do you really not know who he is?'*
>
> *'I have no idea at all,' I replied.*
>
> *My wife Esther added that it was something that had puzzled her for a long time too.*
>
> *'He is your brother!' Brenda blurted out.*
>
> *'What? That's impossible. How can that be?' Esther and I asked at the same time.*

Brenda told us that my mother had married a Mr Linkerman and that Cecil, now known as Carl, was born about two years after the wedding. She knew little more than that the marriage had not lasted, as my mother and her husband divorced when Cecil was young.

Esther and I were determined to get as much information as we could without embarrassing either my mother, who was by now 74 years old, or my much younger father, who apparently did not know of this prior marriage. The one person we could speak to was Cecil.

Carl and Esther in Cape Town, 1980

I was visiting Johannesburg quite regularly on business. On my next trip I made contact with him by telephone. I said that Brenda had told me of our relationship, and he was relieved that a secret he had kept for so long was at last out in the open. We both resolved not to embarrass our mother and we met whenever I was in Johannesburg. Our relationship was warm and respectful, but always a little restrained, and we were guarded in what we said to each other. He and Michelle, his third wife and business partner, visited Esther and me in Cape Town.

Cecil and I were seldom alone when we saw each other in Johannesburg, as Michelle was inevitably present. Consequently, we somehow never got the opportunity of discussing his and my mother's past. I could not resist asking him why he said he was my 'cousin' and my mother's nephew. His answer revealed a great deal about our Bobba (Leah Rachel) and came as a shock to me.

Cecil told me that on arriving in Cape Town in 1949, he had stayed with our grandparents. It was only then that he found out that his mother, Mae, had remarried. Our Bobba also told him that my father did not know our mother had been previously married and divorced, or that she had a son. What is more, my father also was not aware of Mae's real age; as I have already outlined, she had given her date of birth as 21 June 1914 and not 5 July 1904.

Bobba asked Cecil not to ruin things for Mae, as she was now very happy. To account for his visit to our home, he pretended to be Mae's nephew. Cecil explained that the whole charade was very painful, particularly since it made him feel rejected by his mother. I was surprised at how angry this revelation made me.

At that point, I took no steps to get any official documentation of the prior marriage or of the divorce and Cecil's birth. It was not that I was not interested, but rather that both Esther and I were focused on our plans to leave South Africa and did not want to divert any of our energy. Cecil and I did not discuss the Linkerman marriage, the divorce or his early years. It just seemed too painful for him and embarrassing for me.

Some years later, in February 1995, my father passed away suddenly at the age of 80. By then Esther and I were living in London, and we had resolved to bring my mother, who was then 91 years old, to live with us. My mother had a South African passport, on which she could enter the UK, but was unlikely to be granted permanent residence. I decided to ask for Cecil's help in obtaining a British passport for her, to which she was entitled by virtue of having been born in the UK.

This proved to be much more difficult than I had ever imagined. The British government required me to prove that the Mary Dorfman born in Glasgow on 5 July 1904 was the same person as Mary Kapelus, whose date of birth on her current marriage certificate and her Book of Life was shown as 21 June 1914. There were no official documents in South Africa to show that Mary Kapelus (née Dorfman) was born on 5 July 1904, that she was a divorcée, having married a Mr Linkerman in Glasgow, Scotland, and that she was the mother of another son.

I needed Cecil's help. By 1995, he was living in Murfreesboro, Tennessee, USA and had divorced Michelle some years earlier. Luckily, we were still corresponding on an irregular basis, so I had his address.

I decided to ask a firm of solicitors in Edinburgh to obtain copies of the marriage certificate of Mary Dorfman and Hyman Linkerman, the birth certificate of Cecil Linkerman and proof of the divorce. I was in South Africa at the time and the documents I needed were in Scotland. It took some three weeks to get what I required.

The marriage certificate showed that Hyman Linkerman, aged 22, waterproof cutter, bachelor, married Marie Dorfman, aged 21, both of 40 Regent Park Square, Glasgow on 6 June 1925. (The spelling of her first name is different to that on her birth certificate (Mary). Her age is incorrect as she was not yet 21, her birthday was a month later on 5 July 1925.) Their son, Abraham Cecil Linkerman, was born on 19 December 1926 at 102 South Portland Street, Glasgow.

Obtaining proof of the divorce was somewhat more difficult. As I did not have any information about where or when or what court had granted the divorce, the search took some time. The Register of Corrected Entries for the District of the Gorbals in the Burgh of Glasgow recorded: '1 February 1936: Decree of Divorce was pronounced by Lord Wark, Ordinary, in an action at instance of Hyman Linkerman otherwise Lincoln, Tailor's Cutter, 26 Dundreman Road, Langside, Glagow: against Mary Dorfman or Linkerman otherwise Lincoln, 41 Regents Park Square, Glasgow.'

This still did not prove that the Mary Dorfman mentioned in all of the above documents was my mother, Mary Kapelus née Dorfman. The only person who could establish that link was Abraham Cecil Linkerman/Lincoln, now known as Carl Linkerman. I drafted an affidavit in which Carl traced the history as set out above with the certified marriage, birth and divorce certificates attached. In addition, he gave evidence of his mother's migration from Scotland to South Africa and her marriage to Arnold Kapelus, my father.

Cecil and I had worked together to put our mother's official record straight. For the first time, we shared an experience as (half) brothers. It was now much easier to speak of the difficult past, which we did when I visited him in Murfreesboro in June 2001. Sadly, he died suddenly in his sleep in September of that year, three months before his 75th birthday.

What I learnt from Cecil then was that the Linkerman family had lived in Glasgow, but Bobba, Rachel Dorfman, interfered in their affairs, causing friction and tension. An otherwise happy marriage became increasingly unhappy. The terms of the religious divorce (*Get*) were that Mae would have custody of Cecil until he was 10 years old, whereupon custody would revert to his father so that he could prepare for his barmitzvah.

Cecil and Mae lived in Edinburgh with Bobba and Zeida, where they were very happy. Shortly after his 10th birthday, men in suits arrived at the family home and took Cecil, bewildered and confused, to live with his father, who had by this time remarried. Cecil described this to me with tears in his eyes. He said that Mae was hysterical, sobbing bitterly. Her sister Celia (Cissie) tried to comfort her, but Bobba and Zeida played no part. Cecil could not remember anyone preparing him for this shocking event.

Luckily, his father, Hyman, was a kindly man, as was his wife, and Cecil was nurtured and well cared for. He turned 18 on 19 December 1944, while the Second World War was still raging. Like all young men of that age, he was subject to conscription. He entered service in the Merchant Navy and travelled to South Africa as soon as he could after his discharge.

Mae, now divorced and without Cecil, was free to pursue her own happiness. However, as we shall see, she still seemed to be very much under the influence of her mother Rachel.

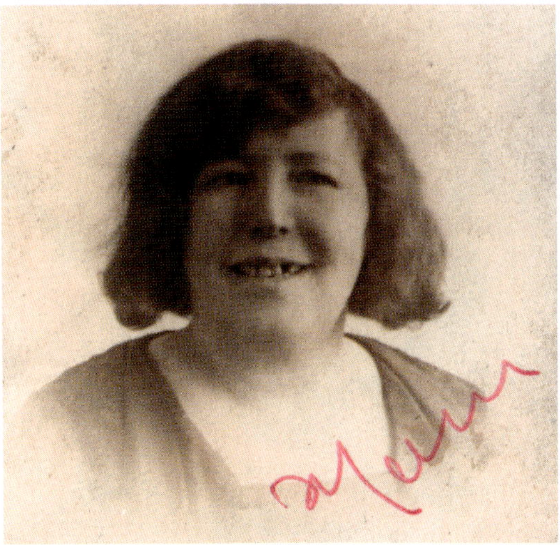

An undated photograph of Rachel Leah Dorfman as a young mother living in Glasgow, Scotland

Louis and Rachel Dorfman walking in Edinburgh, dated 1934 by my mother, Mae

George, seated fourth from the left in the third row, with his hands on the shoulders of the soldier in front of him.

A young George

Hendry

Celia [undated]

Celia and Mae, 1960

The Dorfmans
Back L to R: Alex, Ida (Alex's wife), Unknown, Polly (Morris's wife), Morris
Middle L to R: Brenda (Alex and Ida's daughter)
Front L to R: George (Israel Isaac) holding Max (Morris's son), Evelyn (Alex and Ida's daughter)

Danny and family

Taken at Balloch. 1946.
Geo - his wife Gladys
his child Jean &
my Evelyn the
nice looking child.
& myself.
Alex

PART II

Jewish Life in South Africa

A Basic History of South Africa

By the time Leib Kapelus arrived in Cape Town in July 1897, South Africa had moved from being an agrarian society to having the beginnings of an industrial economy, after the discovery of diamonds north of the Orange River at Kimberley (1867-71) and gold in the Transvaal Republic (ZAR) near Johannesburg (1886). The exploitation of these resources started the industrialisation of the country and resulted in a sea change in its socio-economic and political structure.

South Africa had also changed from a society with no professing Jews during the period 1652-1806 to one with a fast-burgeoning Jewish population.

In the 50 or so years before Leib's arrival, the political, economic and social life of South Africa had thus undergone major changes. It had moved from a slave-owning white population to a society that had banned slavery; and from a population living primarily in the Western and Eastern Cape to one where the hinterland was occupied and settled by Afrikaners in two waves of mass movement known as *Die Groot Trek*, the Great Trek.

The origins of South Africa's racial, cultural and language tensions undoubtedly were sown soon after the Dutch occupied the Cape in 1652. Those first Dutch settlers were not alone in southern Africa; in fact they had invaded the space of those already living there, as did the *Voortrekkers* (those who participated in *Die Groot Trek*). These tensions were exacerbated by English-speaking immigrants from Britain arriving in the Cape after 1820, who did not assimilate into the existing Afrikaner society.

Inevitably, there are differing interpretations of and great sensitivity about many of these events. In common with all the people of South Africa, the lives of the Kirsch, Kapelus, Hotz and Dorfman families were shaped by the course of the country's history and by the political and social issues that flowed from it. To appreciate their acculturation and their attitude to South African life, it is therefore necessary to look at some of these events.

The Portuguese Search for Spices and the Cape They Found

Europe's first direct contacts with the East had been over land and not sea. Spices for cosmetic, medical and culinary uses and related products from India, Ceylon

(Sri Lanka), the Moluccas (Indonesia) and the Malay Peninsula were imported by the caravan routes overland to ports accessible from the Mediterranean and the Black Sea, as was the silk brought in from China. Gold from the Niger region of Africa was transported by the trans-Saharan caravans to Alexandria on the Mediterranean.

By 1400, these overland routes were no longer secure or available. The rise of the isolationist Ming Dynasty in China severely disrupted the silk trade. The spice trade was adversely affected by the insecurity of the steppe route via Muscovy, Novgorod and the eastern outposts of the Hanseatic League, caused by plague, banditry and hostility to Christians with the rise of Islam in the Mongol Khanates. To find and pioneer the new ocean routes needed to reach the East Indies, the trading nations would have to overcome their fear and superstitions that the oceans of the world were not navigable.

Portugal, despite having a long Atlantic coastline, needed an alternative route to the gold, spice and silk so desired by all in Europe, as its overland route westwards had been blocked by Spain. Its use of the Mediterranean was severely curtailed by the might of the Italian states, thus the only option open to Portugal was via the Atlantic Ocean. It also needed political will and drive as well as sufficient capital to invest in better technology for sailing the oceans.

By the 1400s, new ships and new techniques of long-range navigation for oceanic sailing had become available. Portugal also had a person of power who could drive and finance the research and exploration of the Atlantic: Prince Henry. Dom Enrique, the fourth son of the King of Portugal, Joao I, established a school of astronomy and navigation at Sagres in 1418. Here he began a systematic, government-subsidised programme of research and improvement of navigational techniques, as well as financing and encouraging expeditions.

Prince Henry brought together some of the finest mathematicians, astronomers and geographers, including the most famous cartographer of the time, Jehuda Cresques. Called the 'map Jew', Cresques, subsequently known as Mestre Jacome, became director of the Academy. After Prince Henry's death in 1460, his brother King Joao II and his successor Manuel II pressed on with his work and continued to employ Jews.

A commission of five specialists on maritime matters was set up, including Joseph Vecinho, a Jewish astronomer, and Moses, a mathematician. It was to this commission that Columbus put his plan for finding Cathay by sailing west, subsequently complaining that the 'Jew Joseph' had rejected his proposals.

To find the sea route to the East Indies, the Portuguese had to explore further and further south along the west coast of Africa. In 1473, they crossed the equator; in 1487, Bartholomew Diaz left Portugal on an expedition to find a southern route to the Indian Ocean. Later that year he reached Angola, landed at present-day Walvis Bay in Namibia and in 1488 rounded the Cape of Good Hope and was in the Indian Ocean, where he found that the coast runs northeast.

On 8 July 1497, Dom Vasco da Gama set sail from Lisbon with a fleet of four ships and twenty cannon, with Bartholomew Diaz as pilot as far as the Canary Islands. On 7 November 1497, the party landed at St Helena Bay, 200 kilometres north of the Cape of Good Hope. Two days later, they rounded the Cape and landed at Mossel Bay, where they traded trinkets for an ox. On 25 December 1497, they sighted land and named it Natal. On they sailed and reached Calicut on 20 May 1498. Da Gama followed the same route back to Portugal, although due to a loss of men he was down to two ships. He rounded the Cape on his way home on 20 March 1499, arriving back in Lisbon on 18 September 1499.

The voyages undertaken by Bartholomew Diaz and Vasco da Gama (and also Columbus) did much more than discover the Cape of Good Hope and the route to India via the Atlantic and Indian Oceans. In 1522, a mere 23 years after Da Gama's return to Lisbon, Magellan circumnavigated the world and demonstrated that all the great oceans were interconnected. For the first time, maps reflected the basic structure of the oceans and continents of the world as it actually existed. These voyages heralded a new age of discovery and exploration made possible by the development of new maritime skills and an enhanced knowledge of geography. Europe now saw the shaping of the age of the professional explorer and navigator.

This period of discovery had changed the course of history. The world no longer came to Europe; the Europeans, particularly those with direct access to the Atlantic, Spain, Portugal, France, Holland and England, went out to the world and took possession of it. Discovery would be followed by conquest and colonisation.

Ironically, at the very time these momentous journeys were being planned and undertaken with a real and substantial contribution from Jewish cartographers, mathematicians and astronomers, the Jews of Spain (1492) and Portugal (1495) were being forcibly expelled.

Once the Portuguese reached Africa, their settlements and interests on the West Coast went from Elmina in the Gulf of Guinea, founded and fortified as early as 1481, southwards to Sao Tome, the Congo and Luanda in Angola, which became an important slave-trading post. From Sofala, at the mouth of the Zambezi River, they occupied by 1505 all the way up the east coast, including Mozambique, Mombasa and well north of Malindi in the north of Kenya. For approximately 100 years, Portugal dominated and virtually controlled trade in the Indian Ocean through its navy and the ports under its command, extorting tolls and duties from local shipping. The Portuguese trading monopoly was not only with Europe but also between Asian countries.

Having a base at the Cape of Good Hope played no part in the Portuguese scheme of things, however, since they saw the slave trade along the western seaboard and the trading opportunities of East Africa with Asia and the Gulf as preferable.[54]

The Dutch East India Company Moves In: 1594-1795

Because of their successful European trade, Dutch merchants had acquired substantial amounts of capital and were seeking new investment opportunities. In 1580, Portugal and Spain united, denying the Dutch their lucrative re-export trade of oriental goods from Lisbon to northern Europe. This galvanised the Dutch to venture into establishing an Eastern trading base. They were well placed to do so with their powerful navy, years of trading experience and access to capital to finance new business opportunities.

After an initial successful foray to the East Indies in 1594, so many Dutch merchants tried their luck in this area, which had been dominated for 100 years by the Portuguese, that the competition thus generated posed a risk to the ventures' profitability. To protect the advantages gained in the East, as well as to promote further expansion, the States-General of the Netherlands in 1602 stepped in and promoted the creation of the United East Indies Company (Vereenigde Oostindische Compagnie, VOC). This combined the competing companies into a single, well-capitalised entity and was to become known as the Dutch East India Company. The States-General granted the VOC a 21-year monopoly to carry out colonial activities in Asia. It was obliged not only to trade but also to protect the national interests of the Netherlands by fighting its enemies in the region and preventing other European nations from gaining a foothold in the East Asian trade.

From the outset, the VOC was a successful enterprise,[55] achieved through diplomacy with the indigenous rulers to shut out opposition and thus gain monopolies, which were exploited through an extensive network of trading stations throughout the region. These monopolies were ruthlessly enforced by warships and men under arms.

The Cape, although well known through the accounts of Portuguese explorers and the journals kept by shipwreck survivors of the sixteenth and early seventeenth centuries, was not attractive, as it offered no opportunity to trade. It could supply fresh water and meat, but it could not compete commercially with Congo, Angola and the East African ports. In contrast, Mozambique was a prize that the Dutch tried and failed to capture from the Portuguese in 1609-10.

In 1611, a VOC captain discovered a new direct route from East Africa to the Straits of Sunda. When using this route, the Cape was almost halfway between Europe and Asia. This resulted in ships sailing to and from the Indies using the Cape more often for provisioning, increased activity that convinced the VOC to establish a station there. Johan Anthoniszoon 'Jan' van Riebeeck was requested to take command of establishing the first Dutch settlement at the Cape of Good Hope. He commanded a fleet of three ships, *Drommedaris, Reijger* and *Goede Hoop,* with a complement of 82 men and 8 women, including his wife, Maria de la Queillerie. They landed at the Cape on 6 April 1652 charged with building a fort, improving the anchorage in Table Bay, establishing a fruit and vegetable garden and obtaining livestock to establish a breeding herd from the indigenous inhabitants, the Khoikhoi. The energy and ability that Van Riebeeck applied to the task brought quick results.[56]

The VOC had not intended to colonise the Cape and had very narrow aims for the station, as it was not self-financing. However, the cost of maintaining it began to grow. There was also an increased need for labour and skills to give effect to the VOC's original aims. Two of the decisions made to alleviate this position were to have a deep and lasting effect on the development of the Cape, its inhabitants and eventually on South Africa.

The first was to release nine employees from their contracts in 1657 in an effort to arrest rising costs. They became burghers, citizens who were granted land for farming. The first free full-time farmers were given Khoikhoi grazing land in the Liesbeck valley, which led to the first war (1658-60) between the Khoikhoi and the Dutch settlers. As the VOC released more and more employees from their contracts, a new social class developed: land- and slave-owning free citizens with a particular view of themselves and, as we shall see, of their relationship towards slaves, servants and blacks. These were the ancestors of the Afrikaner nation.

The second decision was to import slaves to provide the necessary labour. The first slaves arrived at the Cape in 1658. Unlike America, Brazil and the Caribbean, the Cape did not have a plantation system and most slave owners had a small number of slaves who performed a variety of tasks. The slaves owned by the VOC were used to build and maintain the Cape's infrastructure. Those in private ownership performed diverse activities such as domestic service and being market gardeners, fishermen and artisans. In keeping with the VOC's policy of maintaining the Dutch character of the Cape, slaves and Khoikhoi alike were taught to speak Dutch. The majority of the slaves were of Malagasy origin, with a fair number from India and Indonesia. Many of them were Muslims.

By 1676, the VOC directors agreed with Commissioner Verberg 'that a good Dutch colony should be planted and reared here'. This decision marked the start of a new era at the Cape, an age of immigration, expansion and colonisation beyond the confines of the Cape flats and the Drakenstein Mountains. It led eventually to the birth of a new nation – the Afrikaners – and to conflict, initially with the indigenous Khoikhoi and San people, and eventually with the Bantu tribes of the hinterland.

Not all the settlers were wealthy or successful. An underclass of landless white settlers was developing who were unwilling or unable to do manual labour, which was performed by slaves or Khoikhoi servants. The white settlers' attitude of superiority stemmed as much from their view of themselves as European Christians and thus better than the heathen black slaves and indigenous people as from their status as burghers.

How were such settlers to be accommodated in the economy of the Cape? Many younger sons of farmers who could not afford farms of their own, as well as many others, who could not or would not work as farm employees, were moving further inland to become pastoralists and hunters. They were acquiring livestock from the Khoikhoi and competing with them for grazing land. This movement was accommodated by the VOC by allowing grazing land to be acquired cheaply and easily.

So throughout the eighteenth century the *trekboer* (stock farmer), as these semi-migrant pastoralist/hunters were known, led a migration of whites northward from the shadows of Table Mountain up to the Orange River and eastward into the Great and Little Karoo. By the 1770s, this expansion had come to a halt in all directions, stopped in the north by the semi-desert conditions of Namaqualand, some 300 miles from the Cape Peninsula; in the northeast by the ferocious fighting with San hunters, who occupied the Sneeuberg Mountains; and in the east by the Bantu-speaking Xhosa at the Fish River.

By now, the white settler community of the Cape had become self-perpetuating and knew no other country. They considered the Cape as their home. They referred to themselves, and others referred to them, as Afrikaners, rather than as burghers or as Dutch, German or French. A new language was also developing, Afrikaans, initially a dialect of Dutch, which became creolised as it was the language used by the slaves, Khoikhoi servants and their masters to communicate with each other. In addition to considering themselves Afrikaners, the settlers also increasingly saw themselves as white people compared to the slaves, Khoikhoi servants and others who were black.

It was in the rural Western Cape that the model crystallised of a racially exclusive white burgher community with special political and social privileges. This formed the basis of the attitude and philosophy that these settlers took with them when they migrated north of the Orange River.[57] These *trekboers* and their descendants were to be the pioneers who settled the three towns that became home to the Kapelus family, Ceres, Calvinia and Van Rhynsdorp.[58]

The British Take Over: 1795-1838

The Cape of Good Hope was not immune to the momentous events taking place throughout the world as the eighteenth century ended. Developments started with the Declaration of Independence by America and the outbreak of the American War of Independence in 1776. Soon to follow was the French Revolution, with its philosophy of Liberty, Equality and Fraternity. In Britain, a strong movement for the abolition of slavery was gaining ground. All of this sent shock waves through slave-owning economies around the world.

In the Cape, slave owning was widespread and slaves formed an integral part of a burgher's assets and wealth, just as much as his land or livestock did. Any changes to the system would inevitably be forcefully opposed by this class.

The wars that erupted in Europe because of the French Revolution resulted in the British taking possession of the Cape of Good Hope. In January 1793, the French King Louis XVI was beheaded and at the end of that month the French Convention decreed the annexation of the Austrian Netherlands to the French

Republic. The next day France declared war on Great Britain and Holland. The House of Orange fled from Holland to the safety of Britain and Dutch republicans established control over what was to become the Batavian Republic.

The French occupation of the Flemish coast threatened England, endangering trade with Europe, as the English Channel was no longer safe. If the French took control of the Cape of Good Hope as well, the only sea route to the East Indies, they would threaten the English East India Company's growing trade with Asia and particularly India. To protect this trade route, a British expedition took the Cape from the VOC in September 1795 and forced the company into surrender. It was during this brief period of British military rule that the large Cape Malay community was for the first time allowed the right of public worship as Muslims.

The Batavian Republic

The British withdrew from the Cape in 1803, when, by the terms of the Treaty of Amiens, they restored the Cape to the Batavian Republic, the area that had been Holland. With the arrival of the Batavians, the atmosphere changed. The new regime under Commissioner-General J.A. de Mist and Governor J.W. Jansens planned reforms in the spirit of European Enlightenment, especially in the fields of religion and education. De Mist's *Kerkenorde* of 1804 granted the protection of the law on equal terms to 'all Religious associations which for the furtherance of virtue and good conduct respect a Supreme Being'.

There had been no freedom of religion during the period of VOC control of the Cape. All employees and burghers were obliged to be members of the Dutch Reformed Church; in the early years under Van Riebeeck, people were obliged to attend church, with harsh penalties for missing Sunday worship. In the Netherlands, although it was not a state church, the Reformed Church (DRC) following the Calvinist doctrine was in a privileged position. In the Cape, however, for approximately 150 years it was the only church allowed. The Lutheran Church had to wait until 1778 to be granted permission to form a congregation, even though it followed the Calvinist doctrine. Now, because of the *Kerkenorde,* all monotheistic faiths could worship in public and the Catholic Church immediately did so.

Even though Jews were VOC directors, the company only employed members of the Dutch Reformed Church. Any Jews fleeing from the devastation wrought in Eastern Europe by Bogdan Chmielnicki had to be baptised before coming to the

Cape. In fact, it was not until 1841 that the first Jewish community met there for divine worship.

Return of the British

The rule of the Batavian Republic in the Cape was short-lived, as by May 1803, hostilities between Britain and France had resumed and the two countries were again at war. To protect their access to the East Indies and particularly India, the British retook the Cape in 1806. Britain and its allies remained at war with France until the defeat and abdication of Napoleon on 3 April 1814. Europe now prepared itself for the struggle for peace at the Congress of Vienna of 1815. In the Peace of Paris, the outcome of the Congress, Britain expressed its concerns about safeguarding its trading routes and obtained agreement that the Cape would become a British colony.

This new colony spread over a large area, from Cape Town in the south to the Orange River in the north and northwest and the Fish River in the northeast. It was a complex, slave-owning society, with the white European burghers, by now an Afrikaner population, varying from the urban dweller in Cape Town and its immediate vicinity to the isolated and very rural *trekboer* of the Cape hinterland. The indigenous population of the Khoikhoi had been largely subjugated and were treated as no better than indentured labour.

By now, the burghers had met the Xhosa farmers and pastoralists in the northeast. Like the burghers, these people were cattle-owning farmers. They were black people with their own culture, social mores and political system of clans, tribes and chiefs. The *trekboers* were in competition with them for their territory, grazing, water and farmland. The *trekboers* had the advantage of guns, however, so conflict was inevitable.

To deal with the turbulence on the eastern frontier, it was decided to settle some 6,000 British people (known as the 1820 Settlers) on small farms in this troublesome region. The 1820 Settlers and other immigrants from Britain added to the already complex society. Unlike all the other immigrants – French Huguenot, German and Dutch – who easily acculturated and assimilated into the burgher community by speaking Dutch and accepting the Dutch Reformed Church, the British settlers were culturally far removed from the burghers by their language, traditions, religion and experiences. They were the first white immigrants who did not assimilate with the host white population.

This cleavage between Afrikaans and English speakers was to grow and be present in the South African landscape as an ethnic issue for generations to come. The Kirsch, Kapelus, Dorfman, Broude and Hotz families all experienced the rift at first hand.

The attitude of English officialdom and English speakers was that the rural Afrikaners were their inferiors. Giliomee expresses the following view: 'In many ways the Afrikaners, ironically, were being subjected to the same rituals of subjection and degradation as those they employed to keep the Coloureds and blacks in their inferior place.'[59]

The Afrikaners felt marginalised and powerless to influence the authorities. Their perception was that the government abused and did not protect them, nor did it meet its obligations to them. This feeling of being marginalised and placed on an equal footing with former slaves, Coloureds and blacks led to two mass movements away from the Cape colony into the hinterland of South Africa. The first wave occurred between 1835 and 1840, when approximately 6,000 people (10% of the colony's whites) moved across the Orange River north of the Cape's border; and the second between 1840 and 1845, when 2,308 families, about 15,000 white people accompanied by approximately 5,000 servants, left the colony, in *Die Groot Trek*. This resulted in the establishment of two Afrikaner republics, the Orange Free State (OFS) and the Zuid Afrikaanse Republiek (ZAR), as well as the occupation of Natal, later annexed by the British as a colony. In all the areas of South Africa there were now whites living among the indigenous blacks.

Perhaps the statement in the memoirs of Anna Steenkamp, the niece of Boer leader Piet Retief, when writing about the emancipation of the slaves, best sums up the attitude of the *Voortrekker* community to race:

> *It is not so much their freedom that drove us to such lengths, as their being placed on an equal footing with Christians, contrary to the laws of God and the natural distinction of race and religion, so that it was intolerable for any decent Christian to bow down beneath such a yoke; wherefore we rather withdrew in order thus to preserve our doctrines in purity.*[60]

Jewish Life in South Africa: 1806-1860

How different the very south of Africa was to be from the north when it came to Jewish history and tradition. The first book of the Torah, Genesis, ends with Jacob and his family settling in Egypt. Exodus, the second book, describes the Jews departing circa 1275-1250 BCE after a stay of some 400 years. Alexander the Great conquered Egypt in 332 BCE and again Jews settled in the land. Their number swelled when Ptolemy I attacked Palestine in 301 BCE and sent large numbers of Jewish prisoners to Alexandria, where they practised their ancient faith and established a community that flourished, lasting until modern times.

In stark contrast to Alexandria, the Cape had no Jewish community to take advantage of the freedom of worship granted by the *Kerkenorde* (1804). The reason for this was simple: as mentioned previously, the VOC did not employ Jews as a matter of policy.

We know that a number of Jews were baptised during the period 1669 to 1795; indeed, the earliest record of Jews in the Cape is found in the baptismal registers of the Dutch Reformed Church. These records that on Christmas Day 1669, 'after confession of faith two adult persons were baptised who were formerly Jews, the one named David being 22 years old and the other Samuel being 20 years old'. The VOC muster rolls for 1669 reveal that the two persons referred to were David Heijlbron, who was stationed on Robben Island, and Samuel Jacobson, who served as a shepherd.[61]

Professor Gluck of the UNISA Department of Semitics believes that even earlier baptised Jews came with Van Riebeeck, because they named one of the Khoikhoi with whom they traded 'Osinghkhima', 'Schacher', or later even 'Prince Schacher'. There was no Dutch equivalent for this word, which could have been the Yiddish for 'merchant' or 'black'. The humour of the name could only have been appreciated by Yiddish-speaking sailors.[62]

The reality of the Cape under the VOC was that non-conformity was not tolerated in any form, particularly insofar as religion was concerned. One needed to be baptised, married and buried by the church. Consequently, any Jews eventually assimilated, leaving only their Jewish names, particularly as there were very few if any Jewish women in the colony.

Even after British rule was established and immigration was encouraged without any religious restrictions, the Jews who migrated to the Cape from Britain, Holland and Germany soon assimilated. There was no Jewish communal life that would enable them to worship according to the laws of Judaism and so bind them to their faith.

The most notable of these early immigrants hailed from St Helena, a rocky island in the Atlantic where Saul Solomon, an English Jew, settled and established a thriving commercial and trading enterprise. He later became known as 'the merchant king of St Helena', where he was the sheriff. Saul Solomon gathered his relatives by blood and marriage around him on St Helena, where they too were involved in the family enterprise and maintained the traditions of their faith. Somehow, however, their adherence to their faith did not last once they settled in the Cape.

The first of the Solomons to arrive was Benjamin, a younger brother of Saul, who had joined the family business in St Helena as a youth from England. In September 1806 he settled in the Cape, shortly after it was re-occupied by British forces. Benjamin married Johanna Petronella du Plessis in 1809 and assimilated. His nephew Nathaniel Isaacs followed him to the Cape in 1825. Then Saul Solomon (1829), the son of Joseph, named after his uncle, and his brothers Edward and Richard (1830) arrived to attend the South African College in Cape Town. Their parents Joseph and Hannah and their siblings Margaret, Isabella and Benjamin followed them to the Cape in 1831. Of these, only Joseph and Hannah remained Jewish. Their children were all baptised in the Church of England. Saul became an illustrious politician in the Cape. Nathaniel recorded his adventures in Natal in his book *Travels and Adventures in Eastern Africa (with a sketch of Natal).*

Siegfried Fraenkel was the first settler who was a professing and practising Jew. He arrived in the Cape in 1808. During the Napoleonic Wars, he was obliged to do military service, so his studies at two medical schools in Europe were interrupted. Fraenkel thus never attained a medical degree, but so impressed was the Supreme Medical Committee by his knowledge and skill that it granted him a licence to practise as a surgeon in the colony in 1808. Everybody in the Cape referred to him as doctor, although he always signed his name simply as S. Fraenkel. He practised as a surgeon from 9 Roeland Street until, in 1816, he moved his surgery to Marktplein. He was to play a leading role in the formation of the first congregation of the Cape. Although he married a non-Jewess, he attended services regularly once the congregation was established.

The tide seems to have turned, albeit slowly and on shaky foundations, with the advent of the 1820 Settlers. A party of settlers from London, under the initial leadership of Thomas Wilson and accompanied by a Church of England clergyman, Reverend William Boardman, sailed out of Deptford on the *Belle Alliance*, arriving in Simon's Bay (Simon's Town) on 2 May 1820, when Thomas Wilson abandoned the party, absconding with the money that had been deposited with him. Reverend Boardman became head of the group, but did not get a government stipend, as it was soon discovered that they were not all members of the Church of England.

Of those 307 prospective settlers, a number were Methodists and at least 18 were Jewish. These were Morris (33) and Phyllis Sloman (24) and their three children, Mark (5), Rosetta (3) and Julia (2)[63]; John (25) and Sarah Norton and their two children, Lewis (4) and Joshua (2); Philip Simons (38) and his two sons, Samuel (10) and Ralph (8); Benjamin Simons (18); and Benjamin Norden (22) and his brothers, Joshua, Marcus, Samuel and Harry.[64]

The *Belle Alliance* sailed on from Simon's Bay to Algoa Bay, where the settlers disembarked in May 1820. In keeping with its policy, the government immediately allocated them farms in the Eastern Cape. Like many 1820 Settlers, these Jews were not farmers by profession and after struggling for some time all but one gave up farming and settled in the towns.

By 1840 there were certainly sufficient professing Jews in Cape Town to have established a regular basis for prayer with a *minyan* (a quorum of ten men) for Sabbaths or Jewish festivals, yet they had not done so despite several attempts. Nor had they established any formal community structure. The reason might be that the nature of their businesses as traders and merchants required them to travel into the hinterland and they were often away from home. In addition, many had not practised their religion and traditions for some time, while others had assimilated.

A dedicated and strong personality would be required to galvanise this nascent Jewish community into being formally organised. That man was Benjamin Norden, one of the 1820 Settlers.[65] His brother Joshua carried on farming, but Benjamin soon left his farm in the Albany district of the Eastern Cape in 1829 to become an auctioneer and merchant in Grahamstown. His exploits as an ivory trader, a pioneer of trade in Natal, his meetings with the Zulu chief Dingane on behalf of the Governor of the Cape, Sir Benjamin D'Urban, as well as the role he played in the civic affairs of Grahamstown and Durban have been well documented.[66]

By the time Norden settled in Cape Town in about 1840, he was in his 50s, a well-known figure in business and civic affairs with an extensive knowledge of southern Africa. He and Aaron de Pass (a fellow Jew) were partners in an enterprise, and Norden quickly became involved in public affairs and was an active Commissioner for the Cape Town Municipality.

It was Norden, who on Friday, 25 September 1841, the eve of Yom Kippur, the Day of Atonement (5602), succeeded in raising 17 adult males to form a *minyan* for the Kol Nidrei service at his home, 5 Helmsely Cottages, Helmsely Estate, Hof Street; now part of the Mount Nelson complex, where a plaque records the event.

This was the first meeting of Jews for divine worship in South Africa.[67] There was no minister and they did not have a Sefer Torah (Scroll of the Law), so the congregants had to lead the services from their prayer books (*machzorim*). From the records, it is clear that the congregation had several capable readers who did the honours.[68] Dr Siegfried Fraenkel read Nehilah (Concluding Service), which he continued to do each year until his death in 1846.

On Sunday morning, 10 October 1841, the worshippers met at the invitation of Simeon Marcus at his home in Loop Street to found a permanent congregation 'for services on Sabbaths and Holy Days and the maintaining of the Jewish religion in South Africa'. They named the congregation the Society of the Jewish Community of the Cape of Good Hope, in Hebrew Tikvath Israel (Hope of Israel).

A donation of £100 opened the subscription list. All those who had attended the first service subscribed. Nathan Birkenruth, Joseph Mosenthal, Gabriel Killian and his partner Stein made additional subscriptions.

A number of Jews also subscribed who did not care to join the congregation but nonetheless wished to show their support for its establishment. 'Old Moses the money changer' was one of these. The community elected Messrs Norden, Sloman, Horn and Canstatt as Elders 'to act for the whole body of Jews here in all matters having in view the establishing of the Jewish religion in this Colony'. The treasurer was Simeon Marcus and Canstatt acted as Secretary.

The founding members in turn made their homes available for services. It was not easy to be Jewish in the Cape Colony. There was no Sefer Torah, no *tallit*, no rabbi, no *mohel*, no *schochet*, no *mikveh*, no kosher food and no *cheder*. The tiny community could not afford a minister and many of the rituals observed by

Jewish communities, such as the provision of kosher meat, the circumcision of male babies and marriage ceremonies, were not possible.

By 1875, some 34 years later, there were 495 Jews in the Cape spread across the Colony, Cape Town (169), Port Elizabeth (123), Kimberley (120), Graaf-Reinet (36), Grahamstown (25) and Victoria West (22).[69] Six years later, this would change dramatically when the gates of Russia opened and the Eastern European Jews began to pour out, including the ancestors of my family and Esther's.

Significant firsts for the Tikvath Israel Congregation

1. Acquiring a burial ground for Jews in Albert Road, Woodstock that was in use until 1887, where the first Jewish funeral took place in December 1844 with the interment of Abraham Horn, an attendee at the first service held at Helmsley Place.
2. The first Sefer Torah arrived in June 1848. It was a gift from a Mr P. Salaman and was brought from England to the Cape by Aaron de Pass.
3. The first birth recorded in the new register was of Charles Horn, the son of Abraham Horn, born posthumously (1845). There was then no *mohel* in the Colony, so we do not know who performed the traditional rite of circumcision. Perhaps it was Dr Siegfried Fraenkel?
4. On 19 June 1844, all the members of the congregation and their families were invited 'to celebrate the Nuptials' of Michael Benjamin and Amelia Marcus, the daughter of Mr and Mrs Simeon Marcus, one of the founding fathers of Tikvath Israel congregation. There was no *shul*, so they held the ceremony at the home of the bride.

   It was an unusual occasion, as only a clergyman could perform marriages in the Colony at that time and there was no Jewish clergyman to do so. In the circumstances, the Jewish congregation asked Reverend George Hough, the Senior Colonial Chaplain of St George's Church, to perform the official ceremony in a manner that would not cause offence to the Congregation.

   Before acceding to the request, Reverend Hough sought the advice of the Attorney General as to whether the marriage would be legal if he omitted all reference to the Trinity. The Attorney General gave a written opinion that it would be legal for the minister to omit all such reference and to direct the couple to make their responses after the word 'Father'.

   The records show that Reverend Hough performed the official ceremony 'liberally and handsomely according to the English law, leaving out every part objectionable to our religious feelings'. Immediately afterwards, afternoon prayers (*mincha*) were read and the marriage ceremony was again performed 'according to our ancient law of Moses and Israel'.

At the time of giving the opinion, the Attorney General promised to introduce an ordinance in Council making marriages a purely civil contract and allowing Jews to be legally united in marriage by a Jewish layman until the congregation appointed a minister.[70]

5. R.J. Joseph, a qualified *mohel*, arrived at the Cape in 1846 and the first circumcision he performed was on his own son in October 1847.
6. Reverend Isaac Pulver, the first minister to the Tikvath Israel community, arrived in Cape Town with his family on 8 August 1849.
7. The son of Amelia and Michael Benjamin (the first wedding) was the first barmitzvah boy in 1858.
8. He was not the first boy of 13 to be called to read the Torah, however. That honour fell to the son of Morris Sloman, also one of the founders of the first community, when the Reverend Pulver called him to the Torah in 1849 at the first public reading in South Africa. This brave young man had his *bris* the year before when he was 12 years old, because there had been nobody in the Cape qualified to do it before then.
9. On 6 April 1849, the community purchased a property consisting of two houses situated in Bouquet and St John's Streets for the sum of £800. A plaque commemorates the site. This is not very far from the site of the Gardens Synagogue (Old and New) in Hatfield Street today. The houses had formed part of the Good Hope Lodge. The larger of the two houses was converted into a synagogue; the other was to serve as the residence of the minister, when one was appointed.
10. The *shul*, formerly the larger of the two houses, was consecrated at 4 pm on Friday 15 September 1849.
11. The first Jewish bride to be married in a synagogue was one of the eight daughters of the Slomans. The synagogue had at the time no marriage canopy (*chupah*), so they took down the ark curtains to serve the purpose.
12. By 1861, the congregation had outgrown the small synagogue. With the encouragement of their minister, Reverend Rabinowitz, a house, stables and a large garden extending back from St John's Street onto Government Avenue was purchased, where the first purpose-built synagogue, now the South African Jewish Museum, was constructed. It was duly consecrated on Rosh Hashanah, 13 September 1863, which coincided with the fourteenth anniversary of the opening of the Bouquet Street Synagogue.

Some views of Cape Town 1869-1895

Cape Town – St Georges Street 1869

Cape Town – Greenmarket Square 1870

Cape Town – Post Cart

Cape Town – Van Riebeeck Square 1880

Diamonds and Gold Bring Riches and War

The explosion of the diamond and gold mining industry onto the South African scene, in the deepest hinterland, in the most underdeveloped and least stable part of the region, brought about a sea change in every aspect of life. Immigrants rushed there from all corners of the globe, including Eastern Europe. These were young, mostly unmarried adventurers seeking a quick buck, a fast life and a stiff drink. They brought with them new ideas, new languages and new socio-cultural mores. These were not those of the deeply religious conservative Afrikaans agriculturalists.

Diamonds

'Gentlemen, this is the rock on which the future success of South Africa will be built.' So said Sir Richard Southey when displaying the first diamond in Parliament in Cape Town in 1867.[71]

He was right; only his timing was wrong. It took another three years before the world grasped the significance of the diamond, found in 1867 and displayed in the Cape Parliament and at the Paris Exhibition. The discovery in 1869 of the 'Star of South Africa', a diamond of 83.5 carats, triggered the first rush to the alluvial diamond fields along the Vaal/Harts and Orange Rivers.

The reality of the discovery of diamonds was perhaps more charming in its innocence than the later sordid political manoeuvring and financial intrigues used by Britain to annex the diamond fields.

By 1867, many *trekboers* had settled along the banks of the Orange River. Daniel Jacobs and his family had made their home on a farm, De Kalk, on the southern bank of the Orange, near the hamlet of Hopetown that had been established in 1858, some 834 kilometres north of Cape Town.

Here they raised their sheep and cattle and engaged in growing crops for their own needs. The children were, as was customary, required to fulfil certain farming and household duties, but for much of the time were left to their own devices. They amused themselves by playing on the river banks, creating their own entertainment and playthings. A favourite pastime was collecting colourful stones of all shapes and sizes from the gravel. Sometimes these stones were taken home and, when the children became bored with them, they were thrown in the yard.

On one such occasion, while the children were playing with their newest collection of stones (*klippies* in Afrikaans), Mrs Jacobs noticed that her son Erasmus had a particularly bright and shiny stone that seemed different to the others in its whiteness and sparkle. It clearly made an impression on her, as she told her neighbour Schalk van Niekerk about it when he visited the farmstead a day or so later. He asked to see the stone. Mrs Jacobs looked for it in the house but could not find it. So she searched in the yard, where she found it lying in the dust.

Van Niekerk wiped the dust off the stone and was also taken by its brightness and sparkle. He offered to buy the stone from Mrs Jacobs. She was amused by the thought of selling a stone (*'n klippie*) and, laughing heartily, gave it to him.

Putting it in his pocket he made for home, vaguely thinking that this lovely stone might have some value.

Some days later, a travelling salesman, John O'Reilly, visited the Van Niekerks' farm. During their conversation, Van Niekerk showed O'Reilly his shiny stone and asked him to find out whether it had any value and could be sold.

O'Reilly's first stop was in nearby Hopetown, where he showed the stone to the brothers Leopold and Martin Lilienfeld, Jewish traders from Germany, who had been in the town since the 1850s. In fact Martin Lilienfeld had been appointed a Justice of the Peace. They were not interested in buying it.

John O'Reilly went to Colesberg, some 186 kilometres southeast of Hopetown, where he showed the stone to Tiberius Benjamin Kisch, the local pharmacist and nephew of Aaron de Pass, a prominent member of the Cape Town Jewish community. He, too, thought it was pretty but of no value.

Kisch suggested that the stone should be shown to the acting Civil Commissioner in Colesberg, Lorenzo Boyes, who carried out a simple experiment by scratching his initials on a window pane in his office with this shiny stone. It made clear cuts in the glass. Boyes, with all the seriousness of a Civil Commissioner, announced that he thought it was a diamond. Kisch was there at the time, but was not convinced. So Kisch bet Boyes a new hat that it was a topaz and not a diamond. Boyes accepted!

To settle the bet, it was decided to send the diamond by ordinary post to Dr W. Guybon Atherstone, a well-known mineralogist in Grahamstown, some 337 kilometres from Colesberg. A covering letter was enclosed with the little stone and off it went by regular post cart in an unsealed envelope. It would have taken several weeks to reach its destination.

Atherstone carefully examined the stone and wrote to Boyes as follows:

> *I congratulate you on the stone you have sent me. It is a veritable diamond, weighs twenty one and a quarter carats, and is worth five hundred pounds. It has spoiled all the jeweller's files in Grahamstown, and where that came from there must be lots more. May I send it to Mr Southey, Colonial secretary?*

So Boyes won his bet!

We do not have the reply that Boyes would have sent Atherstone, but we do know that the diamond reached Cape Town (887 kilometres from Grahamstown) and that at the behest of Sir Philip Wodehouse, the Governor of the Cape Colony it was once more examined to verify its authenticity. This time the expert was Louis Hond, a Jewish diamond cutter who had migrated from Holland to Cape Town. Hond confirmed Atherstone's finding and valuation. Sir Philip paid £500 for the stone and, through the French consul in Cape Town, immediately arranged for it to be exhibited at the Paris Exhibition. There it attracted some attention as a large diamond, but sadly did not arouse any interest in the area of Hopetown and its environs as a diamond field.

The discovery of diamonds was the catalyst for the economic development of South Africa and played a significant role in the development of Ceres and Calvinia, the two towns in which Leib Kapelus made his home.

It was the discovery of the 'dry' diggings in 1870 that sparked the major diamond rush. Flocking would be a more precise description, as the infrastructure was primitive and it took months to get from Cape Town to the diamond fields, a distance of some 955 kilometres. A journey from Cape Town to Kimberley took the travellers through the towns of Ceres and Calvinia. Even travelling from Colesberg, 370 kilometres away, would take several weeks. Nonetheless, thousands of people made their way to these dry diggings in New Rush, which became known as the town of Kimberley.

By 1872, some 20,000 whites and 30-50,000 blacks had moved into the area of New Rush. Most of the blacks were itinerant workers who would work for as little as three months and as long as nine months.

The diamond fields created a host of economic opportunities and it was in this milieu that those who are now legends of the diamond industry worked and made their fortunes. It was in truth the start of the industrialisation of South Africa. It was also the place and time in which the basic system of racial discrimination against blacks, which was to be a feature of South African life for the next 120 years, was put in place by the pressure of white workers and the needs of the mine owners.[72]

Southey's prophetic words were vindicated. The development of the diamond mining industry pulled the Cape out of an economic downturn. With Kimberley being situated in the centre of the country, far from the ports and populated areas, the development of an infrastructure to service the mines resulted in large areas of the interior being opened up to trade and commerce. This benefited people of all races, as they now had employment opportunities beyond agriculture and domestic service.[73]

Gold

The myth of fabulous gold wealth had come to the Cape with the arrival of Van Riebeeck in 1652. He was convinced that the fabled gold city of Monomotapa was somewhere in the middle of the continent. As we shall see later in the history of Van Rhynsdorp, he sought this fabled city in Namaqualand.[74]

Two hundred years later, little was Southey to know when he addressed the Cape Parliament in 1867 that by 1886 there would be an even greater discovery of wealth. This time it was in Paul Kruger's sovereign state of Zuid Afrikaanse Republiek (ZAR), north of the Vaal River near what is today Johannesburg.

Prospecting for gold in the ZAR was not new and deposits had been found in 1834, 1852 and 1853, but had not been financially viable. This all changed with George Harrison's discovery in 1886 of a gold reef on the farm of Langlaagte, some 40 kilometres from Pretoria, the capital of ZAR. Further prospecting revealed a reef that extended nearly 50 kilometres to the east and west through Langlaagte.

A gold rush ensued. A tent town of eager prospectors, all white, descended on the area in their thousands; this was unlike the Kimberley diamond fields, where there were prospectors of all races.[75] The deposits were certainly plentiful, but were spread thinly on the ground before dipping and going deep underground. It seemed that the gold rush would peter out, but a confluence of circumstances ensured that this would not occur. Within a few years, the tent city in the middle of literally nowhere had metamorphosed into the complex, dynamic and volatile city of Johannesburg.

To understand why this happened, it is important to remember that international currencies had been fixed to the gold standard and the price of gold was fixed. Every industrialised country therefore wanted gold to underpin their currency. At that very time a new technology, the MacArthur-Forrest process, was also developed, involving cyanide amalgamation in the refining process of the raw gold that made deep-level mining of the gold deposits on the Witwatersrand possible.

Thus there was a demand for gold as well as available technology to refine the raw product. However, two further elements were necessary to make the mining industry a reality: capital investment in the industry, and sufficient technical knowledge of mining coupled with the administrative capacity to make the mines operate effectively.

London was the financial capital of the world and it provided the capital needed to exploit the riches. The magnates of the diamond industry of Kimberley provided the gold fields with the knowledge, experience and administrative capacity for mining. All of these factors came together at the same time.

The ZAR had been on the brink of bankruptcy, with the Standard Bank refusing to lend Kruger's government any more money. In a mere four years, however, the ZAR went from a beggar state to one of untold riches; from a rural backwater to an area at the forefront of modern industrial development.[76]

Historian C.W. de Kiewiet succinctly illustrated the extent to which the discovery and mining of gold changed the financial fortunes of ZAR when he wrote:

> *In 1884 the Transvaal was barely solvent: three years later, in 1887, its revenue of £683,000 approached that of Natal; two years later again its revenue of £1,500,000 was in hot pursuit of that of the Cape. For every reluctant pound which the ZAR had to spend in 1883, it had twenty five pounds.*[77]

The Road to War

The glitter of gold was tinged with the tinsel of trouble, however. This trouble lay in political and social changes that would shake the ZAR to its very foundation. These were engendered by mass immigration, which resulted in immigrants far outnumbering Afrikaners.

In 1886, when George Harrison found the first gold deposits at Langlaagte, the whole area was desolate and uninhabited *veld*. Within a year, a village of tents and corrugated iron buildings had arrived housing some 3,000 diggers, speculators and traders. By 1896, just ten years later, the first census taken by the Johannesburg Sanitary Board (basically its town council) showed a population of 102,078, with 61,292 people living within the jurisdiction of the Sanitary Board (within three miles of the Market Square). By the turn of the century the population had swollen to 166,000.

Moreover, new mining towns along the Reef seemed to spring up overnight.[78] The municipal boundaries of Johannesburg expanded just as rapidly. In 1898, the city occupied some 5 square miles; by 1901, it was 9 square miles; and by 1903, a massive 82 square miles.[79]

The population explosion was not limited to the ZAR. Between 1870 and 1900, some 400,000 white immigrants entered South Africa, coming mostly from the UK. By far the majority settled on the gold fields, increasing the non-Afrikaner population even more.

The call of the diamond and gold fields was also heard in Eastern Europe, where the poverty-stricken and persecuted Jews were now allowed to leave. Some 40,000 Jews migrated from Lithuania to South Africa during the period 1881-1914, many of whom sought their riches on the gold fields.

The number of Jews in Johannesburg was thought to be around 100 in 1887, but within a year there were 500 and by 1890, 2,000. According to an article by Meir David Hersch, by 1893 the Jewish population had reached 10% of the white population of the city, 4,000 out of 40,000; by 1895 it had increased by half again to 6,000 out of 60,000.[80] These early Jewish inhabitants were not beholden to any 'establishment', either Jewish or Gentile.[81]

Thus the Afrikaners in Johannesburg were soon substantially outnumbered by non-Afrikaners. By the late 1890s, there were some 44,000 white non-Afrikaners or *uitlanders* in the ZAR. Some estimates claim that there were now more *uitlander* males eligible to vote than burghers. Kruger, who was narrowly elected President of the ZAR in 1883, believed that there were some 60,000 to 70,000 *uitlanders* whereas there were only 30,000 burghers.[82]

The Volksraad felt that it had to act, so it changed the constitution of the ZAR in 1890, granting the franchise in presidential and Volksraad elections to naturalised citizens only if they had lived in the Republic for 14 years. By effectively disenfranchising the very people who were responsible for the state's economic prosperity, Kruger had created an issue that imperialists and some of the mine owners (randlords) could use in their effort to control the gold fields. The disenfranchisement was probably more apparent than real, however, as most of the *uitlanders* did not care too much about the franchise. The majority would be most unlikely to give up their British nationality for citizenship of the ZAR – they were there to find riches! [83]

British imperialism played a major role in the drama that was to unfold in South Africa. The stick that the British would use beat the ZAR with was constituted by the disenfranchisement of British nationals, the language issue, as well as the Republic's use of railway tariffs to free itself from any dependence on the British.

In addition, there was a European dimension. Tension was growing between Britain and Germany. The British perceived the German occupation of South West Africa (later to become Namibia), situated as it was right on the doorstep of the huge gold deposits in the ZAR, as a threat to their supremacy in the area. This was another incentive for the British to seize and control the gold riches. To prevent German access to ZAR or the ZAR itself expanding, Britain annexed Swaziland and Bechuanaland (Botswana).[84]

The Jameson Raid

Cecil John Rhodes, Prime Minister of the Cape Colony, believed that he could foment a revolt against the Kruger government by a group of *uitlanders* (the Reform Committee) in Johannesburg. Rhodes could not be seen to be interfering in the affairs of a sovereign state, however, so he concocted a plot whereby Leander Starr Jameson would enter the ZAR with a troop of armed men to assist the internal revolt.

The Reform Committee started to quarrel on tactics and by 27 December 1895, it was clear that there would be no revolt. Both Chamberlain and Rhodes were informed of this. Rhodes sent a telegram to Jameson commanding him not to move on the ZAR. Nevertheless, Jameson ignored Rhodes' instructions and invaded the ZAR from Bechuanaland on 29 December 1895. The Reform Committee then assumed control of Johannesburg, but entered into negotiations with Kruger. Jameson surrendered to ZAR forces on 2 January 1896.

What became known as the Jameson Raid was an unmitigated disaster for Rhodes in particular and he had to resign. In the event, Kruger was magnanimous in his victory and showed mercy to the four leaders, who had all been sentenced to death, by commuting their sentence into fines of £25,000 each.

This fiasco demonstrated and underlined the polarisation in South African white politics. British South Africans felt humiliated and the Afrikaners were now convinced that the British could not be trusted. Thus the Jameson Raid destroyed Anglo-Afrikaner co-operation in the Cape Colony.[85]

Sir Alfred Milner, an avowed imperialist and High Commissioner of South Africa, decided to meet Kruger and Jan Christian Smuts (Attorney-General of ZAR and later Prime Minister of South Africa) at Bloemfontein in an attempt to force them to accept British demands in respect of the *uitlander* question. Kruger and Smuts tried in vain to find a compromise solution, conceding to most of Milner's demands on condition that the British drop their claim of suzerainty and refrain from further interference in the ZAR's affairs. Milner refused. At this point Kruger retorted:

> *'It is our country you want.'*

The Outbreak of the Anglo-Boer War

These events only strengthened support for the Pretoria government in the Orange Free State (OFS). War was now unavoidable and the Republics were keen to strike before reinforcements arrived from Britain, so at the beginning of October 1899 the ZAR and OFS presented Britain with an ultimatum, demanding that Britain consent to a neutral arbitration of their political differences.

At last, Milner and Chamberlain (the British Foreign Secretary) had what they wanted: a war to attempt to take the ZAR and OFS as colonies. On 10 October 1899, Great Britain rejected the demands of the two Republics. The Afrikaner Republics of ZAR and OFS were thus at war with Great Britain.

The build-up to this conflict is important, as many of the issues that gave rise to the Anglo-Boer War continued to play a role in South African politics for many years and so inevitably touched the lives of the Kirsch and Kapelus families. All three of the towns in which these families lived were involved in the war, although they were a long way from the ZAR. Ceres suffered because of its support for the Afrikaner Republics. Boer forces occupied both Calvinia and Van Rhynsdorp, before the British retook them. Leib was then working between Ceres and Calvinia and was therefore right in the thick of the action in this area.

Where did the Jews of the Transvaal, the OFS and the Cape stand on the Anglo-Boer War? It is clear that many Jews fought on the side of the Republics and the Afrikaner community considers many of them as heroes. *Boerejode: Jews in the Boer Armed Forces 1899-1902* by David Saks gives a full account of this. Some Jews fled the Transvaal and OFS for the coastal regions of Cape Town, Port Elizabeth and even Durban, where they sat out the war. Others joined the Imperial forces and fought for the British. There was no communal Jewish attitude to the conflict.

Leib Kapelus Arrives in South Africa

What Leib would have seen on his arrival: Some photographs of Cape Town from around 1897

Cape Town – first railway 1890

Cape Town harbour

Cape Town – St Georges Street 1895

Cape Town – Adderley Street 1895

Cape Town – Roeland Street 1900

The Kirsch Family

When Leib Kapelus finally arrived in the Cape after a long sea voyage, he headed for the town of Ceres, some 130 kilometres from Cape Town, where three of his six first cousins in the Kirsch family – Joseph, Raphael (Folie) and Max – were already living. It was much easier for an immigrant to learn the ropes in new surroundings supported by family or *landsleit* to help.

Raphael was the first Kirsch to settle in Ceres. Born on 12 February 1877 in Plungyan, Raphael Abraham was the third son of Hersch (Girsch in the records, as the Russian alphabet does not have an *H*) and Feige-Ente Kirsch (née Kapelus, sister of Movsha Itsko). There were five boys in the Kirsch family and one girl; Mordechai, the eldest, never left Plungyan and worked with his father, a flour trader, later trading in grain and flour on his own.

The second child, Rachel, who became Mrs Holtman, migrated to the USA and published her memoir *Mein Lebns-Weg* (*My Life)* in 1948. In it, she wrote that Raphael was 15 when he left home. She also said that Mordechai died young, the father of five children.

Ceres would not have been on Raphael's mind when he arrived in South Africa in 1892 with £30 in his pocket – a considerable sum of money for a raw 15-year-old. He wanted to go to the gold fields. He took a coach to Johannesburg and found lodgings in a tent with other Litvaks. It was a rough neighbourhood and it did not take him long to find that he no longer had his £30. Fortunately, Raphael found some *landsleit* from Plungyan and told them his tale of woe. They gave the boy some money to get back to the Cape, a route that took him through Calvinia and on to Ceres.

On seeing Ceres, his response was, 'This is a beautiful place! Here anyone could live forever.'[86] He might have been young, but he had learnt some lessons and was old enough to see good commercial possibilities. The diamond rush had turned the sleepy village into a bustling staging post for the transport of people and goods on wagons loaded to bursting. The long road from Ceresweg (Wolseley) to Kimberley and Barkley West passed through Ceres, Calvinia, Sutherland and even Beaufort West. Cape Town was the most developed commercial harbour that afforded access to the diamond fields and the transport infrastructure inland had developed substantially.

Map showing the towns and villages where the Kapelus, Dorfman and Hotz Litvaks settled

Ceres became Raphael's home, where he became a smous, a peddler, with a horse and cart, selling goods to and buying produce from the farming communities in the Bokkeveld.[87] By 1904, he had become a general dealer and he applied for Letters of Naturalisation on 19 May 1904. He stated that he was 26 and had resided in the Cape Colony for 12 years. In Ceres and the surrounding district, Raphael – often referred to as Folie (by some as Pollie) – became a farmer of some note.

Soon after he had settled in Ceres, he encouraged his brothers to join him. Joseph was the first to do so. We do not know when he left Plungyan, but the records of the Poor Jews Temporary Shelter show that J. Kirsch aged 27 years entered the Shelter on 16 June 1896 and left for the Cape on the Warwick Castle on

18 June 1896. On the same page (194) the record shows that M. Kirsch (Matatiahu or Max) entered the Shelter on 12 November 1896 and sailed for the Cape on the *Greek* on 27 November 1896 (coincidentally the same ship as his cousin Leib sailed on seven months later). His youngest brother Shmuel remained in Plungyan and migrated to South Africa many years after his brothers, settling in the village of Kopjes in the Transvaal.[88]

Although Raphael started life as a *smous*, like many Litvaks before and after him, he was well established by 1904, as his son Leon confirms, and became friendly with many prominent families in the town and district.

One of these was the Zulch family. Mrs Zulch met a Mrs Ettman, accompanied by her 16-year-old daughter, in a hotel in Ceres. The Ettmans were also immigrants from Russia and lived on a farm near Matjesfontein (the family later moved to Piketberg). During their conversation, Mrs Zulch said to Mrs Ettman

> *'You know, I have a wonderful Jewish friend, Folie Kirsch. I would love to introduce your daughter to him.'*

Mrs Zulch made the introduction and Lena Ettman soon became Mrs Lena Kirsch. They had six children, who grew up in Ceres and later on the farm Ou Stasie at the foot of Michell's Pass.

Raphael also experienced hard times. In 1922, the price of wool dived in the short period of six weeks from 120 pennies to 6 pennies a bale. Raphael owed the National Bank £47,000; to repay his debt he had to sell properties, including his farm Roggevlei on Gydopass for £6,000 (about eight years later, the same farm changed hands for £250,000). The worry and heartbreak caused him to have a stroke and he lost the use of one hand.

Raphael nevertheless flourished, but he never forgot his humble origins and his selfless and unpublicised generosity became legendary in Ceres. He died at the comparatively young age of 58 on 2 September 1934, then a farmer at Ou Stasie.[89]

Max Kirsch lived to a ripe old age, dying a month before his 75th birthday on 30 June or 1 July 1954. Having arrived in Ceres in 1896, he worked diligently to establish himself before going back to Lithuania to marry his sweetheart Augusta Jafshits (Hebrew name Gusta bat Pinchas) in Ponevezh on 2 February 1915. They returned to Ceres, where they were childless but fully involved with their family, being godparents to Russel Kirsch (son of Raphael) and David Kapelus (son of Mokey). Max and Augusta were close to my uncle Mokey, so much so that they stipulated in their joint will that 'the survivor of them shall consult M. Kapelus in regard to his/her affairs'.

Joseph, who also arrived in Ceres in 1896, never married, as his loved one back home in Plungyan married another man. Joseph died and was buried in Ceres on 20 July 1938.

Ceres

The town of Ceres came into existence a little over 40 years before Raphael's arrival. It was the genius of the road builder Andrew Geddes Bain and the administrative capability of Charles Michell that opened up this beautiful valley. In a letter to his friend and fellow geologist, Bain ventured that the pass he was about to build, Michell's Pass,

> *... is a magnificent undertaking and will reflect high honour on its projectors. It will open up all the interior parts of the Colony, many of them formerly – as it were – hermetically sealed up from all communication with the Capital.*[90]

Using 240 convicts to do the heavy manual work together with artisans, Bain commenced work in October 1846 and completed the pass in two years at a cost of £21,000.

In early February 1849, even before the sale of the first plots that were to become Ceres and only some two months after the opening of Michell's Pass, Bain commenced work on another pass from Wagenmakersvallei (Wellington) through the *kloof* (ravine) to the Breede River Valley beyond. It took four years to complete. Bain's Kloof, opened in September 1853, was a masterpiece of engineering and road building, rightly immortalising the engineer who brought it into being.

The opening of Michell's Pass on 1 December 1848 by the Governor of the Cape, Sir Harry Smith, made access to this area significantly easier, thereby opening the valley for settlement. It was at the opening ceremony that Andrew Geddes Bain apparently declared that in England people considered the wheat from the 'Bokkeveld' as the best in the world. It seems that officials of the Cape Colony used this statement to name the new town Ceres, after the Roman goddess of cultivating plants, especially the grain named after her, cereals. Bain thus not only built Michell's and Bain's Kloof Passes, which certainly led to the establishment of the town, but it now seems that he also named it in honour of its grain production.[91]

Bain's Kloof Pass

Early Ceres

Main Road in early Ceres [Photographs by courtesy of the National Archives, Cape Town, South Africa]

The sale by public auction of the first 20 *erven* (plots) on the western bank of the Dwars River took place on the pavement outside the Magistrate's Court of Tulbagh on 21 July 1849. The document proclaiming the sale referred to the village as Ceres.

In 1863, the railway line from Cape Town reached Wellington at the foot of Bain's Kloof Pass, making the market of Cape Town more accessible to Ceres. Thus within a space of 15 years the 'hermetically sealed' Breede River valley had become accessible both by road and by railhead.

However, the mountain ranges beyond Wellington, including the formidable Hex River Mountain, halted further progress. All talk of the railway passing through Ceres met with strong resistance. The locals feared that a rail line would adversely affect the livelihood of those involved in the transport industry and disturb the tranquillity of the town. An alternative route for the railway had to be found.[92]

With the completion of the rail line to Kimberley in 1885, Ceres feared that the traffic by road through the town would fade away, although the reality was the contrary, it seems. With the discovery of gold in 1886, the need to get supplies to the north was even more pressing, so the town continued to thrive. The rail link from Cape Town to Johannesburg was opened in 1892, just when Raphael made Ceres his home, part of the construction of railway lines linking together the whole of South Africa. The building of stations along the various routes opened much of the hinterland and provided it with a link to the industrial and commercial heartland, as well as to the ports of Cape Town, Port Elizabeth, Durban and Delagoa Bay.

Ceres soon had postal services, as one Kensington Edwards ran a post office from his home by 1850, for which he received the handsome sum of £6 per year. By March 1857, Mr N.G. Vos, the first official postmaster, had received his appointment. His successor, James Warren, took over in 1861, earning £30 per annum as well as commission on all the stamps he sold.

The Early Jewish Community of Ceres

The Kirsches were not the first Jews to settle in Ceres. Adolf Arnholtz, a practising Jew, had started the Inland Transport Company, which provided regular passenger-carrying wagons from Ceres to the diamond fields. Arnholtz hailed from Germany, as so many of the early Jewish settlers did. He and his wife Mary were living in Ceres shortly after the town was established and he was a founding father, one of the original commissioners who constituted the first Town Council in 1864, becoming mayor in 1873.

Reverend Joel Rabinowitz, minister to the Tikvah Israel congregation in Cape Town, circumcised the Arnholtzes' son Harry in Ceres in 1868. By 1870, B. Arnholtz, Adolf's brother, who also became mayor of Ceres and later a Justice of the Peace, was living in the town.

The diamond rush did not only open Ceres to opportunities to sell goods and provide transport to people en route. Some of those travelling to the diamond fields made money by entertaining the locals on the way. One such was Barnett Isaacs, who sailed for the Cape to join his brother Henry and cousin David Harris in Kimberley. Henry had adopted the stage name of 'Signor Barnato, the Great Wizard from London' when he gave conjuring performances in South Africa. When Barnett joined him, he also adopted the surname Barnato. The world knows him as Barney Barnato. When Barnett's transport to the diamond fields stopped overnight in Ceres, he approached Mayor Adolf Arnholtz for permission to rent the Town Hall in order to perform conjuring for a paying public. Little did Adolf or anyone else in the audience imagine that the performer would in a short time become one of the magnates of the diamond industry (more on this later).

At this very early stage of the town's existence, the Jewish population, like the rest of the Cape, was primarily of German origin. We have seen the role the Arnholtzes played in the establishment of the town. Other Jews appear in the records, such as Baumann (1870s) and Ring (1880s). Ludwig Weiner, also a German Jew, traded in the Tulbagh-Ceres area from 1850 to about 1870, when he settled in Cape Town, devoting himself to public affairs. During this time he won a seat in the House of Assembly as a member for Cape Town and after serving in this capacity for 15 years he became a Senator. He has the rare distinction of having had a public holiday named after him: the first Monday in October was Weiner Day, although this was abolished in 1953.

Ceres by now had a fair number of practising Jews. The Tikvah Zion Society in the town was established in 1898 by Abraham Miller and Lazarus Goldberg. It became one of the first societies to affiliate to the South African Zionist Federation, also established in 1898. It is interesting that the community set up a Zionist society several years before it founded a religious congregation; the Ceres Hebrew Congregation did not commence until 1903. Services were held in the homes of various congregants, as the *shul* was built only many years later in 1923, when it also served the Jews living in the neighbouring towns of Wolseley, Tulbagh and Prince Alfred's Hamlet.

By 1904, there were 59 Jews living in Ceres. Many of the newcomers were part of the Lithuanian migration to South Africa. David Cohen and family (his son Losky served on the Ceres Municipal Council for many years and his grandson David became a celebrated racehorse breeder), Joseph Sarembock and his brothers Louis and Jack had joined the Kirsch, Sebba, Daneman, Goldberg and Miller families in the town. These are all names that were to become synonymous with the Jewish community there.[95]

Raphael (Folie/Pollie) Kirsch and his son Theo, David Cohen, Jockey Levin, Wolf Metter and the Sarembock family have become part of Ceres folklore. François Botma, in his book *Ceres van Gister en Eergister (Ceres of Yesterday and the Day before Yesterday),* gives a charming insight into life in the town, but also the Jewish community and their acceptance within it.

In a short piece headed Mnr (Mr) Isaaac Raskin, Botma relates how the Raskin family who owned the *koeldrangfabriek* (cold drink factory) in Ceres soon found themselves in financial difficulties because of their large family. The Jewish community faithfully stood by the Raskins and helped them over their financial problems. In conclusion Botma says,

> *Dit het vir ons andergelowiges as 'n voorbeeld gedien om te sien hoe naasteliefde en – hulp uitgeleef moet word.* (This served as an example to us of other religions how love of one's fellow men and neighbourly help should be given; uitgeleef, literally 'lived out').

Raphael Kirsch and his partner Abraham Elterman traded as general dealers under the name of F. Kirsch & Co. Their premises were on the northeastern corner of Vos- and Voorstrate. Max, Raphael's younger brother, was also a general dealer and his shop was directly opposite Raphael's on the northwestern corner. Botma does not give a date for these events, but it was probably in the early 1900s, as the farmers at this time still used a horse and cart to visit the town and used to barter farm produce such as eggs, butter and live chickens for their groceries and other household necessities.

A farmer and his wife would draw their cart up opposite Raphael's premises with baskets laden with eggs and butter at their feet. Raphael would approach them and, as was his wont, start to bargain with them on price. While this exchange

BARNEY BARNATO

Born on 5 July 1852 in Whitechapel in the East End of London to Isaac and Leah Isaacs, well-established Jewish shopkeepers, Barnett Isaacs joined his brother Henry on the diggings as a diamond broker or *koppie-wal loper* (hill bank walker). Later, Henry and Barney went into partnership under the name of Barnato Brothers – Diamond Brokers. Within two years, even during the worst of times on the diggings they were able to accumulate £3,000 capital.

In Chapter II of his memoirs, his cousin David Harris (later Sir David) relates how Barnet Isaacs, now Barney Barnato, got started. Harris had learnt about diamond buying while employed by a fellow Jew, Marcus Hayman. Barney spent his early days on the diamond fields shadowing Harris in his new office. One day Harris had used all his available capital in buying stones and asked Barney to mind the office while he attempted to sell his merchandise to the merchants. It was not long before a digger came into the office and asked for Mr Harris. Barney advised the digger that Mr Harris would be back shortly and asked if he had anything to show, as he was Mr Harris's partner. The digger wanted £150 for a dirty stone, but Barney agreed a price of £120. Not having any money, Barney advised the digger that the 'firm's cheque book was in the safe and Mr Harris had the key.' Could he return for payment? Barney was very excited and quite nervous at having bought a stone with his limited knowledge, although Harris says, 'I examined the stone and was highly satisfied with the transaction.'

Luckily for Harris, he had disposed of his stock for cash, which enabled him to pay the digger when he came to collect his money. In the meantime, Barney could hardly wait for the digger to leave to find out what Harris thought. 'I indicated my satisfaction, and this seemed to take a load off his mind. I placed the diamond in acid, cleansed it thoroughly, and held it in my hand – a perfect gem,' wrote Harris. '"What is it worth, Dave?" inquired "Barney" anxiously. "About £15 or £16 a carat," I replied, "and whatever it realises you will get half of the profits."'[93]

The diamond in fact fetched £300, earning Barney his first £90 on the diamond fields and providing him with the start he needed. Later, when Cecil John Rhodes and Alfred Beit wanted to consolidate the claims in order to gain control over production, the price of the remaining claims soared as Barnato competed with them. Beit and Rhodes obtained funding from Jewish financiers N.M. Rothschild and Sons of London to acquire almost all the shares in the De Beers Mine, with Barnato owning the major share of the Kimberley Mine. After protracted negotiations, Rhodes persuaded him to sell his holdings to De Beers Consolidated Mines and to become a life governor of the company; Rhodes paid £4,000,000 for the control of Barnato Diamond Mining Company, reputedly the largest cheque ever presented for payment at that time.[94] This gave De Beers Consolidated Mines and thus Rhodes control of the production of diamonds. One of the conditions imposed by Barnato was that Rhodes would secure him membership of the Kimberley Club, which did not admit Jewish members.

was taking place, Max would stand on the veranda of his shop, arms folded and leaning against the doorpost. He would listen to his brother offer 'one and three' and the farmer counter with 'one and four'. They went back and forth and, just as it appeared that Raphael would get his price accepted, Max would saunter across the road, pick up the basket and say,

> *'Kom maar na my toe, Mister, ek sal jou one and four gee'* (Rather come to me Mister, I will give you one and four).

Some years later, Max built a little shopping centre to which he moved his business. A Mr Baum of Prince Alfred's Hamlet took over Max's old premises and after his death his son Sammy and his brother-in-law Cyril Sarembock ran the business.

Grand Levin's Hotel

The Grand Hotel or, as the large sign over the front entrance proclaimed, 'Grand Levin's Hotel', became a favourite holiday destination for many Jewish families from Cape Town in the 1950s for their April or September breaks. For our branch of the Kapelus family, it has very special memories.

We lived in Van Rhynsdorp, some 210 miles from Ceres. From 1954, my parents, my sister Yvonne and I used to spend about a week to ten days at the Belmont Hotel in Ceres, opposite the synagogue. Faan and Betty Conradie created a space with beautiful and spacious gardens, a swimming pool and a little zoo, in which was situated the main hotel building with a luxurious dining room. Near the tennis court and only a short distance from the main building were *rondawels*, round, thatched-roof cottages of two double bedrooms and a shared bathroom. We used to live in one of these for our stay. On Friday evenings, my father and I would attend services at the synagogue and then my mother and sister would join us as we walked at a leisurely pace to the Grand Hotel for Shabbat dinner. The last time we did so was in December 1964.

The Ceres Synagogue[96]

The owner of the Grand, Jockey (Jack) Levin, bought the hotel in August 1929 and ran it until it was destroyed by the earthquake of 29 September 1969, when it was, sadly, irreparably damaged. After demolition it became Andrag Motors. The earthquake, measuring over seven on the Richter scale, wrought havoc throughout the area. One of the other casualties was the Ceres Synagogue, which also had to be demolished. Luckily, the three Sefrei Torah were rescued unharmed and were used for Simchat Torah.

Jockey became a character in Ceres, a man of small stature, impeccably dressed with a red flower, preferable a mountain rose, pinned to the lapel of his jacket. He always seemed to be in a hurry. He preferred to serve his customers personally in the hotel's well-frequented bar. On the occasions when some regulars became boisterous, they would lean over the counter and pull Jockey over to drink among them. Jockey would swiftly move to the end of the counter where there was a flap, duck beneath it and return to his post behind the counter, calmly calling out,

'Gentlemen, gentlemen, please behave yourselves.'

Jockey was renowned for his good heart and his generosity to the Jewish community of Ceres. He ordered the curtain for the Holy Ark of the synagogue from the USA. His sister, Bertha Epstein, brought it to South Africa after one of her visits to America.

Miss Beth van der Merwe, formerly a teacher, was known as the cantankerous spinster of the village. She used to walk to the Grand Hotel every evening for a drink and sit in one favoured spot. Jockey sensed her loneliness and knew that she was not well off. After she had been coming for a while, the waiter would approach her and casually ask,

'Your usual?'

She would nod. The drink would duly be served – on the house.

I married my second wife, Cynthia, on 3 September 2003. When I first met her parents, Mary and Julius Solomon, we inevitably indulged in some South African Jewish geography. Lo and behold, I discovered that Mary (née Epstein) was the niece of Jockey Levin and that we shared the Ceres experience. Mary knew the Kirsch family and remembered Augusta and Max well.

Leib Kapelus in Ceres: 1897-1910

On arriving in Cape Town in July 1897, Leib made his way to Ceres. We do not know for sure how he travelled that part of his journey. What is almost certain is that he would have chosen the cheapest mode of transport.

Once in Ceres, he could depend on his first cousins, Joseph, Raphael and Max, for support and advice. Raphael, as we have seen, was by then reasonably well established, but Joseph and Max had only arrived a year earlier. They were not the only Jewish traders in the town, so the 18-year-old Leib would have had a helping hand from others as well. The Litvaks were by now arriving on a regular basis and quite a few settled in Ceres. The families Sebba, Daneman, Goldberg, Miller, Fisch, Green and Katzen became well known in the town and its immediate vicinity.

Like most of the young men from Lithuania who arrived in the country towns of the Cape as Yiddish speakers, Leib had to learn to speak English and Afrikaans as well as how to buy produce and sell all manner of supplies, from household goods to small farm implements. He started out working for Raphael in his store and once he was able to conduct a simple conversation, Raphael fitted him up with goods and he too set out as a *smous*, at first for Raphael and later for others of the more established Jewish shopkeepers. Leib had a horse and cart, which formed his transport and his store. His stomping ground was the farming community and smaller villages on the Hantam, an area of the escarpment known as the Warm Bokkeveld from Ceres to Calvinia and west of Calvinia as far as Nieuwoudtville.

Life as a smous

We can get an idea of what it was like for Leib from the description by a journalist, Hoffman, who had himself been a peddler, in his *Book of Memoirs*, published in Yiddish in 1916, the first Yiddish book in South Africa:

> *The first journey of the togger took a few weeks and was the most difficult of his career as a peddler. When he had learned the language of the Boers and had become accustomed to their food and their ways, his lot became easier. When he had sold his stock, he returned to town. Here he would pay his debts to the merchant, then buy larger stock, and return to the road.*
>
> *It was sheer hell for the togger walking around with a heavy pack on his back, uphill and down dale, in the valleys and the bush, under the relentless*

South African sun. As soon as he had acquired enough money, the togger bought a donkey from a Boer. A donkey, which is common in South Africa, is a small animal slightly larger than a goat. He divided his large pack in two and tied it on to either side of the donkey's back. In this way he led the donkey as Haman led Mordechai on the King's horse. He went from farm to farm peddling his wares and earning himself a few shillings.

It did not take long for the peddler to exchange his donkey for a horse and cart. He now considered himself fortunate since he no longer needed to go on foot. Having a horse and cart enabled him to trade with the Boer on a larger scale. He was able to exchange goods with an equivalent value for articles such as sheep skins, buck skins, bundles of ostrich feathers, ostrich eggs, rolls of tobacco, bars of soap, chickens, eggs and vegetables. He loaded all these 'Seven species' onto his cart and headed for the nearest village where he would sell these goods to the shopkeeper. He would rest for a few days, replenish his stock and go back to the Boers.

This description gives some idea of the loneliness and rough circumstances that a *smous* endured. The area that Leib covered is to this day one of the most sparsely populated areas of South Africa. The stretch from Ceres to Calvinia through the Warm Bokkeveld is 260 kilometres, the longest distance in South Africa between towns without any other settlement or village.

Between 1899 and 1911, when Leib would have been traversing this area, visiting farms all along the way to trade, feed and water his donkeys or later his horses, there would also have been 'outspans' used by the many ox wagons, post coaches and mule- and horse-drawn wagons travelling the route from Ceres via Calvinia, Williston, Carnarvon, Prieska and on to the diamond diggings in Kimberley.

On leaving Ceres, Leib would have travelled in the direction of the Theronsberg, some 1,090 metres high, which he would have had to traverse. Then he would have headed north, with the impressive blue granite mountains of the Sneeuberg and Cederberg range on his left. These would have been his companions for most of his journey, until they gave way to an almost continuous outcrop of high hills, like lonely sentinels, seemingly always ahead of him. Luckily, he would not have had to attempt those.

After crossing the Doring (Thorn) River, his gaze would have been drawn to his right, as the Roggeveld Berge and later the Hantam range would now dominate the landscape almost as far as Calvinia. Some 40 kilometres from Calvinia, Raphael would have had to cross the Bloukrans (1,083 metres). Now he would have been within touching distance of Calvinia, as he would have seen the stately Rebunie Mountain on his right, with the huge Hantam range in front of him, almost forming a frame behind the village of Calvinia.

This journey would have taken a month or more, as he would stop and trade along the way. On his outward journey he would have some goods ordered by his customers as well as wares that he thought could sell. On his return journey, his wagon would be loaded with skins, pelts and similar farm produce that he would sell on to his principal.

This was a lonely, tough and uncompromising life for a young man who in Lithuania had lived in a small village surrounded by family and friends and was accustomed to a flat land with green forests, lakes and rivers, snowy winters and balmy summers.

One can only imagine what his thoughts were on his first journey into this mountainous and barren *veld*. Ceres could get hot in summer, but he certainly would not have experienced the intense dry heat of the long summer of the Ceres Karoo and the Hantam, where temperatures would reach the mid to high 40s centigrade on a daily basis.

The approach to Theronsberg, which Leib traversed many times

The Warm Bokkeveld (Ceres Karoo) in summer

The hilly sentinel-like outcrops

Leib seems to have been reasonably successful, as by 16 June 1902 he applied for Letters of Naturalisation. In his application, he stated his occupation as general dealer and his place of residence as Ceres. He confirmed that he had resided in the Cape Colony for five years at the time of application. His naturalisation was approved by the Executive Council on 4 July 1902. He must have been more concerned about regularising his stay than Raphael, who only applied for his naturalisation two years later, in May 1904.

To the question 'Age Next Birthday' Leib replied 23. We know from the Lithuanian birth records that he was born on 23 November 1878, so by June 1902 he would have been 23 years old, turning 24 in November. His lack of understanding of the language might be an explanation for this error.

A Taste of the Courts

By 1902, Leib had had his first experience of the courts in his new homeland. The Executors of the Estate of Johannes Marquard (Colonial Orphan Chambers) issued a writ against Lewis Kapelus for goods sold and delivered, interest and costs in the sum of £123.6.5. The defendant did not file a Notice of Appearance to defend the claim, so the Plaintiff obtained judgment for the sum claimed. Leib did not pay when called on to do so and the plaintiff issued a Writ of Attachment on 5 February 1902 to attach goods owned by Leib, sufficient to pay the sum due. No attachment was made, as Leib seems to have paid the total sum, the Writ of Attachment having been withdrawn at Ceres on 18 February 1902.[97]

What assets could Leib have owned that the bailiff could attach? The records of the Deeds Office show that he was the owner of half of 'a certain piece of land situate in the village of Prince Alfred's Hamlet being part of Erf No 57, Plan 1, measuring 39 square roods and 9 square feet', as well as a half share in Plot 57 marked 'B'. The transfer to Leib occurred on 22 May 1902. A first mortgage bond was registered over the property in favour of Estate Late William Marsh in the sum of £400, loaned to Louis Kapelus and Abraham Katzenellenbogen jointly and severally to enable them to pay the balance of the purchase price.

On 8 August 1902, Leib borrowed £300 from Abraham Katzenellenbogen at 6% interest per annum paid half yearly. A second mortgage over Kapelus's half share of the plots secured this loan. It seems as though Leib used the proceeds of the loan to repay some, if not all, of his debts. I have not yet been able to establish when the first and second mortgages were cancelled.

The Arrival of the Kapelus Siblings

No letters have survived between Leib and his family or between the Kirsch brothers and theirs in Plungyan, but between 1902 and 1906 Leib was joined in South Africa by his brother Abel, his sister Khave (Eva) and her husband Wolf Brickman and their children.

Eva and Wolf Brickman were married in Plungyan on 5 June 1898, when Eva was 22 years old and Wolf 21. By 1902, they had three children aged 4, 2 and 1. Wolf left Plungyan for South Africa in 1902 and brought out Eva and the three children a year later. They sailed from Southampton for Cape Town on the *Gaika* on 26 December 1903. The Brickmans did not go to Ceres, but stayed in Cape

Town. Wolf rented a shop at 67 Caledon Street as a workshop for his cleaning and dying works.

We do not know when Abel (Abe) arrived in South Africa, but we do know that in June 1906 he too was living with Leib in Ceres. I discovered this in the most unlikely way – through the record of a Supreme Court case![98]

On 2 October 1906, Michaelis Baumann, a merchant, issued at Ceres a summons against Louis Kapelus. The summons was served personally on Leib on 6 October 1906.

Baumann's case was that on 28 May 1906, Leib had requested Baumann to lend him £50.5.0 so that he could purchase donkeys for the German government, which had stipulated certain terms about the condition of the donkeys. The arrangements seemed to have been that donkeys of a certain class had to be delivered in Ceres by 3 June 1906. Leib would be paid at the rate of £19.0.0 per donkey. Payment would only be made after the German government had inspected the donkeys and agreed that they were acceptable, so Leib bore the sole risk of the transaction. Leib failed to deliver the donkeys on the due date, but on 6 June 1906 his brother delivered six donkeys to Baumann. The German government accepted two of the donkeys and paid Baumann £9.10.0 for each, instead of the original sum agreed of £19.0.0.

Baumann pastured the remaining four donkeys at Leib's risk, at a cost of £3.0.0. Baumann thus claimed £34.5.0, being £53.5.0 less £19.0.0. Leib did not defend the action and Baumann duly obtained judgment for the capital sum claimed and costs. How and when Baumann was paid we do not know.

Thus from this court record we know that Abe was in Ceres in June 1906. He was still there on 21 December 1906, since attorney Evelyn William Krige stated in an affidavit that, being unable to serve documents on Leib as he was not in Ceres at the time, he duly served the documents on 'Leib's brother, Abe Kapelus, who occupied a room jointly with him.'

So when did Abe get to the Cape Colony? It was probably in 1902, the year he left Plungyan with his sister Roche.

Rachel's Journey

Rachel was born in 1888, the very year her father died. We also know that her mother Pese was six months pregnant when her husband, Movsha Itsko, died (the posthumously born son, named Movsha Itsko after his father, died aged six months). On 12 July 1902, Rachel, then 13 years old, set off for London with her brother Abel. She travelled from Hamburg to London on the ship *Olivia.* The passenger list gives her Yiddish first name Roche, her surname as Kapalus and her approximate age as 11 years old. Rachel stayed in London, where she became a seamstress/tailor.

On 14 October 1907, Wolf Brickman submitted an application for a permit to allow his sister-in-law, Rachel Kapelus, to enter the Cape Colony. He undertook to support her. Initially this application was turned down, however. A note on the application dated 4 October 1907 records:

> *Mother living in Russia. The girl is 19 years. Lives in London. Working as a tailor. She went to London 4 or 5 years ago with her brother. Permit cannot be granted.*

Nevertheless, Wolf persisted and eventually Rachel received permission to enter the Cape Colony. She left London for Cape Town aboard the *Goorkha* on 20 March 1908.

From the note on the record that she went to London with her brother, we can infer that this was Abel. There is no record of him being on the same vessel from Hamburg, but he probably was. He appears to have gone on to the Cape while Rachel remained in London.

Thus, by the end of April 1908, Leib had his brother Abel with him in Ceres, and two of his sisters, Eva and Rachel, living in Cape Town. Their mother Pese was still in Plungyan with her son Shmuel Movsha (born 10 October 1880) and his two sons Morris and Nathan, as well as her daughter Mere-Mine (born 13 February 1887).

It was not long before Mere-Mine also decided to leave Plungyan. She was ready to go in the summer of 1911 and hoped to head for the Cape in South Africa, as it was by then. She was 24 years old and unmarried. Family folklore has it that she met a young man who was on his way to the USA and decided to follow him. Whether there is any truth in the story, we do not know.

Mere-Mine certainly went to America, though. The records of the *SS Rhein*, which sailed from Bremen for the USA on 19 August 1911, show her as a passenger. She lied about her age, stating that she was only 20. Unfortunately, the US Port Authorities detained her when the ship arrived in New York on 31 August 1911. She had stated that she was going to join her cousin G. Garb, but he did not arrive to meet her at the docks. She is recorded as having $25 on her person. According to the Record of Detained Aliens, the cause of detention was stated as 'No Cousin.' Mere-Mine was lucky, however. She was able to contact another cousin, Chaie Kaplan, and was released to her.

Leib and Sarah Marcus Get Married

Sarah and Leib Kapelus

Despite the setback of losing the case with Baumann, Leib continued to trade in Ceres and on the Hantam, where he became quite well known. He now apparently felt ready and able to be married. How and where he met Sarah Marcus we do not know. The Marcus family apparently hailed from Kovno, but they lived in Camps Bay in Cape Town, quite a long way from Ceres.

While searching through the records of the Poor Jew's Temporary Shelter, I found the details of a Miss Sarah Marcus. She had sailed from Libau, arriving in London on 7 July 1898. The only personal details given are that she was born in Kovno and was 22 years old.

The records of the Shelter show that she departed for South Africa aboard the *Greek* on 8 July 1898. The passenger list, Schedule B, of the *Greek* shows Miss S. Marcus travelling steerage for the Cape. However, it gives her age as 20. Amazingly, Leib and his future wife travelled to South Africa on the same boat one year apart. This inevitably raises the question of whether they knew each other back home and whether she followed him to the Cape.

Leib (now called Lewius) and Sarah entered into an ante nuptial contract dated 30 September 1908. The contract itself had no special provisions and simply recorded that the parties were married 'out of community of property' and thus were not answerable for each other's debts.

They were also married in 1908, although I have not been able to find the marriage certificate. Sarah was a stately, beautiful woman, as the photograph on the previous page shows. They made their family home in Ceres where their first child, Morris Isaac (Mokey to his family), Moshe Yitzchak ben Mordukh Leib, was born on 20 March 1910. He bears the name of his paternal grandfather, Movsha Itsko.

The Changing Landscape of South Africa: 1897-1911

In his first 14 years in South Africa, Leib saw and experienced profound changes: the Anglo-Boer War from 1899 to 1902, the first signs of anti-Semitism with the introduction of the Cape Immigration Restriction Act of 1902 and the creation of a new state, the Union of South Africa, in 1910. He had also grown from a callow youth of 18 to a married man with two sons.

Leib and the Anglo-Boer War

Within two years of Leib's arrival, South Africa was engulfed in the Anglo-Boer or South African War, the origins and build-up to which were briefly described above. Leib could never have imagined that he would personally be caught up in the conflict that to him seemed so far away, in the Transvaal.

By 1898, he was 'smousing' between Ceres and Calvinia. His clientele were almost entirely Afrikaner/Boer farmers on remote farms in the Warm Bokkeveld. Twice a year, at Nagmaal (Holy Communion), they would all make the pilgrimage to the nearest town with a DRC congregation. For most of Leib's clients this would be Calvinia, but for some it was Ceres.

A visit to Ceres or Calvinia for Nagmaal would also be a time for shopping, socialising with their fellow farmers, talking politics and business. Everybody was by this time acutely aware not only of the riches that gold mining had brought to the ZAR, but also of the escalating political situation that was developing between the ZAR and Britain. This was even more so after the calamity of the Jameson Raid, resulting in Cape Afrikaners strongly voicing their support for the cause of the Republicans.

Leib – a newcomer in the country, Jewish and in the eyes of his Afrikaner clientele a foreigner – would have experienced the anti-British feeling from the very start of his business life in South Africa. By the time hostilities in the South African War started, Leib knew many of the farmers and their families who supported the Boer Republics. Some of these farmers and their sons left their farms to join the Boer Commandos, who had started to enter the Cape by November 1899.

By 1900, the Commandos had taken Kenhardt, Prieska and Gordonia (Upington) and were threatening towns further south and westwards. Republican sympathisers in the Afrikaans farmer community in the small towns were anticipating with relish the arrival of their compatriots. Sir Walter Hely-Hutchinson, Governor of the Cape, believed that 50% of the white population was effectively pro-Boer. It is estimated that between 6,000 and 7,000 Cape Afrikaners joined the Boer forces.[99]

It was different for the Coloured communities of the Cape towns under threat. News had quickly spread from the towns taken by the Boer Commandos of how they had enforced their racial policies. The Coloured communities feared the loss of the rights they enjoyed under British rule, such as a qualified franchise as well as equality before the law.[100]

For Leib, the activities of these Commandos in the areas of Calvinia, Nieuwoudtville and Van Rhynsdorp were real and formed part of his early years in South Africa. Calvinia and other nearby towns expected to be taken by the Commandos during the winter of 1900. In the light of the Boers' invasion of the Cape and the level of support they enjoyed, the Cape government placed virtually the entire colony under martial law. In Ceres, martial law came into force on 3 January 1901, although the Boer forces were some 260 kilometres away.[101]

The people of Calvinia were sharply divided in their loyalties. The Afrikaner farmers and town dwellers were almost entirely pro-Republican. The Coloured population of the town were fiercely pro-British, and as they learnt of the fate of their fellow Coloured citizens in the towns taken by the Boer Commandos, they became fiercely anti-Boer/Afrikaans. A few of the white town dwellers were pro-British, as were several of the Jews.[102]

This divisive atmosphere in Calvinia was clearly demonstrated on 19 May 1900, when Adam Esau, a Coloured blacksmith in Calvinia and a leader of that Coloured community, led a victory parade and rally consisting almost entirely of Coloured men and women, to celebrate the relief of Mafeking. The tension between the Boer (Afrikaner) and British (mainly Coloured) supporters was exacerbated in September 1900, when the Coloured community feared that a Boer attack on Calvinia was imminent and, led by Abraham Esau, petitioned the local magistrate, Peter Dreyer, to issue them with arms. He refused, fearing that the arming of the Coloured inhabitants could lead to a rebellion by the embittered Afrikaans community.[103]

Leib was then living in Ceres and travelling to Calvinia to service his Boer clientele. In Ceres, he was subject to martial law. On the road and at every farm he stopped at, he was with Boer families who were pro-Republican. In Calvinia, he was acutely aware of the sharp division between the white Afrikaners and the Coloured community. By now, there were several Jewish traders living in Calvinia. As they relied on the trade and business of both these communities, they were careful not to offend either of them.

The attack on Calvinia, when it came on the evening of 7 January 1901, was sudden, swift and over before sunset. A force of some 50 OFS Commandos entered the town unopposed. Within an hour, 100 Commandos on horseback had joined them. There was some sporadic resistance from the Coloured community, but the Union Jack flying over the magistrate's office was torn down and by nightfall it was all over.

The senior Boer officers in Calvinia were now Judge James Barrie Munnik Hertzog (later Prime Minister of South Africa, 1924-39) and Kommandant Charles Nieuwoudt, who entered the town on 12 January 1901. By the next day there were some 600 Boer Commandos billeted there. They immediately declared martial law, enabling them to requisition buildings, clothing, food, horses and valuables from local inhabitants. Nieuwoudt declared himself *Landdrost* of Calvinia and duly promulgated Republican native law, thereby robbing the Coloured community of their right to equality.

JAMES BARRIE MUNNIK HERTZOG

Hertzog's godfather, James Barrie Munnik, was the son of the child (James Barrie Munnik) born in the first successful Caesarian section operation in South Africa. The operation was performed by the British army surgeon Dr James Barry, who served at the Cape from 1816-28. Barry suggested that in lieu of a fee and in celebration of the miraculous delivery, the child should be named after the doctor. Barry was physician to Lord Charles Somerset, Governor of the Cape, but it was only on Barry's death in 1865 that it was discovered that the doctor was actually a woman!

The Boers issued warrants of arrest for those whom they thought were British loyalists before they took Calvinia. On 13 January 1901, they launched a manhunt for those loyalists. They duly arrested 14 men in all; of these, 9 were from the Coloured community, with Abraham Esau top of the list. He is said to have been found in a hiding place 'which was in a cellar underneath the shop of the English Jew, Cohen.' After torturing Abraham Esau, the Boers murdered him on 5 February 1901.

The next day the Boer occupation of Calvinia ended as suddenly as it had begun. They apparently fled from an advancing British force.[104]

Arrested

The Commandos may have left the town, but they continued to roam over the countryside between Ceres and Calvinia as well as the area to the west, towards Nieuwoudtville and Van Rhynsdorp.

It was during this period, while Leib was 'smousing' between Calvinia and Nieuwoudtville, that he was confronted and apprehended by the Boer Commandos who had occupied Calvinia. After some preliminary questioning and on hearing that he lived in Ceres, a town controlled by the British and under martial law, they decided to arrest him as a British spy. The senior officers, including Charles Nieuwoudt, made the decision to shoot Leib! All his pleas and frantic explanations that he was a *smous* who served many of the families of those in the Commandos were ignored and all seemed to be lost.

Leib was kept prisoner in a tent. One of the men was instructed to take him some food. He entered the tent and as his eyes adjusted to the light, he recognised Leib, who had often been a guest at his farmstead.

> '*Goeie genugtig klein Kappie wat maak jy hier?* (Good gracious little Kappie, what are you doing here?)' the man asked.

At last, Leib felt some hope. The farmer had known him for about three years. Leib explained that the Commandos had arrested him and the Kommandant had condemned him to death for being a British spy. The farmer knew that Leib was generous and supportive of the wives left alone on the farms and certainly was not involved in espionage.

It now transpired that several other farmers with the Commando knew Leib and they all came to greet him. A deputation of these farmers approached the Kommandant and explained that they knew Leib well, and that he supported their families while they were on Commando activities. Nieuwoudt listened with interest and agreed to release Leib, who was allowed to continue on his way.

He spent the rest of his days working and living among these farmers and their families. My father and uncle never mentioned the name of the farmer who saved Leib's life.

Leib seems often to have been engaged in litigation. In following his life through courtroom records, I have come across an interesting case, Lewis Kapelus versus Van der Byl and De Villiers 1924 (an appeal). According to the record of appeal, Van der Byl and De Villiers had obtained a judgment against a Mr Burger for £118.8.5 plus costs. When the Messenger of the Court attempted to attach 450 sheep and goats, Kapelus claimed that the livestock belonged to him. He then began interpleader proceedings claiming the livestock. The court found against Burger and Kapelus, however.[105]

Why did Leib take this risk to save Burger's livestock? There could obviously be many reasons for this action, but I have not found any reasonable explanation. Who knows, perhaps this was Leib's way of repaying the Burger family for saving his life during the Anglo-Boer War?[106]

Anti-Semitism Rears its Head

By 1875, the small, mainly Anglo-German population in the Cape numbered about 495 souls. These Anglo-German Jews were largely secularly well educated, and assimilated easily into the Victorian culture of the day. They felt comfortable and at ease in their surroundings as Jews. Sir Henry Barkly, Governor of the Cape, in his speech at the laying of the foundation stone of the synagogue in Kimberley in 1875, praised the Jewish community for their 'wholehearted loyalty'. He went on to say:

> *I have had opportunities of becoming acquainted with them in many colonies, and I have ever found them as a body obedient to the law, ready to take their part on all occasions as good citizens and to co-operate in works of benevolence and mercy.*[107]

Jews and Gentiles seemed to have got along well, as is illustrated by a resident of Kimberley, who is reported to have said:

> *'generally Jews are much respected by the other inhabitants.'*[108]

All this was to change dramatically from 1881 onwards with the arrival of Jewish immigrants from Eastern Europe, mainly Lithuania, from the provinces of Kovno, Vilna, Grodno and Northern Suwalki.[109] As we saw above, the assassination of Alexander II was followed by a wave of state-sponsored pogroms and repression of Jews in Russia, which led to a mass migration of Jews to the USA, Great Britain, Argentina and South Africa. The first wave of these migrants to South Africa, some 40,000 of them, arrived between 1880 and 1910.[110] The Kirsch brothers, Leib and Abel Kapelus, their sisters Eva Brickman and Rachel (later Mrs Feldman) and David and Leah Hotz were all part of this stream of immigration.

The Lithuanian immigrants had a significant impact on the existing Jewish community. In 1880 there were some 4,000 Jews in South Africa, most born in Britain but with a significant German-born minority. Inevitably, the question arises of whether those Jews in South Africa would have maintained their faith and culture without the arrival of their Eastern European fellow Jews; or whether the lack of Jewish brides would have resulted in intermarriage in such numbers that they would have become assimilated.

By 1904, the Jewish population had swollen to 38,101; after the first census of the newly formed Union of South Africa in 1911, their number was recorded as 46,926. (Despite the passing of the Cape Immigration Restriction Act, which will be discussed below, the 'Russian' Jews kept coming to South Africa, so that the 1936 census showed 90,645 Jews and ten years later the 1946 census recorded their number as 104,156.[111])

Unlike their Anglo-German co-religionists, the Eastern European Jews were not secularly well educated. They spoke Yiddish, and later heavily accented English and Afrikaans, dressed differently and were altogether more orthodox in their religious practices. The majority of them settled in the cities, but a great number of them, like the Kirsches, Kapeluses and David Hotz, chose to start their new lives in the *dorpies*, small villages in farming areas or towns along the transport routes where they had family, kinsmen or *landsman*, people from the same village or town back home in Lithuania. Here they would feel comfortable, as the small villages were much like those back home.

A number of the Lithuanians were tradesmen, tailors, carpenters and glaziers, but by far the majority had to learn new skills, often allied to their traditional role as traders back home. As did Leib Kapelus, they often learnt their new business skills from their first employer and many began life in South Africa as a *smous* before moving on to become a trader, general dealer, shopkeeper or businessman. Just as in Eastern Europe, they became the intermediaries between the new markets of the towns and growing cities and the producers, both black and white. In fact, they were instrumental in the significant economic change that took place in the rural areas of the country in the late nineteenth and early twentieth centuries by providing producers with access to the markets on the one hand and by offering a wide array of goods to the emerging country consumer on the other.[112]

Many Afrikaners with poor education had been displaced from the land due to the industrial and commercial changes that had occurred in the country after the discovery of diamonds and gold. Subsistence farming was no longer viable. Competition for manual jobs came from the black workforce, who could be paid substantially less than a white worker. English was the commercial language of the cities and many Afrikaners from the rural areas at that time spoke no English. To make matters worse, the population of South Africa had increased by some 400,000 white immigrants between 1870 and 1900. These migrants came mostly from the UK. The Dutch Reformed Church as well as the Cape Colonial government recognised the 'poor white' problem.[113]

The 1880s and 1890s also saw a significant downturn in the economy of the Cape, and the perceived success of the Litvaks, particularly in the rural areas, started to draw the attention of those seeking an explanation for the woeful lot of the growing Afrikaner poor white population, consequently the pressure to stop the immigration of 'Russian Jews' began to grow. Newspapers of the day reported that the Commission of Enquiry into Labour in the Cape Colony of 1893, which had nothing to do with immigration, was:

> *... wholly unanimous against the introduction of Russian Jews ... a most undesirable people, as already found in the Uitenhage District, where these people have pushed out many poor shopkeepers and have obtained property intensively.*[114]

This negative and stereotyped image of the Eastern European Jew was fast becoming pervasive in country and city newspapers and weeklies. The Cape Town weekly *The Owl* was one of the more virulent anti-Semitic papers. All this resulted in the 'Russian Jew' being stigmatised as 'undesirable', 'unassimilable' and 'the scum of Europe'.[115]

After the Anglo-Boer War ended in 1902, large numbers of Jews from Lithuania continued to arrive in the Cape and it was not long before the anti-alien and anti- Semitic lobby was again vocal and challenging. Now it was not only *The Owl* that purveyed these sentiments but the *South African Review* and even the *Cape Times*. Unemployment was exacerbated by the returning soldiers, and this undoubtedly fuelled the more general anti-alienism.

On 11 November 1902, Colonial Secretary Sir Peter Faure introduced the Cape Immigration Restrictions Act in the Cape Parliament and it duly passed into law the following day. The section of the Act that had a direct bearing on Jewish migration from Eastern Europe was the definition of 'prohibited immigrant', which was as follows:

(a) Any person who, when asked to do so by any duly authorised officer, shall be unable, through deficient education, to himself write out and sign in the characters of any European language an application to the satisfaction of the Minister;

(b) Any person who is not in possession of visible means of support, or is likely to become a public charge.

The implication of clause (a) of the Act for Jewish immigrants from Eastern Europe was immediately obvious. These were Yiddish-speaking people who wrote Yiddish using Hebrew characters. Would Yiddish be accepted as a European language? It seems that if one was in possession of £5, one satisfied the provisions of clause (b).

The Act came into force on 30 January 1903. Shipping companies and intending migrants had received very short notice of its provisions and thus had little time to adjust to its requirements. This caused great consternation and confusion. Following representations made by the shipping companies and after action by the Cape Town community in raising funds and providing employment for passengers who were initially refused permission to land, the government decided that the provisions of the Act would not be strictly applied or enforced for the first three months (February to April 1903).

The passing of the Act galvanised the Jewish communities, both in the Cape and in London. In the UK, the Anglo Jewish Association as well as the London Committee of the Board of Deputies of British Jews intervened with the government to have Yiddish recognised as a European language. The Jewish Board of Deputies in England decided that their chairman, D.L. Alexander, should have direct discussions with the Agent-General for the Cape Colony, T.E. Fuller. As a result of these representations, a letter dated 27 April 1903, a copy of which is shown on the right, was sent by Fuller to the Colonial Secretary in Cape Town.

In Cape Town, Reverend A.P. Bender, who referred to himself as Head of the Jewish Community, worked assiduously on two fronts: to obtain a liberal and tolerant interpretation of the Act and an acceptance of Yiddish as a European language. Bender also made representations to Faure as well as the Attorney General, T.L. Graham, for Yiddish to be accepted as a European language. Graham indicated that he was willing to do so and agreed to have an official conversant with Yiddish and German to deal with those passengers who did not speak English. Bender expressed himself satisfied that British goodwill and justice would be applied.

Others, such as Lionel Goldsmid, owner/editor of the *South African Jewish Chronicle*, Morris Alexander KC, a prominent advocate at the Cape Bar, and David Goldblatt, a Yiddish-speaking journalist, were not so ready to rely on the goodwill of an individual, even if he were the Attorney General. They wanted an amendment to the Act that specifically stated that Yiddish would be accepted as a European language so that it would take a change in the law through Parliament to alter the situation. Alexander expressed the need for an amendment to the Act by asking:

> *'What happens when there comes a Pharoah who does not know Joseph?'*

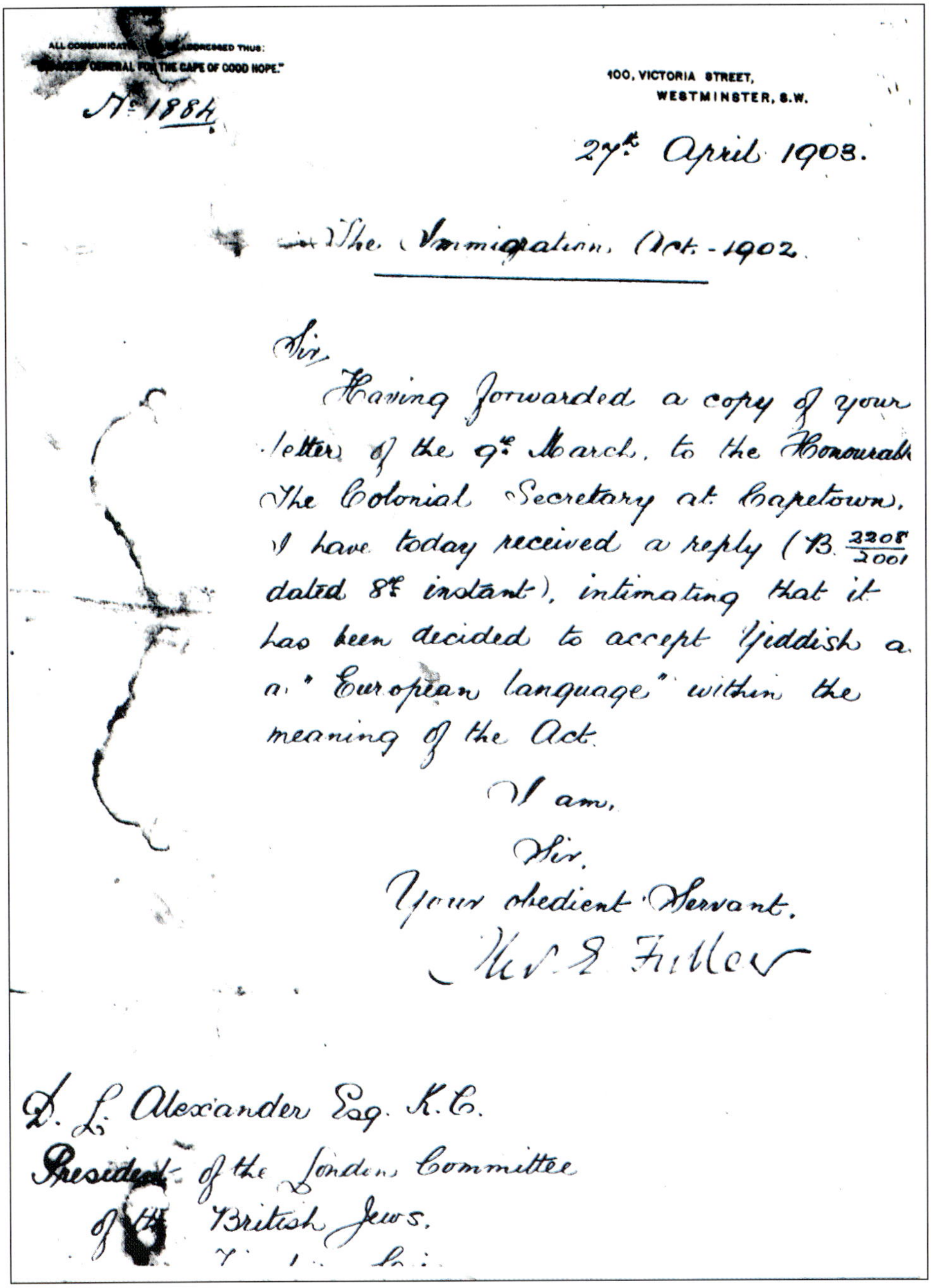

ALL COMMUNICATIONS TO BE ADDRESSED THUS:
"AGENT GENERAL FOR THE CAPE OF GOOD HOPE."

No. 1884

100, VICTORIA STREET,
WESTMINSTER, S.W.

27th April 1903.

The Immigration Act - 1902.

Sir,

Having forwarded a copy of your letter of the 9th March, to the Honourable The Colonial Secretary at Capetown, I have today received a reply (B. 2208/2001 dated 8th instant), intimating that it has been decided to accept Yiddish as a "European language" within the meaning of the Act.

I am,

Sir,

Your obedient Servant,

T. E. Fuller

D. L. Alexander Esq. K.C.
President of the London Committee
of the British Jews.

A letter by the Agent-General for the Cape Colony, T.E. Fuller, to the Colonial Secretary in Cape Town regarding the question of Yiddish being recognised as a European language within the provisions of the Cape Immigration Restrictions Act of 1902

Furthermore, Goldsmid, Alexander and Goldblatt believed that it was time to establish a secular body representing Jews in the Cape, a Jewish Board of Deputies, although as we shall see this was not achieved until later.

In furtherance of their dual purpose, Alexander and Goldblatt decided that a deputation consisting of representatives of the various Jewish congregations in the Cape should be formed and that this body should meet with Graham to press for an amendment to the Act. They succeeded in organising a deputation representing thirteen congregations and nine other Jewish organisations to meet with Graham on 28 May 1903, despite the opposition of the Cape Town Hebrew Congregation, led by Bender, and a number of other congregations. The deputation handed Graham a resolution expressing their appreciation for the sympathetic and liberal enforcement of the Act and for appointing a Jewish official, proficient in Yiddish, to meet incoming migrants. Nonetheless, it called on the government to amend the Act specifically to state that Yiddish was a European language within the meaning of the Act. Graham agreed to put such an amendment before Parliament at the first opportunity.

That opportunity did not immediately arise, however, as shortly after the meeting with Graham a new government under Dr L.S. Jameson came to power. It too continued to accept Yiddish as a European language, but did not introduce any change to the law.

How did the deputation persuade the government to accept Yiddish as a European language? They organised for a non-Jewish German translator who did not know any Hebrew to translate an article in Yiddish (written in Hebrew characters) on the philosopher Agassiz as it was read by David Goldblatt (so that its resemblance to German was clear). A full report on this demonstration was published the following day in the *Cape Times*.[116]

This was significant for the Lithuanian Jews in South Africa, but in fact it did not have any impact on the Kapelus family. By the time the Act came into force, Leib was a naturalised citizen of the Cape of Good Hope (4 July 1902). His brother-in-law Wolf Brickman was the next family member to arrive. According to the records of Find My Past, Wolf left London for Cape Town in 1902. I have found a copy of the manifest page recording his name, but it does not give the exact date of sailing or the name of the vessel. However, we do have the exact record of the route and vessel on which his wife Eva (née Khave Kapelus) and their eldest three children travelled. They arrived via Hamburg to Southampton and sailed to Cape Town on board the *Gaika*, which departed from Southampton on Boxing Day 1903.

When Wolf tried to get permission for Eva's sister to enter the Cape, not from Lithuania but from London where she had been working for six years, he initially encountered difficulty, as we have seen. There is no explanation in the file why. By then she could speak some English and she had a trade, being a seamstress/tailor. After reconsideration, she was given consent to enter the Cape, however.

David Hotz arrived in the Cape in 1901 and was naturalised as a citizen on 13 March 1905. The Act clearly did not affect him at all. His wife, Leah Abramson, sailed in steerage on the vessel *Scot* that departed from the UK bound for Cape Town on 7 February 1903. She gave her age as 22 and her occupation as a tailor, a trade, so she too managed to enter the Cape without difficulty.

In June 1906, the Cape Parliament considered a new Immigration Law, in an effort to control more effectively the entry of people from other colonies to the Cape. Alexander, now President of the Cape Jewish Board of Deputies, and a Mr Abrahamson, a Member of the Legislative Assembly, met with the Colonial Secretary to push for the amendment on the acceptance of Yiddish. The government agreed and introduced a proviso to Section 3(a) of the Act, which 'provided that for the purposes of this subsection, Yiddish shall be accepted as a European language'. It was passed without any problems.

The Formation of the Jewish Board of Deputies

There is little doubt that the coming into law of the Cape Immigration Restrictions Act was the catalyst for the formation of a secular body that would represent the Jews of the Cape Colony to protect and champion Jewish rights and interests. On 4 September 1904, representatives of a number of congregations held a meeting in Cape Town and unanimously passed a resolution constituting themselves as a Jewish Board of Deputies for the Cape Colony, with the power to add representatives of the remaining Jewish congregations and organisations throughout the Colony.

The organisation, later known as the Cape Board of Deputies, elected Morris Alexander KC as president. Their first task was to assist in the naturalisation process of their fellow Jews. Unfortunately, Alexander never won over the recalcitrant members of the oldest and most prestigious congregation in the Colony, the Cape Town Hebrew Congregation, and others that took their lead from it. By 1907, Alexander so dominated decision-making that he seemed to be the lone face of the Cape Board, which after Union in 1910 merged with the Transvaal and Natal Board in 1912.

The South African Board of Deputies (SAJBD) played a leading and key role in monitoring events that affected the Jewish population of South Africa and defending their rights. Its objectives were:

(a) This Board shall watch and take action in all matters affecting the Jews in the southern portion of the continent of Africa.

(b) That the Board shall make observations of all proceedings relative to legislative and other enactments, and shall use such means as they may deem requisite in order that no infraction of the religious rites, customs and privileges of Jews may ensue therefrom.

The SAJBD is still the guardian of Jewish interests in South Africa, interacting with the government of the day as well as other institutions in the country. There has lately been much soul searching about the role played – or, more accurately, not played – by the SAJBD in opposing the racial policies and Apartheid legislation of the National Party government of South Africa after it came to power in 1948. My generation of the Kapelus family has grappled with this question since the late 1950s and we shall visit the debate later in the book.

The Forging of the Union of South Africa, 1910

We can safely assume that the first generation of the Kirsch, Kapelus and Hotz families would have wholeheartedly endorsed the sentiments expressed in a Union Day address by Morris Alexander KC, who had worked assiduously for the creation of the new state:

> *Today marks the end of the old, and the beginning of the new South Africa, the youngest of the daughter nations of the Empire. Under the British Flag we Jews have enjoyed civic, political and religious freedom to the full throughout South Africa. Let us resolve here and today so to serve and guard the best interests and the true development of this young country of our adoption, as to repay in unstinted measure the tolerance and broadmindedness with which we have been treated.*

What is more, history shows the significant and lasting contribution made by Jews to the new state in every sphere of life, out of all proportion to their number.

MORRIS ALEXANDER KC

It was said of Alexander that:

> *'nothing rouses him to anger more than privileges, ring fences, colour bars, race prejudices and all obstacles to freedom of action and thought ... Make the test one of a standard of civilisation and Morris Alexander is with you all the time. Make it one of race or colour or creed and he will perish in the last ditch as a minority of one rather than give way. He has the moral courage to back the unpopular cause.'*

His influence was not only felt in South Africa. Alexander was one of the very few whites who succeeded in winning the confidence of Indians as a man who would listen. When Alexander stood for Parliament in 1908, he stated that he was in favour of 'the free right of British Indians to enter and settle as long as they conform with the laws of the country' throughout the Empire. In 1909, Mahatma Gandhi spent his last night in South Africa under the Alexanders' roof.

Alexander also stated:

> *In speaking and thinking of today, we should fail in our duty as Jews and as men if we forget that section of the community which cannot with self-respect rejoice over Union wholeheartedly as we. I refer to the Coloured people, who by the Act of Union suffer serious and unmerited injustice. Let us trust that this 'blot on the scutcheon,' this stain on the honour of our young country, will speedily be wiped out.*[117]

These noble and wise sentiments did probably not register as readily with the majority of the Litvaks in South Africa as the earlier quoted thought on Union. The Kirsch, Kapelus and Hotz families, like most other newly arrived Litvaks, were then so occupied in providing for themselves and their young families and establishing a home in their new environment that they steered clear of politics that did not directly affect them.

The second generation of these families were all born during the period leading up to the formation of the Union of South Africa and the end of the First World War. The social, political and economic differences and attitudes between the language and racial groups that make up South Africa inevitably influenced how they acculturated in their new country and their attitudes to the issues of the day.

For this generation of the Kapelus family, who lived, grew up and were educated in the midst of the Afrikaners, these differences were even more real. My father and his siblings lived and went to school in Nieuwoudtville and Calvinia shortly after the establishment of Union and during the First World War. My parents moved from Calvinia to Van Rhynsdorp in 1941 and my sister and I lived and initially went to school in the village. We both attended English boarding schools in Cape Town, I at the age of 9 and my sister at 10. We spent all our school holidays in the village with our Afrikaans friends. Being Jewish, we straddled three of the white groups in South Africa: the Jewish community, the Afrikaners among whom we lived and the English speakers at school.

We experienced the hostility of the Afrikaners towards the English, as well as their fierce nationalism from an early age. Our mother was from Scotland, so we spoke English at home but Afrikaans to everybody else. We observed our Jewish traditions and everyone in the village knew us as Jews; the Afrikaans children and some adults often referred to us as *Jood* (Jew).

Why was there this hostility and even hatred of the English? Why was the point of reference for the Afrikaners what one was – English, Jew, Hotnot (a disparaging term for Coloured people, abbreviated from Hottentot) or Kaffir (an equally disparaging term for black people)?

That notwithstanding, the English speakers were as prejudiced against the Afrikaner, treating them with disdain. As Giliomee puts it: "In many ways the Afrikaners, ironically, were being subjected to the same rituals of subjection and degradation as those they employed to keep the coloureds and blacks in their inferior place." The English South Africans created their own exclusive clubs, not allowing Jews, Afrikaners, blacks or Coloureds to become members. It was as if South Africa developed into a 'silo society', labelling each group, restricting them to living and socialising with their own, and by doing so reinforcing the differences between them. It felt as if there were at least three white societies, Afrikaner, English and Jewish, and three non-white societies, black, Coloured and Asian.

In the cities of South Africa where both English and Afrikaner had substantial communities (Johannesburg, Cape Town, Port Elizabeth and Bloemfontein), they by and large lived among their own and sent their children to separate schools, clearly illustrating this concept of the 'silo society'.[118] There appeared to be no desire to create an inclusive South African nation. Why was the division between the white communities so bitter and final?

Effect of the Anglo-Boer War on Ethnic Attitudes

The attitude adopted by the British in the Anglo-Boer War exacerbated this animosity and in turn influenced the social, economic and political development of South Africa until 1994.

Britain had rejected the ultimatum of the Boer Republics on 10 October 1899 and by June the following year both Boer capitals were under British control. The annexation of the Transvaal and Orange Free State swiftly followed in December 1900, and before the year was out British commander-in-chief Lord Roberts had returned to England. The British thought the war was over and won.[119]

What seemed to be the end was only the beginning, however. An intensive, country-wide guerrilla war ensued. Far from capitulating, the Boers made use of the one resource they possessed in abundance, the open *veld*, as well as local support wherever they found themselves, to provide food, fresh horses and fodder, men, weapons and ammunition.

Roberts' successor Lord Kitchener's response was twofold: deporting captured Boers to prison camps in St Helena, Bermuda, Ceylon (Sri Lanka) and India, as well as a 'scorched earth' policy to prevent the local population from resupplying the Boer Commandos. To achieve this, British troops rounded up and incarcerated Boer women and children in concentration camps run by the military. They also placed blacks who acted as *agterryers* (driving wagons, tending horses, and so on, behind the fighting Boer forces), as well as the servants and farm labourers of Boers, in separate concentration camps.

The British military held 154,000 Boer and black civilians in the camps, including some 116,000 Boer women and children.[120] The conditions were appalling. The tents in which the inmates lived were of poor quality and provided scant protection or warmth in the cold Highveld winter. Rations were meagre and the conditions unsanitary. This was a combination that was bound to result in diseases ravaging the inhabitants. Some 27,000 Boer women and children died of typhoid, measles, dysentery, pneumonia and whooping cough. By October 1901, the death rate had reached 344 per 1,000.

The seriousness of the situation was not lost on High Commissioner Sir Alfred Milner, who wrote to then Colonial Secretary Joseph Chamberlain that the death rate was 'a very dark spot'. Yet nothing changed. Attorney General Smuts estimated that about 10% of the Boer population of the Republics died in the camps. Almost every Afrikaans family lost a mother, child, brother, sister or relative.[121]

Kitchener's strategy had worked and the bedraggled Boer forces were staring defeat in the face. Milner wanted unconditional surrender, but Kitchener realised that preserving the dignity of the Boers in the peace negotiations was paramount to having the Afrikaans people as part of a new white settler nation. Peace finally came when the parties signed the Treaty of Vereeniging in Pretoria on 31 May 1902.[122]

In a speech shortly before his death (26 March 1902), founder of Rhodesia Cecil John Rhodes was prescient in telling a Loyalist gathering in Cape Town:

> *You think you have beaten the Dutch [the Afrikaners]. It is not so. The Dutch are not beaten. What is beaten is Krugerism, a corrupt and evil government, no more Dutch in essence than English. No! The Dutch are as vigorous and unconquered today as they have ever been; the country is still as much theirs as yours, and you will have to live and work with them hereafter as in the past.*[123]

The seeds of the Afrikaners' bitterness, resentment and hatred of the English (lumping the British and English-speaking South Africans together) were sown and fertilised by their defeat and further encouraged by the devastation of their lands, and the incarceration of their women and children in the camps, with the death toll that followed. No sooner had they returned to their lands than drought, crop failures and economic depression drove many of them, proud landowners, off their land and into the cities to seek work for which they had little or no training. They felt that the same villain, the English, had inflicted on them military defeat followed by economic subjection.

It is against this backdrop that Afrikaner nationalism arose again. In January 1906, Louis Botha, leader of the Transvaal Boers, announced the formation in the Transvaal of the political party Het Volk (The People), with Jan Smuts as his deputy; in May 1906, the Boers of the Orange River Colony formed the Orangia Unie (Orangia Union). In the same year, Britain granted the defeated Republics self-government. In the Cape, the Afrikaner Bond, despite its association with the Boer forces, maintained its position as a political force and was at the forefront of establishing the South African Party (SAP) under the leadership of John X. Merriman and J.W. Sauer.

Between 1906 and 1908, in a long exchange of correspondence, Smuts and Merriman prepared the ground for a South African constitution. Having decided on a unitary state, the one issue that occupied their minds was the franchise for blacks, Coloureds and Asians. The Cape wanted a qualified franchise that would bring the blacks into the political arena. This was anathema to the Transvaal and the OFS. The agreement reached was that in the Transvaal, OFS and Natal, only whites would have the vote, while in the Cape, Coloureds would have a qualified franchise and blacks, also on a qualified franchise, could vote for special white representatives. Only whites could sit in Parliament and English and Afrikaans were the two official languages of the country.

The Union of South Africa came into existence on 31 May 1910. For a short while, the proponents of the 'forgive and forget' philosophy (Botha and Smuts) and those who wanted to unite whites into an Afrikaner nation, such as James Barrie Munnik Hertzog and General De Wet, put aside their differences and all joined the National South African Party. It won the first election in 1911, with Boer general Louis Botha as its first prime minister.

The 1910 census showed the following population figures:

Blacks	3,956,000
Whites	1,257,000
Coloureds	517,000
Asians	148,000
Total	5,878,000

Afrikaners constituted some 700,000 out of the 1,257,000 whites.[124]

The exclusion of blacks from the vote led in January 1912 to the formation of the South African Native National Congress, which in 1923 became the African National Congress (ANC), which today governs South Africa.

By December 1912, tensions and differences between Botha/Smuts and Hertzog had come to a head, Hertzog famously saying that he would rather live on a dunghill than stay in the palace of the British Empire. The inevitable split came in November 1913, when at the SAP conference the delegates decided by 131 to 90 that Botha should continue without Hertzog. The result was that in January 1914 a special congress of Hertzog supporters established the National Party.

The decision of the South African government to enter the First World War exacerbated the rift between the English and Afrikaans speakers, as well as between Afrikaners themselves. The government of the day easily quashed a rebellion by Afrikaans rebels against the war and dealt leniently with the participants. The Afrikaners felt economically suppressed, culturally isolated and confused. The economic downturn made matters that much worse for the mainly agrarian and rural Afrikaners who had to seek work in cities dominated by English. They were by now a dispirited people.

In June 1918, a violent mob broke up a political meeting of the National Party in Johannesburg, addressed by Dr D.F. Malan, leader of the Cape Party. The next day, four young Afrikaners met on a *koppie* (hillock) in Kensington, a suburb of Johannesburg, and decided to form an organisation that would defend 'Afrikanerdom' and restore its pride.

It was against this background that, on 5 June 1918, the Afrikaner Broederbond (Afrikaner Brotherhood) came into existence. This organisation played a pivotal role in South African politics, education and social groupings for the next 75 years. It started as a cultural organisation for Afrikaners, but by 26 August 1921 had transformed itself into a secret society. Its aims were to expand to be an elite organisation with the specific aim of implementing a master plan making the Afrikaners the rulers of South Africa. It was the driving force in keeping Afrikaners and English speakers apart, thus creating the 'silo society' to which I have already referred.[125]

Thus the political entities that dominated South African politics for almost the next century were all in place within eight years of the creation of the new state, the Union of South Africa.

The Move to Calvinia

A Family Tree of the Kapelus Family of Calvinia

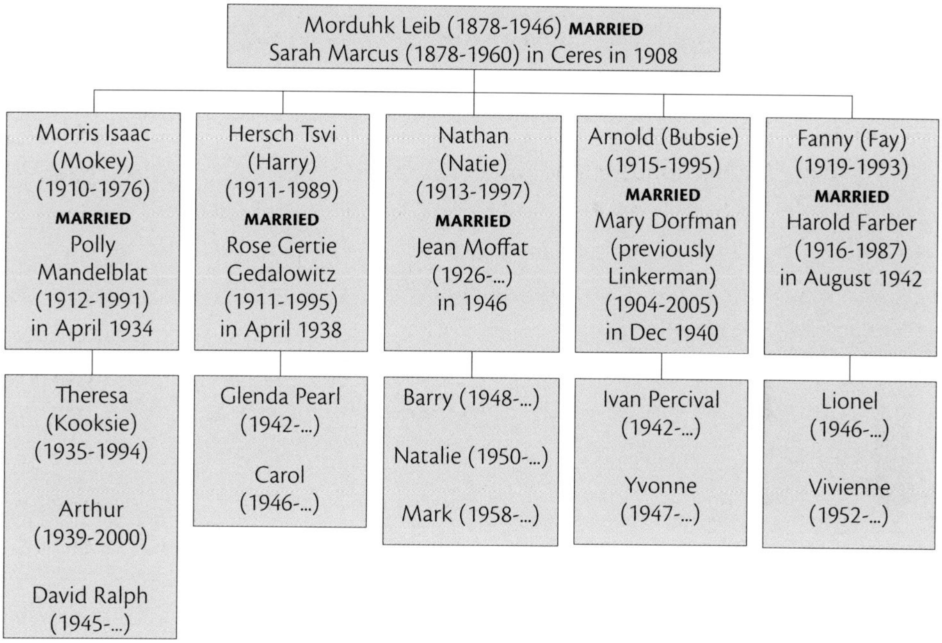

Leib Kapelus was spending more and more time in Calvinia and its environs. As we saw earlier, the journey between Ceres and Calvinia was an arduous and long trek of 260 kilometres through dry, sparsely populated and dusty territory. In the circumstances, the decision to move the family home to Calvinia seemed sensible. He lived in and around Calvinia for the rest of his life.

Calvinia – A Short History

The town of Calivinia in the Northern Cape (now), or Northwestern Cape as we knew it, played a significant part in the lives of the Kapelus and Dorfman families. A look at its history would not go amiss.

Hantam was the original name given to the area and later the town that was established on the northern bank of the Oorlogskloof River. The word *hantam* is of Khoi origin, *!Han\ami*, which apparently means 'mountain where the red bulb grows'. Hantam is the corrupted version of *!Han/ami*, as the mountain to the north of the town is still called today. Another explanation is that *Han* in Khoi is the plural of father and *t'a* the Khoi word for reed. The Hantam's River appears on old maps as *Vaderlandsche Rietfontein*, a Dutch translation of the Khoi name. The Hantam and Rebunie, a mountain to the south of the town, are the two outstanding landmarks in the area.[126]

The view as one approaches Calvinia, with the Hantam mountain range as a backdrop to the town

Rebunie, as seen from the road leading to Calvinia

This is a winter rainfall area, very dry and dusty in summer. Since the earliest times it had been a hunting ground for the nomadic San people, as well as the grazing ground for the Khoi, nomadic sheepherders. There were no boundaries and no one person or tribe owned the land. Both the San and the Khoi would criss-cross the area hunting or grazing their flocks. Their heritage is still to be found in the rock paintings of the San and the utensils and stone walls of the sheep pens built by the Khoi. The only whites who visited the area in the early eighteenth century were hunters, who would also have bartered with the Khoi for skins, ivory and livestock.

By 1750, the first *trekboers* had settled in the area and applied for licences to graze on and occupy tracts of land. By 1813, the Cape had introduced a system of quitrent, allowing *trekboers* to establish themselves on farms on a permanent basis. The first quitrent farms leased to *trekboers* in the Hantam date from between 1832 and 1838. The occupants created boundaries to their properties, preventing the Khoi and San from roaming freely over all of the area. This inevitably led to clashes, particularly with the Khoi, who were also stock farmers.[127]

The San resented the occupation of their hunting grounds and moved north, but the Khoi, who over time had had their social and political system undermined by the whites, succumbed, lost their independence and finally became part of the system. Many of the Khoi in the Hantam settled on white farms as herders, with some even keeping their own livestock.

The town of Hantam is some 420 kilometres from Cape Town. In the 1830s, there would have been two viable routes for the *trekboers* to get to the area. The first would have been to cross the Witzenberg Range from *het land van Waveren*, present-day Tulbagh, and then the Skurweberg Range as well as the Breede River several times. The second would have been to travel north by passing Piekenierskloof, which lies between Piketberg and Citrusdal, and proceeding on the eastern bank of the Olifants River near Clanwilliam, then crossing the Pakhuis Pass. Neither of these routes had roads or bridges, so the ox wagons on which they travelled had to be dismantled and hauled on the backs of the oxen, to be reassembled once they had reached passable terrain.

The farming community in the environs of Hantam grew and prospered and by 1826, this community fell under the jurisdiction of the magistrate at Jandisselsvlei (later Clanwilliam), where they would also have attended church. It would have taken some 20 hours on horseback or 60 hours by ox wagon to reach Clanwilliam through Pakhuis.

On 19 January 1847, at a meeting held on Tygerhoek farm, those present decided to found a community of the Dutch Reformed Church. The church authorities duly gave their approval and Hantam became the 33rd community of the DRC in the Cape of Good Hope.[128]

Within six years of this decision, two feats of engineering gave Hantam much easier access to the market of Cape Town: Michells Pass, connecting Tulbagh and Ceres, opened on 1 December 1848; Bain's Kloof Pass, between Wellington and the Breede River Valley, in September 1853. Travellers could now cross the previously impassable passes with greater ease, thus opening the route through Ceres to Calvinia.

The first predikant (minister) of the DRC, Reverend N.J. Hofmeyer, made a request to the DRC Synod to change the name of Hantam to one that would honour John Calvin (1509-64), whose Calvinist teachings form the basis of the DRC. The Synod agreed and an announcement in the *Government Gazette* of 30 October 1851 gave notice of the change of the town's name to Calvinia.[129]

In 1858, T.E. Bains completed the pass through Piekenierskloof between Piketberg and Citrusdal, initially called Grey's Pass in honour of Sir George Grey (now known as Piekenierskloof Pass), and later Van Rhyn's Pass between Van Rhynsdorp and Nieuwoudtville, through the Bokkeveld Mountain. This route travelled a long way next to the Olifants River, making the journey from Calvinia to Cape Town less arduous. It also gave travellers the option of using Pakhuis Pass over the Cederberg, between Clanwilliam and the escarpment to Calvinia.

Views of Calvinia
[Photographs courtesy
of the National Archives,
Cape Town, South Africa

The Jewish Community of Calvinia

Even at this early stage in the existence of Calvinia, it had at least one Jewish resident. Louis Heilbrun, who appears to have been the first trader in the town, settled in Hantam some time between 1839 and 1843. It seems that he rented his first store from two other Jews, Goldschmidt and Sussholtz. Goldschmidt became a magistrate in Calvinia and went on to be a member of the Cape Parliament. Heilbrun hailed from Germany and soon took in a partner, Gustav Wetzlar, a German Jew who had arrived at the Cape in 1861. How and when Wetzlar settled in Calvinia we do not know. It is clear that Louis Heilbrun later moved to Cape Town, as he was a warden of the Cape Town Hebrew Congregation from 1859 to 1864. It is probable that Wetzlar worked in Calvinia and Heilbrun visited from time to time. This is all the more likely as in 1863 another German Jew, Louis Rosenblatt, bought out the partnership. In 1873, Wetzlar also left Calvinia, settling in East London, where he made a mark in public life, being elected to the East London Town Council in 1881 and becoming Mayor in March 1889 and a Justice of the Peace a month later.

By the time Wetzlar left Calvinia in 1871, other German Jews had made their way onto the Hantam and settled in Calvinia and the surrounding area. D. Bauman as well as Bernhardt and Anna Heilbrun settled in Calvinia during the 1860s. Julius Rosenblatt, Louis' son, soon joined him, as did his sister and brother-in-law, Joseph Hammerschlag, who arrived in the town in 1871 to join the family business. Julius' son Max was the third generation of Rosenblatts in the business. L. Rosenblatt & Co traded in Calvinia with a family member in control for 106 years.

In a letter to Reverend Joel Rabinowitz written in 1878, Louis Rosenblatt complained that it would be impossible for him to celebrate Rosh Hashanah 'except to the ruin of my business,' as Professor Hofmeyer of the Stellenbosch Seminary was travelling to Calvinia to celebrate the September Nachtmaal (communion), which fell on the same day as Rosh Hashanah. Rabinowitz, in a letter published in the *Jewish Chronicle* of 6 December 1889, reports that he wrote to Hofmeyer asking him kindly to postpone the Nachtmaal so that the Jews of Calvinia could celebrate Rosh Hashanah. Hofmeyer agreed and wrote to the DRC Council of Calvinia to make the appropriate arrangements.[130] A similar situation arose in 1932 and the DRC community agreed once more to postpone the Nachtmaal so that the Jews of Calvinia and the district could celebrate Rosh Hashanah without being concerned that their livelihood was threatened.[131]

From the 1880s to the turn of the century, Calvinia's Jewish population grew as migrants from Lithuania and other parts of the Pale of Settlement arrived in South Africa and many made their way to towns where *landsleit* had settled.[132] Some, such as the Helfet family who became influential in the town and district, had settled in England before venturing to South Africa.[133]

It was during this very early period that one of Calvinia's most famous Jewish sons was born. In 1885, Mr and Mrs Samuel Greenberg had a son called Leopold. When he grew up he studied law and after a successful career at the bar became the youngest judge appointed to the Transvaal Provincial Division of the Supreme Court in 1924, at the age of 39. His rise was meteoric, as by 1938 he was the Judge President of the court and was elevated to the Appeal Court in Bloemfontein in 1943, becoming Acting Chief Justice of South Africa in 1954.[134]

The Jews of Calvinia celebrated the High Holydays of 1894 with services in a private home. By 1899, a special room in the Rosenblatt family's shop had been set aside for regular services.[135] By 1904, the Jewish community had grown to 105 out of a total population of 11,776, of whom 5,830 were white. The Hebrew Congregation of Calvinia officially formed in 1904, purchasing a piece of land from the Dutch Reformed Church for the sum of £10. Moses Cohen and Leon Helfet, as Trustees of the Hebrew Congregation of Calvinia, took transfer of Lot 86a of the portion of Hoogekraal farm by the terms of the deed of transfer dated 9 May 1906. It would seem that this was the burial ground.

There is other evidence of a Jewish presence in the town: the minutes of a meeting of the Town Council of 1 February 1905 show that the Jewish residents of Calvinia had become involved in the civic life of the town from its establishment as a municipality in 1904. In a letter dated 28 January 1905, addressed to the Council, M. Hammerschlag complains that a contractor employed by the Council had not fulfilled his duties. At the same meeting, the council considered and approved an application by Morris Israel to build a shop and dwelling in the town.

At the meeting of the Council of 3 May 1906, M. Cohen & Co. obtained consent to build a hanging veranda without pillars in front of the Royal Hotel, next to the Calvinia *shul*. Many Jews from neighbouring towns stayed at the Royal Hotel when they came to celebrate the High Holydays in Calvinia and the veranda was a popular place to sit and watch the world go by.

After elections in August 1906, the Council at its first meeting welcomed the newly elected members Dr Seton and H. Rosenblatt, the first Jewish town councillor in Calvinia. Two years later, at the elections on 6 August 1908, Leon Helfet became the second Jewish councillor, a position he held unbroken from 1908 to 1918. (Leon Helfet's son, Arthur, became a world-renowned orthopaedic surgeon. His brother Arnold was co-founder and President of the Calvinia Judean Society, formed in 1932.)

In 1919, the congregation, now known as the Calvinia Hebrew Congregation, purchased a piece of ground in the town from Cornelis Adriaan Otgaar, for the sum of £240. Solomon Canter in his capacity as Treasurer, and Leon Helfet and Max Klein in their capacity as Trustees of the Calvinia Hebrew Congregation, Hope of Israel, took transfer of the plot by deed of transfer dated 17 November 1919.

In anticipation of building a *shul*, the congregation had collected sufficient funds to commence building soon after it owned the ground; in addition, it raised a loan of £750 against a mortgage on the property in October 1920 (cancelled on 19 November 1926). The *shul* was duly consecrated and, according to a plaque on its wall, the first service was held on 14 March 1920 and the last on 7 August 1968.

In addition to the Jewish inhabitants, the Coloured community formed an integral part of the town, constituting half of the population. They had the franchise, albeit one qualified by income, the right to own property and an education, mainly in mission schools. They were distinctly loyal to the British, as was seen in their attitude during the South African War.

The Kapelus Family Settles in Calvinia

By the time Leib and Sarah welcomed their second son, Tzvi Hersh ben Mordukh Leib, known in the family as Harry, on Christmas Day 1911, they were living permanently in Calvinia. Like all of Leib and Sarah's children, he had a nickname: Henty.

How long Leib and Sarah had been living in Calvinia we do not know, but from the details given in the declaration of claim in a case instituted against Leib by his cousin Folie Kirsch and his partner, Abraham Elterman of Ceres, on 16 January 1912, Leib is described as a 'trader of Calvinia.' One must assume that the relationship between Leib and his first cousin Raphael (Folie) had become quite fraught for such close family to be engaged in formal court proceedings.

The declaration is interesting because it gives one an insight into the relationship a *smous* had with his principal.

Claim:

Folie Kirsch & Abraham Elterman trading as F Kirsch & Co claims the sum of £49/17/6 being the balance of purchase price of certain goods sold and delivered by Plaintiffs to Defendant during the period 14 May 1909 and 6 July 1909.

Plaintiffs Declaration:

1. *The Plaintiffs are Folie Kirsch and Abraham Elterman trading at Ceres as general dealers under the name and style of F. Kirsch & Co. The Defendant is Louis Kapelus a trader of Calvinia.*
2. *In or about the month of April 1909, the Plaintiffs entered into a verbal agreement with Defendant, whereby it was agreed that the latter should endeavour to obtain orders for Plaintiffs in the District of Ceres and adjoining Districts at a remuneration of 10% on such orders.*
3. *The Defendant was authorised by the Plaintiff to collect so much cash for such orders as he could obtain, he having to supply the Plaintiffs with a list of such collections. By virtue of this authority, the Defendant collected for plaintiffs during the months of April, May and June 1909 the amount of £100/3/2.*
4. *The Plaintiffs debited the Defendant with these collections, permitting him to utilize the same for the purchase of farm products, which it was agreed should be taken over from Defendant by Plaintiffs at their market value at Ceres. In this manner, the Plaintiffs bought from Defendant produce to the value of £78/16/5.*
5. *The Defendant also purchased goods to the value of £57/11/2 from Plaintiffs for his private (household) use, namely during the months of May, June and July 1909 but of these he subsequently returned to the Plaintiffs articles to the value of £20/14/11.*
6. *The Plaintiffs also advanced to the Defendant during the months of May, June and July 1909 various small sums amounting to £16/18/6.*
7. *The commission to which the Defendant was entitled on orders amounting to £16/14/0.*
8. *The Defendant has paid to the Plaintiffs £9 on account there still remaining due by him the balance of £49/7/6, which sum Plaintiffs have duly demanded from Defendant, but he has failed and neglected to pay it.*

Defendant was served with a Notice to Plea served on his attorneys Walker and Jacobsohn on 21 March 1912. There being no timely response, Defendant was barred from Pleading on 16 April 1912.

Judgement entered on Friday 19 April 1912.[136]

How and when Leib paid the judgment we do not know. We must assume that he did, as there do not seem to be any further proceedings against him in the matter.

What the declaration illustrates is the sophisticated and complicated agreements orally entered into by the parties. In the selling of goods and the collection of the money, Leib was acting as an agent. In buying farm produce, he was acting as a principal for his own account. When using the money he had collected as an agent to buy the farm produce, he was acting as the principal, borrowing money for his own use. Presumably, Leib repaid the loan when Kirsch & Co deducted the sum owed from the market price at Ceres, paid to him on the sale of the farm produce to them. It seems that it was Leib's responsibility to keep a record of the money collected by him as an agent as well as such money that he used as a principal for buying farm produce. Little wonder there were disputes that on occasion led to litigation, even between cousins.

December 1913 was once more a time of celebration for Leib and Sarah, as they welcomed their third son Nathan (Natie) to the family on 27 December 1913. Within three years, they had three sons! Natie too had a nickname, Piet.

The family seemed settled in Calvinia and despite the loss of the lawsuit with his cousin, Leib traded throughout the Hantam and Bokkeveld. He still spent long periods away from home as he travelled the area buying farm produce and supplying goods to farmers.

Sarah was pregnant again; since they already had three boys, she and Leib were hoping for a girl. It was not to be. On 16 January 1915, a fourth son, Arnold (nicknamed Bubsie, my father), was born in Calvinia. Still they craved a girl, and the wait, by their standards, was long. On 29 July 1919, Fanny (Fay to us all) was born, to the delight of both parents.

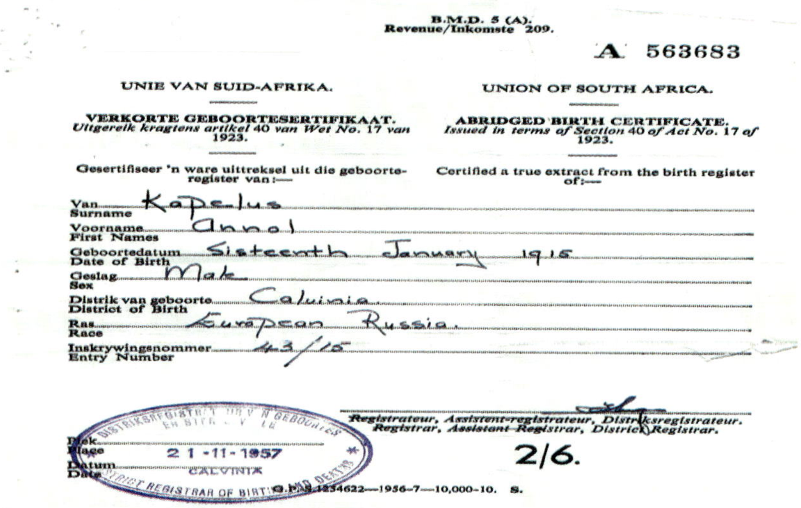
B.M.D. 5 (A).
Revenue/Inkomste 209.

A 563683

UNIE VAN SUID-AFRIKA. | UNION OF SOUTH AFRICA.

VERKORTE GEBOORTESERTIFIKAAT.
Uitgereik kragtens artikel 40 van Wet No. 17 van 1923.

ABRIDGED BIRTH CERTIFICATE.
Issued in terms of Section 40 of Act No. 17 of 1923.

Gesertifiseer 'n ware uittreksel uit die geboorte-register van:— | Certified a true extract from the birth register of:—

Van / Surname: Kapelus
Voorname / First Names: Arnol
Geboortedatum / Date of Birth: Sixteenth January 1915
Geslag / Sex: Male
Distrik van geboorte / District of Birth: Calvinia
Ras / Race: European Russia.
Inskrywingsnommer / Entry Number: 43/15

Plek / Place
Datum / Date
21-11-1957
CALVINIA

Registrateur, Assistent-registrateur, Distriksregistrateur.
Registrar, Assistant Registrar, District Registrar.

2/6.

G.P.-S.1234622—1956-7—10,000-10. S.

Birth certificate: Arnold (Bubsie) Kapelus

By the time Fay arrived, Mokey, Harry and Natie were all attending school in Calvinia, while Bubsie was at home waiting his turn, as children only started school at the age of 6. By 1921 he too was at school in the town, but the family was about to move.

The original Calvinia synagogue now houses the Calvinia Museum. All the Kapelus boys, Mokey, Harry, Natie and Bubsie, had their barmitzvahs in this shul. Bubsie and Mae were married here on 26 December 1940.

The Nieuwoudtville Years

The excitement and thrill of travelling were no longer there for Leib. He longed to be with his children and needed a change of life. His hard work and the time away from home had not been in vain; by now, he had acquired some capital. When the opportunity to change his lifestyle came, he grabbed it with both hands.

Nieuwoudtville, founded in 1897, was and still is a hamlet rather than a town. It lies some 51 kilometres east of Van Rhynsdorp, on the escarpment at the summit of the Bokkeveld mountain range and some 70 kilometres west of Calvinia. The population of the village and district is now some 2,300, but was substantially less in the mid-1920s.

The hotel in Nieuwoudtville was for sale. The price of the land and hotel was £2,650, with the costs of attorneys and transfer somewhat more. Leib was able to borrow on a mortgage the sum of £1,700 plus £100 for costs. He had the balance of the capital to make the acquisition and took transfer of the land and enterprise on 30 August 1924.

The Dutch Reformed Church then owned much of the village, including the property on which the hotel was built. Leib was only the fourth owner of the hotel.

The Nieuwoudtville Hotel during Nachtmaal, 1924

The Nieuwoudtville Hotel, 25 October 2011

Very few Jews lived in Nieuwoudtville and those who did looked to Calvinia and Van Rhynsdorp as their community. When Leib moved to the village in 1924, Albert Fisher, a general dealer, was already established there. Three of his children, Esther, Barney and Julius, were close friends of the Kapelus family. In the early 1950s, Barney and Julius continued to trade from the stone shop adjacent to their beautiful house built from the local stone. Esther married and moved to the copper mining town of O'Kiep near Springbok. All three were close friends of my parents and I remember visiting them at their home when their mother was still alive.

The other family associated with Nieuwoudtville as well as Springbok and Klawer is the Rom family. By the 1940s, Aaron Rom was settled in Klawer, where he owned the Railway Hotel in partnership with a bachelor by the name of Katz. His brother George had by then moved to Springbok and later relocated to Cape Town.

Leib and Sarah Formally Separate

This seems to have been a troublesome time for the family, although the Brickman cousins came to visit them, as recorded by family photographs. In June 1926, shortly after Leib had bought the hotel in Nieuwoudtville, he and Sarah entered into a notarial deed of separation. This was a very unusual step for a Jewish couple. They did not want the stigma of a divorce, so chose the route of a formal separation. No member of the Kapelus family ever spoke of Oupa and Ouma being legally separated, however, nor is there any statement in the document to indicate why the marriage broke up.

When did the split actually occur? We do not know for sure, but it seems from the terms of the deed that the whole family did not move from Calvinia to Nieuwoudtville. In Clause 2, Sarah has guardianship over Fanny, Nathan and Arnold and Leib undertakes 'that whilst the children are at school in Calvinia Louis Kapelus shall be responsible for payment of their school fees and requisites'. The document also states that 'Louis Kapelus shall have guardianship of Moltke [Morris Isaac (Mokey)] and Harry'.

Mokey was 16 at the time, Harry 14 going on 15, Natie 12 almost 13, Arnold 11 and Fay about to turn 7 in July. It seems that Mokey and Harry went to school in Nieuwoudtsville for three years before moving back to Calvinia. Natie and Arnold continued their schooling in Calvinia and did not move to the hotel, but stayed with their mother, as did Fay.

Louis and Sarah both undertook to give the children in their care 'an education sufficient for the purpose for which they may each wish to study having regard to the income of each of the parties concerned'. Each granted the other reasonable access to the children under their care, allowing the children to 'visit alternately and spend some days with their father and mother, respectively'. Sarah received maintenance of £8.0.0 per month.

The terms of Clause 7 illustrate the depth of ill feeling between Leib and Sarah:

> *That neither Louis Kapelus nor Sarah Kapelus shall visit each other or call at each other's residence or lodging without being specially invited so to do; nor write to each other; nor in any way molest, or annoy each other, whether in public or in private; and that either of them so offending shall, at the instance of the other, if so minded, forfeit all further considerations and benefits under this Deed.*

This might have been a standard clause in those days. However, there is not a single photograph of Sarah with any of the children, although there are many of Leib. He seems to have dominated the parental scene. Perhaps the clause does tell us a great deal about their dislike for each other.

The Nieuwoudtville years were brief. In April 1927, Leib sold the hotel property to Izak Albert Nieuwoudt for £3,000, with a further £800 paid for movable property.[137] Leib, Mokey and Harry moved back to Calvinia and all the children were once more attending the same school.

Leib, Mokey, Harry and Natie

Arnold, Fanny, Harry and Natie

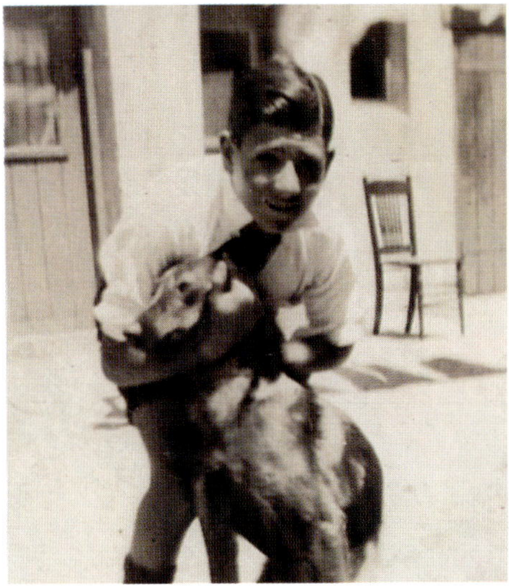

Arnold and his dog Rex

Leib and Fanny in Nieuwoudtville

I have fond memories of Nieuwoudtville and the hotel in particular. During the late 1950s to the mid-1960s, my parents were regular visitors to the Fisher family. Mrs Fisher and her two sons, Barney and Julius, helped her run their general dealer business. The Nieuwoudtville Hotel was then owned by Henry John Stoffberg (Uncle Harry to us), who had acquired it in February 1946, and he lived there with his wife and business partner Petronella Spies (known to us as Miss Spies). Sunday lunch would be enjoyed at the hotel and the men, including Miss Spies, would retire to the bar and play poker for most of the afternoon. In April 1960, the ownership of the hotel was transferred to her.

After a sumptuous tea, the Kapelus family would set off for Van Rhynsdorp. Yvonne and I would inevitably fall asleep on the back seat and be woken on arrival at our home.

Rooi Puts Farm

There is no record of where Leib lived or worked from the time he sold the hotel in Nieuwoudtville in April 1927 until he purchased Rooi Puts, Den Bosch, District of Calvinia by deed of sale dated 4 July 1928. He only took transfer of Rooi Puts on 6 February 1929, but might have been on the farm from the date of the deed, paying occupational interest to the seller.

Rooi Puts is a sheep farm in a winter rainfall area situated just north of De Bosch, some 60 kilometres south of Calvinia on the long and dusty road to Ceres. The farm took its name from the largest of the three pieces of land that made up the whole, totalling 2,287.4 hectares. This is the area that Leib had traversed many times in his early days as a *smous* and consequently he knew it well. Its income was derived from wool, pelts and meat, mutton in the main, sold locally. There were neighbouring farms, but this was a remote part of the Warm Bokkeveld/ Karoo.

By this time his eldest son Mokey had matriculated and was a young man of 19, studying accounting at the Technical College in Cape Town. Harry was in his final year at school in Calvinia, and he too was making plans to leave for Cape Town to study accounting. Natie was 16 years old and about to enter his last two years at school in Calvinia. Arnold (Bubsie), two years his junior and Fanny (Fay) were also at the local school.

Natie, Arnold and Fay lived with their mother in Calvinia, and although Leib had custody of Harry, he too lived with Sarah during the school term, as the farm was too far from the village to enable Harry to get to and from school on a daily basis. I have not been able to establish where the family home was in the village.

Wool, from merino sheep, was South Africa's main agricultural export, so Leib must have taken some note of what was happening to wool prices at the time he bought Rooi Puts. The wool price fluctuated wildly, like that of many agricultural products. During 1920 and 1921 the average price of wool fell from a high of 32.9 pence per pound to 10.7 pence, savaging the earnings of wool farmers. The price recovered steadily and by 1925 was back to 21.6 pence per pound, only to decline steadily thereafter, so that by 1932 it had fallen by 75% to 4.5 pence a pound.[138]

Why was Leib buying a wool farm at the very time prices were declining sharply? Why would he swap the relative comfort and prosperity of a hotel with the only liquor licence in the village for the remote and very basic, if not primitive, surroundings of Rooi Puts? His son Natie once remarked that the worst decision his father ever made was to sell the hotel and buy the farm. We can only speculate on this. Could it have been because the price at which he could purchase it was so attractive that he thought he could at last fulfil his ambition of becoming a farmer? He was paid a total of £3,800 for the hotel and the farm cost £2,530, part of which was financed through a mortgage of £1,000. He would most certainly have been acutely aware of the plight of the wool farmers; his customers of the Nieuwoudtville Hotel would have spoken of little else. We also know he would have been very familiar with Rooi Puts and the neighbouring farms, as he had been there many times over the preceding 20 years.

The farmhouse was and still is some 50 yards from the road on the western side. It faces the road and looks over the land to the east. A whitewashed boundary wall runs the length of the house and creates a garden area in front of the veranda. A gate in the middle of the front wall opens onto a path that leads to what must have been used as the front door.

The house itself is a simple structure, consisting of three rooms, the doors of each opening onto a covered veranda supported by four steel/iron posts. Leading off the room on the right, as one faces the house, is a kitchen with a wood-burning stove and a sink that was supplied with water from a borehole near the house. The bathroom and separate toilet were outside. The door on the right seemed to serve as the front door. The pitched roof of the house is of corrugated iron, leading to a flat roof covering the veranda. The roof is finished with gutters that lead to a corrugated iron tank that stores the rainwater. This served as a back-up to the windmill-operated borehole. The walls on either side have simple gables. A wooden ladder built at the right side led to an attic (solder). The door to the attic still exists, but the ladder is no more.

A photograph taken in December 2011 of the farmhouse on Rooi Puts. One can clearly see the original farmhouse with the sloping, corrugated iron roof and the buildings that were added subsequently on either side of the original house. The door on the right of the original acted as the front door

A giant cactus in the enclosed garden of the farmhouse growing next to a corrugated iron tank, used to catch and store rainwater running off the roof

In 1928 there was no electricity, so there was no fridge. A 'cool room' made of bricks with gaps for the wind to blow through was used to store items that needed to be kept cool. The house is still not wired for electricity. The neighbouring farms are not connected to an electricity grid and have to generate their own power with diesel generators. Rooi Puts has never had this luxury. It does seem now to have a telephone connection, but it certainly did not have one through the 1920s or 1930s.

The view from the house is towards the far-off Roggeberg Mountain range and the trees that grow along the Bos River, which flows across the farm on the eastern side of the road. The river only flows in winter, however; during the summer it is a dry bed of stones and sand. There appears to have been a shed or store on the eastern side of the road, which is now a ruin.

The view from the veranda of the farmhouse with the Roggeberge in the background

The Bos River in October 2011; it is hard to imagine it in flood

Economic Disaster

Without the deed of sale we do not know exactly what Leib purchased in addition to the land, but one must presume that there would have been machinery as well as livestock. What is certain is that in his first five years on the farm, he had to cope with the most severe and difficult financial and climatic conditions South Africa and the world had faced in modern times.

The exuberance, wealth creation and excesses of the Roaring Twenties were brought to a shuddering halt by the October 1929 crash of the New York Stock Exchange (NYSE). On 'Black Thursday', 24 October 1929, share prices plummeted as 12.9 million shares were traded in one day. The fall in prices continued for a month.

On 28 October 1929, known as 'Black Monday', the slide continued as sellers clamoured to get out of the market, causing a record loss of 38 points or 13% of the value of the Dow Jones Industrial Average. The next day, 'Black Tuesday', was even worse, as some 16 million shares were traded and the Dow lost a further 30 points. The volume of shares traded on 29 October 1929 was a record not broken for nearly 40 years. The market lost over $14 billion in value on that day, and the loss for the week was $30 billion.

This heralded the Great Depression, suffered worldwide for almost a decade. As global trade slumped, demand for South African agricultural goods and minerals collapsed dramatically, causing mines, factories, shops and small businesses to close, with the resultant loss of jobs and incomes. All this was exacerbated by South Africa suffering one of the longest and harshest droughts ever experienced during 1932 and 1933.

The macro-economic policy adopted by the then Prime Minister, J.B.M. Hertzog, and his Minister of Finance, N.C. Havenga, made matters worse. They decided not to follow the UK when in 1931 it left the Gold Standard. Hertzog and Havenga based their decision on the assumption that South Africa, as the world's leading producer of gold, would be able to maintain the Gold Standard. The Nationalist government also wanted to demonstrate its economic independence from Britain. As there were at that time no exchange control restrictions on the flow of capital into or out of South Africa, investors withdrew huge amounts of cash to be deposited abroad. This crippled the economy still further.[139]

Leib, like every farmer in the land, had his back to the wall. In a speech on the occasion of his 80th birthday on 16 January 1995, my father, Arnold, spoke extensively about the near-catastrophic effects of this period for Leib.

From March 1929 to the beginning of 1932, Leib had assiduously built up his flock, adding mainly merino ewes for wool and dorper ewes (a South African breed) for producing meat. By the early 1930s he was farming with over 1000 ewes as well as his own merino and dorper rams. As the drought took hold, Leib, in common with many stock farmers, trekked through the *veld* looking for grazing. Nevertheless, he lost 60% of his stock and was facing bankruptcy. His creditors were also suffering from the harsh economic conditions and the drought and they were pushing for settlement of all debts owed to them to enable them to stay in business.

To avoid further disaster and in an attempt to keep farmers and particularly wool farmers on the land, the Government stepped in with legislation and subsidies. A system of Farmers Assistance (*Boere Bystand*) was introduced whereby farmers could apply to court for protection from their creditors, resulting in a form of judicial administration. Their debts were frozen, and they were given the opportunity to trade/farm out of their predicament. Leib took advantage of this legislation in 1933, and over the next five years he rebuilt his stock; he eventually paid his creditors and was discharged from administration.

The Government also heavily subsidised the agricultural sector, particularly wool production, as it had been the country's main agricultural export. The local market was so small that wool prices could only be stabilised above the international price by subsidies. This was done from 1933 to 1937, by which time the annual subsidy to the wool industry amounted to £1,000,000.[140]

All this galvanised Afrikaner institutions such as the DRC, the National Party (Herstigte) under the leadership of D.F. Malan and the Broederbond to create, build and nurture Afrikaans businesses to provide their people with work and financial muscle. An ancillary and important objective was to break what was seen as the Jewish and English domination of commercial enterprise, particularly in the *platteland*, as the rural farming areas were called.

Farmers' co-operatives had been established, but they had not been able to maintain the support of the local farmers, many of whom had longstanding relationships with the general dealers in the local villages and towns. The general dealers were mostly Jewish, and were qualified and recognised graders and traders in agricultural products such as wool, wheat and maize. In the circumstances, farmers and their labourers would purchase their needs from the general dealer on credit during the year and at harvest or shearing time would pay the outstanding debt from the proceeds of the agricultural products graded and sold to that general dealer. This would often occur during the September/ October Nachtmaal.

Previously the co-operatives were partnerships and the farmers were reluctant to become members, as they would be liable for the debts of the enterprise if it failed. A change in the law whereby farmers' co-operatives became limited liability companies created a situation under which farmers were willing to become shareholders. To encourage shareholders to support the local co-operatives, the Government made them agents of the various Agricultural Control Boards, with licences to grade local produce so that farmers would deliver their harvest to them for grading and sale. In addition, the co-operatives provided low-interest loans to farmers, guaranteed by their incoming crops.

The co-operative became a one-stop supplier, as the farmers were encouraged to buy their farm implements and household needs from there, thus cutting out the Jewish general dealers who had previously provided these services. This movement slowly took hold throughout the 1930s and into the 1940s, so that by the mid-1950s the farmers' co-operatives in the *platteland* had largely taken the place of the Jewish general dealers in most villages and towns where they were established.[141]

By the time Leib took transfer of the farm on 6 February 1929, he was 50 years old. He had to support Sarah in accordance with the terms of the Notarial Deed of Separation, as well as support Natie, Arnold and Fay, who were at school in Calvinia. To satisfy his legal obligations, it was imperative for Rooi Puts to be a commercial success.

Leib, through no fault of his own, had an inauspicious start to his farming career, having to seek the protection of Farmers Assistance from the Government to stay in business. He did, however, weather the storm. After 10 years on the farm, now 60 years old, he at last had a profitable enterprise.

LEFT: This photograph of Leib and his children was taken between 1934 and 1936.
Back L to R: Harry, Natie and Mokey
Front L to R: Arnold, Fay and Leib

BELOW: This photograph of the Kapelus family was taken between 1934 and 1936.
(Abe died 20 December 1936.)
Back row from L to R: Harry, Natie, Polly and Mokey
Front row from L to R: Leib, Fay, Abe, his wife Rachel and Arnold

Arnold Chooses a Legal Career

By 1937, the Kapelus boys were no longer in Calvinia. Mokey was by then married to Polly (Mandelblat, married April 1934) and living in Cape Town. Harry, engaged to Rose (Gedalowitz, married 3 April 1938), was also making his mark in Cape Town, as was Natie, who was studying at the University of Cape Town.

Arnold Kapelus walking in Cape Town as a young articled clerk

Arnold (Bubsie) wanted to study law. To do so he had to study Latin as a subject for his matriculation certificate. The school at Calvinia did not offer Latin, so Arnold went to Cape Town, where he lived with his uncle Abe in Woodstock and attended Observatory Boy's High School for two years, matriculating in 1932.

He now had to find a firm of attorneys who would employ him as an articled clerk while he was studying law part time at the University of Cape Town. Arnold was fortunate to obtain articles of clerkship with the firm of attorneys Lazarus and Lazarus. At that time it was not uncommon for articled clerks to pay their principals for the privilege of being articled. Arnold did not suffer this indignity, but did have to work for no salary for the first six months.

Natie Kopelowitz (Kope) and Arnold in Muizenberg in the 1930s, while Arnold was studying in Cape Town

Arnold duly completed his examinations and his articles in 1937 and was admitted to practise as an attorney of the Supreme Court of South Africa, Cape of Good Hope Division on 27 October 1937.

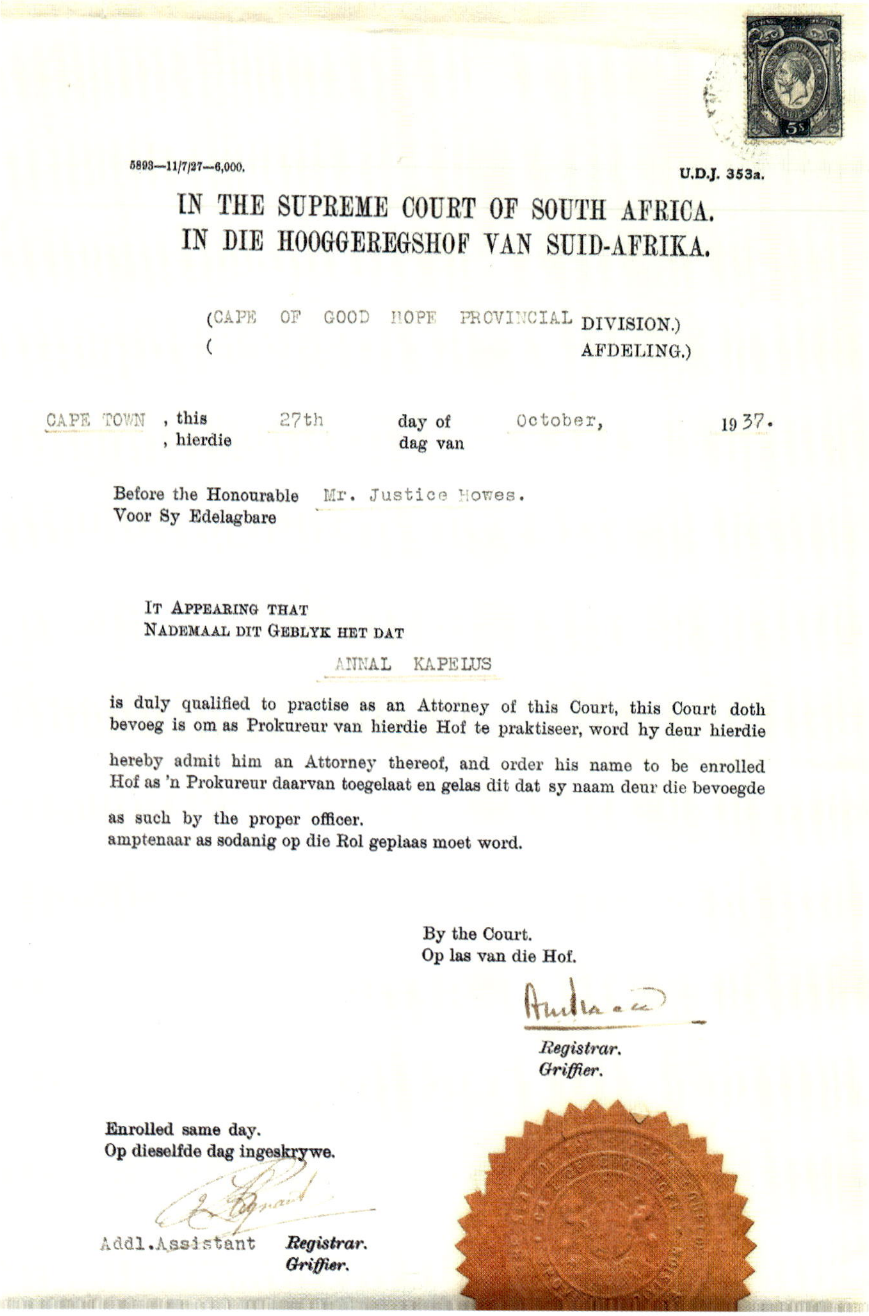

5893—11/7/27—6,000. U.D.J. 353a.

IN THE SUPREME COURT OF SOUTH AFRICA.
IN DIE HOOGGEREGSHOF VAN SUID-AFRIKA.

(CAPE OF GOOD HOPE PROVINCIAL DIVISION.)
(AFDELING.)

CAPE TOWN , this 27th day of October, 1937.
, hierdie dag van

Before the Honourable Mr. Justice Howes.
Voor Sy Edelagbare

IT APPEARING THAT
NADEMAAL DIT GEBLYK HET DAT

ANNAL KAPELUS

is duly qualified to practise as an Attorney of this Court, this Court doth hereby admit him an Attorney thereof, and order his name to be enrolled as such by the proper officer.
bevoeg is om as Prokureur van hierdie Hof te praktiseer, word hy deur hierdie Hof as 'n Prokureur daarvan toegelaat en gelas dit dat sy naam deur die bevoegde amptenaar as sodanig op die Rol geplaas moet word.

By the Court.
Op las van die Hof.

Registrar.
Griffier.

Enrolled same day.
Op dieselfde dag ingeskrywe.

Addl.Assistant *Registrar.*
Griffier.

Arnold's Certificate of Admission as an Attorney of the Supreme Court

Arnold Returns Home

Arnold, like his father, was small in stature, 5 feet 3 inches (1.6 m), with thinning, jet-black hair. He and his brothers were keen sportsmen; Arnold played rugby for his school and university. He was serious by nature, loved reading widely, but was not in any way an intellectual, having little or no interest in music, the arts or theatre. His healthy sense of humour and good nature made him attractive company. He had lived in Cape Town from 1931 to 1937, but retained his love of and attachment to his rural roots.

So when he could not get employment in Cape Town after his admission as an attorney at the end of October 1937, he did not resist when Leib insisted that he return to the farm and take up life as a sheep farmer. By January 1938, Arnold was back in his home town, where he had attended school and knew most of the young whites of his age. Although the farm was some 60 kilometres from Calvinia, he would have visited the village regularly. He certainly knew and was known by all the Jewish residents of Calvinia, Nieuwoudtville, Leoriesfontein and Middlepost.

Arnold and a team mate in their rugby kit. From the background it seems as if this photograph was taken in Calvinia

Calvinia and its environs are dry, dusty and hot during the summer months, from late October through to the end of March/April. Temperatures often reach 40 degrees and higher during the day. At the time of Arnold's return in late 1937, Leib was still working hard to recover from the devastating loss of some 60% of his flock during the drought of 1932/33 and being placed under the administration of the Farmers Assistance Act.

Arnold turned 23 on 16 January 1938 and, in common with young men of his age working on the land, his working clothes were short khaki pants, a khaki shirt and a broad-rimmed khaki hat to protect him from the sun. His footwear was inevitably *veldskoene*, literally '*veld* shoes', actually short, brown boots made of crude leather with thick soles. Arnold had a sallow skin and after a short time back on the farm he was well tanned. He looked much more like a teenager than an adult man.

Leib was turning 60 on 23 November 1938 and for the first time since he had been farming Rooi Puts he had one of his sons working with him on the farm. It must have given him much pleasure and hope for the future. Yet he was very aware of Arnold's desire to practise law.

Some time during 1938 (there is no record of the exact date), Leib had a meeting on the farm with his attorney, Izak Petrus Van der Westhuysen. As they were leaving the farmhouse, Leib casually asked Van der Westhuysen whether he was by any chance looking for a young lawyer to employ in his office in Calvinia. To Leib's delight, Van der Westhuysen answered in the affirmative. They conversed in Afrikaans.

> *'But my son is an attorney looking for a position,' replied Leib.*
>
> *'Where is your son?' asked Van der Westhuysen.*
>
> *'There he is,' said Leib, pointing to Arnold, dressed in his khaki shorts and short-sleeved shirt, working on a piece of machinery in the yard.*
>
> *'But he is still a child (Maar hy is dan nog'n kind),' observed Arnold's future employer.*

Leib was annoyed at the insult. He stormed into the farmhouse and emerged with Arnold's Certificate of Admission as an Attorney of the Supreme Court.

Satisfied as to his credentials, and after a short chat with Arnold, Van der Westhuysen offered him a position as a professional assistant at his firm. So in January 1939, less than a year before the outbreak of the Second World War,

Arnold started his career in law, as an assistant at Le Roux & Van der Westhuizen in Calvinia.[142]

It is striking that it was not Arnold who made the approach to Van der Westhuizen but his father, thereby unselfishly creating the opportunity for Arnold to leave the farm. Leib was once again alone on the farm. By now he was suffering from a heart condition and he was not able to do the physical work demanded from a sheep farmer at lambing time or when the sheep were sheared. He nevertheless wanted to stay at Rooi Puts, so he employed a manager who farmed under his direction.

The Hotz Family in South Africa: 1910-1938

A Family Tree of the Hotz Family of Pniel

David Hotz (1880-1968) **MARRIED**
Leah Abramson (1887-1966) in Paarl in 1910

Jessie (1911-2004)
Abraham (Abe) (1912-1983)
Cecil (1914-1979)
Issedore (Issy) (1917-2005)
Elija (Ellie) (1921-...)

David Hotz, my late wife Esther's grandfather, arrived in the Colony of Cape of Good Hope in 1901 as a 20-year-old and became naturalised on 28 January 1905, some four years later. By then he was a general dealer in Pniel, a hamlet near Paarl.

His future wife, Leah Abramson, sailed steerage on the vessel *Scot* and arrived in Cape Town in about March or April 1903. She gave her age as 22 years and her occupation as a tailor. We know from the death notice filed at the time of her passing that she was born on 7 May 1887, so in fact she would have been only 16 years old in 1903. This was during the period in which the government had agreed not to strictly apply the provisions of the Immigration Act 1902. As she had a trade and could support herself, she managed to enter the Cape Colony without difficulty.

We know very little of Leah Abramson's life in the period between her arrival in 1903 and her marriage in 1910. We know that she was in Cape Town, but not where she lived, what work she did or how she met David. Like many Jewish migrants of their age, mutual friends probably introduced them to each other. We do know, however, that in 1910 they were married in the Paarl *shul* by Reverend J.L. Hilkowitz.

The Paarl Hebrew Congregation was an old community, originally known as Or Israel (Light of Israel), established in 1893. From the following year services were held in a temporary synagogue in Malherbe Street, until 1904 when the construction of the Paarl Synagogue, on the corner of Breda and Synagogue Streets, was completed. The consecration and opening of the *shul* took place on 28 August 1904 and Reverend A.P. Bender of Cape Town and Reverend Weinberg of Paarl conducted the service.

David would have been 30 years old and Leah 23 when they married; quite mature for those days. A photograph of them taken some time between 1913 and 1915 with their eldest two children as toddlers seems to confirm that they were a more mature couple.

David and Leah settled in Pniel, where all their children were born. Their eldest, Jessie, Esther's mother, was born on 27 July 1911, followed very quickly by Abraham (Abe) on 21 August 1912. Jessie and Abe were toddlers when their brother Cecil was born on 31 July 1914. After a gap of three years, Isidore (Issy) came into the world on 14 November 1917, followed by Elijah (Ellie) on 19 February 1921. The family remained members of the Paarl Hebrew Congregation until 1922.

David and Leah with their eldest two children, Jessie standing and Abe on Leah's lap

Villiersdorp

By the time Ellie was born the Hotz family had been living in Pniel for about 11 years and David had lived there for almost 20 years. Yet in 1922 they decided to move to Villiersdorp, a village in the Drakenstein Mountains, where David and Leah once more opened a general dealer's store. Ellie was a baby, but Jessie, 11 years old, now had to attend school in Groot Drakenstein with her brothers Abe (10) and Cecil (8). Issy and Ellie were too young; schooling started at 6 years of age.

While in Villiersdorp, on 18 November 1924 David took and passed a certificate of competence to drive any light petrol-driven vehicle. He obviously lost his original licence, because he applied for a replacement driver's licence, which was duly issued to him in 1943. He and Leah were then living in the block of flats known as Glenhaven at 105 Kloof Street, Cape Town. The replacement licence confirms the issue of the original in 1924.[143]

Villiersdorp is a picturesque village in the heart of the Drakenstein Mountains, where wheat, apples, pears and other deciduous fruit are cultivated. The village did not have a Jewish community, so the Hotz family became members of the Somerset West Hebrew Congregation, which had been established in 1903. The two elder boys, Abe and Cecil, had their barmitzvahs in 1925 and 1927 respectively in the Somerset West synagogue, which was built in 1923.

A view of the mountains in and around Villiersdorp

The Move to Cape Town

In 1928, the Hotz family decided to move to Cape Town and settled in the midst of the Jewish community in Constitution Street. Jessie had completed her schooling, having matriculated from the school at Groot Drakenstein and started to work as soon as they relocated.

The boys had to complete their education in Cape Town. The language of instruction in Pniel and Villiersdorp was Dutch. In Cape Town, however, it was to be English. Cecil, then 14 years old, attended Cape Town Boys High School and Issy and Ellie attended Hope Lodge Junior School and then went on to Cape Town High School to complete their studies.

By the mid-1930s the family had moved to the Tamboerskloof area, first living in De la Ren Street, then at Glenhaven, 105 Kloof Street. David was no longer a general dealer but ran a dairy, situated at the corner of Weltevreden and Kloof Streets. Cape Milk Marketing Organization Limited, of which he owned one fully paid-up 'D' class share, owned the Weltevreden Dairy.[144]

Certificate No. 198

Shares

CAPE MILK MARKETING ORGANIZATION LIMITED

DIRECTORS

David owned one 'D' class share in the Cape Milk Marketing Organization Limited

Abe had just completed his schooling (matriculated 1930) and Cecil was entering his last two years at school, matriculating in 1932.

The family were members of Tikvath Israel, so they attended the Great Synagogue, known as the Gardens Synagogue. This is where Issy (1930) and Ellie (1934) had their barmitzvahs. Ellie sang in the *shul* choir and was quite comfortable on the *bima*.

Issy and Jessie were always considered the academics of the family. Issy completed his schooling in 1935, with Ellie, the baby of the family, matriculating in 1938, just as the clouds of war were gathering.

The Broude Family of Upington

The Broude Family of Upington

Barnet Broude (Riga) **MARRIED** Dvora Isaacman (Zagare)

- Rae B **MARRIED** Benjamin Kessel
  - Daphne
  - Sandra
- Lola B **MARRIED** Julius Huth
  - David
  - Allan
- Solomon Michael **MARRIED** Jessie Hotz
  - Doreen Josephine **MARRIED** R. Penkin
  - Esther Tamara **MARRIED** I. Kapelus
  - Ann Rosalie **MARRIED** H. Whine
- Louis B **MARRIED** Miriam
  - Sheila
  - Leslie
  - Morris

Barnet and Dvora Broude

In the years before the Second World War, Upington, a town on the banks of the Orange River in the North Western Cape situated some 400 kilometres from Kimberley (where diamonds were first discovered) and 809 kilometres from Cape Town, was known for the cultivation of lucerne, grapes and sheep farming. Like so many of the country towns around South Africa at that time, it had a vibrant Jewish community consisting of first- and second-generation immigrants.

The Jewish presence in what became Upington is linked to the early history of the area, particularly after the discovery of the Kimberley diamond fields. In 1871, Reverend Shröder established a mission station on Olyvenhoudtdrift farm, situated on the banks of the Orange River. This was at the request of a local Khoikhoi chief, Klaas Lucas, who had been educated on a mission station himself and thus valued the education it could bring to his people. Lucas hoped that the establishment of the mission would provide protection from marauding neighbouring tribes. By this time there were a number of *trekboers* who had established farms in the area.

To give the mission and those living nearby protection, a police station was established; the safety offered by this development led to a small settlement being founded. The tiny settlement grew steadily, benefiting from the trade generated by the diamond fields. By 1884 it was a town, named in honour of Sir Thomas Upington, then Attorney General of the Cape (later to become Prime Minister), after he had visited it in 1884.

There have been Jews in what is now Upington from its very early days as a mission station. The Hammerschlag brothers, Benjamin and Joseph, opened a trading store at the mission in 1878, just seven years after its founding. Their partner was Morris Nussbaum; in 1879 they were joined by a Mr Benjamin.[145]

The earliest evidence of Jewish communal activity in the area is a report in the London *Jewish Chronicle* of 13 November 1896 headed 'A Remarkable Jewish Congregation in South Africa'. The article starts 'Upington, Gordonia, South Africa, Oct 2, 1896' and goes on to detail how 'Messrs Harris Brothers, who are principal storekeepers in this part of Africa, procured a Sefer Torah and Shofar, and also engaged a Shochet, for the purpose of keeping up the Jewish religion as far as lay in their power'. It explains that Harry Harris was determined to get a *minyan* in order to celebrate the High Holydays of 1896, and helped fellow Jews from as far afield as 100 miles to come to Upington and observe their New Year and Fast. In all 12 men were his guests.

So overwhelmed were the men by the hospitality and largesse of Harry Harris that they wrote him a letter to show their appreciation.[146]

LETTER OF APPRECIATION TO HARRY HARRIS

Upington, Gordonia, C.C.

Sept. 18th 1896

To Harry Harris, Esq. Upington

Dear Sir, We, the undersigned cannot take our leave without first showing you our great appreciation of the kindness and hospitality bestowed upon us by you and your wife on the occasion of the celebration of these great Holidays, Rosh Hashanah and Yom Kippur.

We are here in a vast country, bordering on the great Kalahari Desert, where it is very seldom that we are fortunate to meet members of our race, and we can well believe the very trying times you have occasioned in bringing us together to worship in congregation the Great Creator, and read His commands from the Torah, and listen to the blowing of the Shofar.

We cannot, as we would wish, express to you in words our sincere gratitude for your goodness, but we humbly trust that your prayers will be heard by the Almighty God, and His blessing be bestowed on you and your good wife.

Wishing you and all the members of your family Leahanah Tovah Vetichatemu.

Thomas Jacobson. Jacob Dreiger. S.H. Markus. J. Friedland. S. Jacobson. Lewis Bloom. A. Kohn. M. Greenspan. J. Schaml. B. Katz. S. Edelstein.

By 1898, there were more than 20 Jewish males in the district of Upington and the Harris brothers created 'a properly furnished little synagogue' in a room at the back of their business premises for regular worship. They also employed a *shochet/mohel*, Isaiah Hirsch Matz, who conducted services. After leaving the Harris brothers' employ in 1899 he served the Jewish community of Van Rhynsdorp for a short while.[147]

The Harris family, who had facilitated services and provided a place of worship for the Jewish community, left Upington and the Nurick brothers took over their mantle by 1904, providing a dedicated place for worship at their butchery. Moshe Nurick travelled to Cape Town specifically to purchase a Sefer Torah and *siddurim*. (Presumably the Sefer Torah purchased by the Harris family left with them.)

With the Jewish population of the town growing, it was time for the community to be more formally organised and the Upington Hebrew Congregation appears to have been formed in 1906. A room at the back of the butchery was no longer suitable, so in 1913 services began to be held in a rented building converted for the purpose. Inevitably, money had to be collected for the building of a synagogue with facilities for educating Jewish children. The foundation stone of the Upington synagogue was laid on 27 June 1922 and the building was completed on 19 November 1922 and opened by Reverend Helman, the minister at the time.

Most Jewish immigrants settled in or near the large cities, particularly those close to the mining areas of Kimberley and Johannesburg. A significant number would start their new life in one area and quite quickly move hundreds of miles to another town, where they either had a better support system or an improved chance to establish their own business. Esther's paternal grandparents did exactly that.

Barnet and Dora Broude, first-generation immigrants from Latvia, first lived in Port Elizabeth and then worked their way inland to Upington. Barnet was a jeweller by trade and his wife was a pharmacist. I have not been able to establish when they arrived in South Africa or exactly from whence they came, but by 8 May 1931, when Dvora passed away, they were living in Upington. The records show that Dvora was the first Jewish woman to be buried in the Jewish cemetery there.

A young Mike astride his horse at McTaggarts Camp

The Broude family was soon economically successful and acquired a farm, McTaggarts Camp. Its crops were lucerne and cotton. During the late 1930s tungsten was discovered on the farm, thus significantly changing the family's fortunes.

Esther's father Solomon Michael (always known as Mike) was the third of Barnet and Dora's four children. The two eldest were the sisters Rae and Lola and the youngest was Louis. Most unusually for a Jewish boy, Mike was taken out of school at an early age to work on the farm and to help in the running of the mine.

The Hotz Family in Cape Town

The Hotz Family Tree

David Hotz (1880-1968) **MARRIED**
Leah Abramson (1887-1966) in Paarl in 1910

Jessie (1911-2004) **MARRIED** Solomon Michael Broude (1910-1999) in the Gardens Synagogue, Cape Town in 1937	Abraham (Abe) (1912-1983) **MARRIED** Rachel (Raie) Rose (1916-1979) on 21 December 1939	Cecil (1914-1979) **MARRIED** Sally Solomon (1920-1977)	Issedore (Issy) (1917-2005) **MARRIED** Edith Zolea (née Rueben) in the Gardens Synagogue, Cape Town on 16 August 1953	Elija (Ellie) b 1921 **MARRIED** Bella Muller b 1928 in the Gardens Synagogue, Cape Town in 1949
Doreen Josephine (1938-...) Esther Tamara (1944-2000) Ann Rosalie (1946-...)	Martin (1955-...)	Selwyn (1948-...) Theodore Jeffrey (?-1961) Tanya Judith (?-1961)	Suzanne Elvira (1954-...) Brian Mendes (1960-...)	

The Marriage of Jessie Hotz and Mike Broude

Jessie Hotz in the 1930s

By the 1920s, the first-generation Jewish immigrants were by and large settled and economically viable. Their thoughts turned to the education of their children, most of who had been born in South Africa. It was common for the children to complete their schooling in their home towns and then go on to higher education in the cities. Very few of those who left home to study or train returned, so the young Jewish men and women who remained in rural areas often found it difficult to find Jewish partners. It was thus common for family and friends to make discreet introductions between eligible young people of the second generation.

During August 1936, Jessie Hotz, who was then working in Cape Town, and Mike Broude of Upington met through such an introduction. A romance developed and was kept alive by post.

Just over a year later, on 2 September 1937, they were married in the Great Synagogue in the Gardens, Cape Town, on the slopes of Table Mountain. The young couple established their family home on McTaggarts Camp farm near Upington.

It was not so long before the third generation of these two immigrant families was born. On 26 November 1938, Doreen Josephine was born in Cape Town, where Jessie went for all her confinements so that she could have the support of her parents. As soon as Doreen was able to travel, they set off by train to return to McTaggarts Camp.

Jessie and Mike on their wedding day, with David and Leah Hotz on their left and right respectively

When Doreen was approaching the school-going age of 6, Mike and Jessie decided it was time to move from the farm to the town. They purchased a house at 3 Van Copenhagen Street, Upington in late 1943.

By now Jessie was pregnant with their second child and wanted to go to the city for the birth. However, the Second World War was in full swing. South Africa was a participant and, despite being a long way from the action, suffered some of the privations of the war. Rationing was introduced. Travelling by car required petrol permits. The surfaces of the roads were of gravel and stone, except near the big cities, and the distances to be covered were great. A journey by road from Upington to Cape Town, some 809 kilometres and through at least one mountain pass (depending on the route), was not lightly undertaken, particularly with a very pregnant wife.

The only alternative was the train. Upington was an important junction on the rail route between Cape Town and Windhoek, the capital of South West Africa (now Namibia). Steam trains passed through the town daily. The journey from Upington to Cape Town lasted two nights and a day on what were functional carriages with three classes.

First-class compartments accommodated four passengers, second-class six and third-class, which was for non-whites, also six. On some of the trains there were dining facilities. A waiter dressed in a starched uniform would pass through the first- and second-class carriages with a gong, signalling that the dining coach was open. Those wishing to avail themselves of this service usually booked tables in advance. On other trains there were no dining or cafeteria facilities, and even if there were, many of the passengers took their own food and drink.

Each coach had a little balcony at either end where it was coupled to the others. The door into the coach was situated on this balcony, which was open to the elements. On boarding one entered a long passage with compartments on one side and windows on the other. In the centre there were two toilets and at this point the passage swung round, so that the compartments were on the opposite side to before.

The compartments themselves had two bench seats facing each other. These were hard and covered in green leather, with hard rolled cushions about 30 cm (a foot) long and about 15 cm (six inches) thick, also covered in green leather. To sleep six passengers in the second-class compartment six bunks were needed. The bench seats were used as the bottom bunks. The middle bunk was created from the backrest of the seats, which was pulled out and up to rest on steel pegs; the top bunk was a fixed, wooden-framed cot with a green leather mattress, which sometimes served as packing space if there were fewer passengers. Bedding could be purchased from a bedding attendant for 5 shillings (25 cents). It consisted of sheets, blankets and pillows rolled up like a sleeping bag. Sleeping was actually quite comfortable.

In the centre of the compartment between the two windows was a steel washbasin. A heavy mahogany table, which had flaps so it could be extended on each side, covered the basin when it was down. The table could be stowed by pushing it up and clicking it into a steel clasp.

Each compartment had two large sash windows situated on either side of the basin. At the top of each there was a deep green blind that could be pulled down to give shade and maintain darkness. At the bottom was a wooden slatted blind that could be pulled up, so that the window could be open while privacy was maintained and some protection given from the effect of the steam. Steam meant soot. With the windows open, cleanliness was nothing more than a dream; not even the wooden blinds were much help. In summer the compartment was always too hot and in winter, once the radiator, which switched off automatically at a predetermined time, was off, it was always too cold.

It was early winter, late May 1944, when Jessie and Doreen boarded the train in Upington for Cape Town, travelling second class. It was about 4.30 pm, half an hour before the train departed. Besides the clothes there was the inevitable hamper packed with food and drink to keep them happy for the duration of the journey.

The route took them through the Karoo, where they passed through the towns of Prieska, De Aar and then on to Touws River through Worcester, Paarl and finally Cape Town, where they arrived early in the morning of the second day. They were met at Cape Town station by David, Jessie's father, and driven by car to the Hotz family home in Weltevreden Street, Tamboerskloof, a suburb close to the centre of Cape Town, the same street as the dairy they ran.

It was the middle of winter, cold and rainy, although often there would be the most splendid days of balmy winter sunshine and cloudless skies. On such days Jessie and little Doreen had a clear view of the blue granite majesty of Table Mountain, so close one could almost feel it. When the Northwester blew, the clouds covered the flat-topped mountain like a tablecloth. This signalled rain and storms.

During Sunday night, 2 July 1944, Jessie was taken to the Delherbe nursing home, a maternity hospital in the Gardens, about five minutes by car from Weltevreden Street. The following day Esther Tamara Broude was born, a healthy, sturdy little girl weighing just over 6 lb (2.7 kg).

As soon as Esther and Jessie were strong enough, they and Doreen set out by train to return to Upington. Mike was able to see his little Esther for the first time – she was the image of him.

Mike Broude with Esther on his knee and Doreen kneeling beside him

By the time Esther was 2 years old, Jessie was eight months pregnant with her third child, Ann Rosalie, who was born in Cape Town on 2 August 1946.

Shortly after Jessie and Mike settled in Upington, Reverend Wulf arrived from Van Rhynsdorp to take up his position as minister to the community (1938-41 and 1964-67). This was at the time the Jewish community was at its height, as the census of 1936 shows a Jewish population of 210 out of a total population of 40,107 (16,801 whites). By the end of the Second World War in 1945, the Jewish community had started to decline, so that by 1951 there were 170 Jews out of a total population of 57,579 (17,904 whites).

As soon as Doreen and Esther started at *cheder*, Jessie became involved in community affairs. In the photograph below she can be seen second from the left.

Mike's father, Barnet, passed away and Julius Huth, Lola's husband and Mike and Louis' brother-in-law, took charge of the farm. At about this time, certain business arrangements that Mike and Louis had entered into failed. In the

Jesse can be seen second from the left

Cecil and Sally Hotz

Issy and Edith Hotz

circumstances, Mike and Jessie decided to move to Cape Town and purchased a house at 1 Scholtz Road, Three Anchor Bay, to which the family moved in 1956.

By this time, Doreen had finished school in Upington and started a course at Barkley House, studying to become a nursery school teacher. Esther was about to begin high school (1957) and was enrolled to complete her schooling in Cape Town by attending the Herzlia Jewish day school.

In 1960, Mike and Jessie Broude were divorced. The house at 1 Scholtz Road was settled on Jessie. David and Leah, Jessie's parents, lived with her, as did Esther and Ann. The family was not well off and Jessie worked to maintain them.

Rae and Abe Hotz, Mike and Jessie Broude back right, Ellie left and Issy, wearing glasses, in the third row. David and Leah Hotz are next to Abe

Ellie and Bella Hotz

The Hotz Family in 1958 on the occasion of Doreen and Raymond's engagement, outside No 1 Scholtz Road, Three Anchor Bay

From L to R:
Back Row: Edith and Issy H, Esther B
Third Row: Mike Broude, Bella H (partly obscured), Ellie H,
Raymond Penkin (fiancé of DB), Doreen B, Rae H (wife of Abe)
Second Row: Cecil H, Abe H, Leah H (Granny), David H (Zeida), Jessie B
Front Row: Selwyn H, Theo H, Tanya H (Cecil and Sally), Martin H (Abe and Rae),
Suzanne H (Issy and Edith), Ann B

Influences and Issues for the First Generation of South Africa-Born Jews

The first generation of the South Africa-born Kapelus and Hotz families were all born between 1910 (Mokey Kapelus) and 1921 (Ellie Hotz) in rural areas. As we have seen, the Kapelus children grew up in Calvinia/Nieuwoudtville and the Hotz children in Pniel/Villiersdorp/Cape Town.

Their homes and education were traditionally Jewish. Although they lived in a primarily Afrikaans-speaking environment, they spoke English at home and mostly Afrikaans outside it. It may seem strange that English would be their home language, when their parents, originally Yiddish speakers, had spent all their years in South Africa in Afrikaans-speaking towns. However, the vast majority of Jews in South Africa lived in the cities, where the lingua franca was English, so the newcomers' first objective was to learn that language. This is supported by the findings of the 1936 census statistics on bilingualism, which showed that 60% of Jews stated that they knew both official languages, 35% that they knew only English and there was a mere 0.5% who knew only Afrikaans.[148]

The children had some or all of their education at local village schools, where the majority of pupils were Afrikaans speaking, although the schools were dual medium (tuition was offered in English and Afrikaans). All of them, except for Arnold Kapelus, made their homes in the city: Cape Town in the case of the Hotzes, Mokey, Harry and Fay, and for Natie it was Cape Town when he was a student and then later Port Elizabeth.

As we have seen, divisions within South African society between blacks, Coloureds and whites were well established by the time the first generation of South Africa-born Kapeluses and Hotzes arrived. The situation in the Cape and particularly in the towns was substantially different from the rest of the country (Transvaal, OFS and Natal). In the Cape the people of colour were not black but Coloured, and the Coloured population were on the common voters' roll, albeit via a qualified franchise. Although most country towns had 'locations', areas set aside where Coloured people lived, these people were not subject to a bar on owning land in the towns and cities of the Cape. In fact, Cape Town in particular had a number of suburbs that were of mixed race, in that Coloured and Indian people lived side by side with whites.

However, this generation of the Kapelus and Hotz families grew up knowing that blacks were disenfranchised and were prohibited from owning land, except within areas set aside for them (13% of the South African landmass). Social contact with blacks was virtually unknown to them and even interaction with Coloureds would have been rare. With this background and taking into account that the families were still in the course of establishing themselves socially, economically and culturally, the divide between white, black and Coloured would have been of less importance to them than that between English and Afrikaans speakers.

Through the 1920s and 1930s they were teenagers living with immigrant parents who had suffered anti-Semitism and anti-Semitic legislation in their youth in Lithuania; something that the South Africa-born generation never encountered. Yet as we shall see, the absence of anti-Jewish legislation regulating their lives did not mean an absence of anti-Semitism or, as a Jew, being blamed for the ills of others.

Afrikaner Anti-Semitism

As Arnold Helfet accurately points out in his article in *Buurman* of March 1977, the relationship between Jews in South African villages and their Afrikaans neighbours and customers was poisoned by the anti-Semitic attitude taken by Afrikaners and their political organisations in the run-up to and during the Second World War.

After the end of the First World War, the Baltic States became independent republics for the first time since their annexation by Tsarist Russia in 1795. The emigration of Jews from these countries had all but stopped during the conflict, but by the early 1920s the flight of Jews from Eastern Europe accelerated once more as conditions in these countries deteriorated. Entry to the USA and Australia had become extremely difficult because of changes in immigration rules, which resulted in South Africa becoming a favoured destination – all the more so as many Lithuanians had relatives, friends or *landsleit* already settled there.[149]

It was during this wave of immigration that the last of the Kapelus family from Plungyan, the sons of Shmuel Kapelus, Leib's younger brother, left Lithuania for South Africa. Moses (known as Morris) Kapelus, an 18-year-old, arrived on board the ship *Nyassa* on 21 October 1925; his younger brother Nathan, aged 17, arrived aboard the *Toledo* on 11 December 1929. They, like their uncle Leib, made for Ceres, where the Kirsch brothers, their father's first cousins, were by now well established. They were extremely lucky to have close family who could and would employ them at this very difficult time.

During this period (1925-30), South Africa was suffering a severe economic downturn. The Afrikaners in particular were being pushed off the land and out of the rural regions into the urban areas.

In the general election of 1924, the National Party of J.M.B. Hertzog won power in alliance with the Labour Party. The National Party was mainly composed of Afrikaners, while the Labour Party was predominantly English, with several prominent Jewish members. The Pact Government, as it was called, was faced with growing discontent among its Afrikaans supporters, who were suffering disproportionately in the economic crisis. They did not have the educational, language (English was the lingua franca of commerce) or cultural skills to adapt easily and find work. This was exacerbated by the Afrikaners' view of themselves as white, which influenced the type of work they thought they should do measured against the blacks.[150]

South Africa's economic problems were brought about by both urbanisation and industralisation, which were closely connected. The urban areas expanded due to rapid industrialisation, driven by the sharp increase in the price of gold. Having barely recovered from the devastation and havoc wrecked by Lord Kitchener's 'scorched earth' policy, the Afrikaners felt that the same villain, the English, who had inflicted military defeat on them, was now inflicting economic subjection. This situation was exacerbated by a combination of the Great Depression and the severe drought during 1932 and 1933, which I have already described.

Herman Giliomee in *The Afrikaners* provides statistics that vividly illustration the scale of industrialisation.[151] In 1890, fewer than 10,000 Afrikaners (2-3%) lived in urban areas. This had increased to 391,000 (41%) by 1929, when Leib bought Rooi Puts. By 1936, the number living in urban areas had jumped to 535,000, fully 50% of the Afrikaner people.

The result of all of this was that hundreds of thousands of Afrikaners were reduced to penury. The Carnegie Commission researched the problem and issued a report (1932) concluding that there were 300,000 poor whites (some 17% of the white population), of whom by far the majority, up to 90%, were Afrikaners. This would constitute between a quarter and a third of the entire Afrikaans population of South Africa.[152]

In stark contrast to the Afrikaners, the first-generation Jewish immigrants – who had arrived in South Africa with very little, if anything at all – and their children, born in South Africa, had by and large prospered, both in the cities and in the country villages, where their numbers and financial position were now such that the building of synagogues was warranted: Calvinia (1920), Upington (1922), Ceres (1923) and Van Rhynsdorp (1928).

It was not long after the Pact's election success that a rabid anti-Semitic attack was made by an Afrikaans folk hero, General Manie Maritz, in a speech delivered in the Northern Cape town of Makwassie:

> *We have recently learned a great deal about the poverty of our people in the Northern Cape and Namaqualand. Who are responsible for this? Our arch-enemy, the Jews, who came to this country with a bundle on their backs and always manage to amass a large sum of money. The Afrikaners of these districts were virtually the servants of the Jews. It was similar in all other parts of South Africa, and a people who made their money here out of the suffering of the people usually left the country and spent it somewhere else.*[153]

Although this crude form of anti-Semitism embarrassed the National Party and was repudiated by them, the issue of Jewish immigration was kept to the forefront of politics as a result of a remark by J.E. Holloway (Director of Census) that, for the period 1920-25, the figures showed an increase in poor migrants from Lithuania, the majority of whom were involved in commerce; exactly the type that he stated was not needed or wanted at this stage.[154]

The rhetoric against Jewish immigration was pervasive and supported in influential newspapers such as the *Cape Times, Rand Daily Mail* and *East London Daily Despatch*, as well as *Die Burger*. An added impetus to anti-Jewish immigration was given by the Johnson Act of 1924, under which the USA adopted a strict quota system for immigration. Politicians from both the Afrikaans National Party and the predominantly English-speaking South Africa Party railed against Jewish immigration to South Africa.

Like a chameleon changing colour, so the reasons for the rhetoric against Jewish immigration changed and shifted. The Jews, and particularly those from Eastern Europe, were variously accused of being unassimilable, stereotyped as devious, corrupt and always outsiders because they retained their Jewish identity; if they did integrate and contribute to the economy and society, then they were upwardly mobile and so threatened to dominate the country. When Jews did well and contributed to the country, it was always at someone else's expense.[155]

Yet despite all this agitation for a curb on Jewish immigration, the Pact Government (1924-29) did not change its immigration policy. On the contrary, Dr D.F. Malan, then Minister of Interior, undertook not to interfere with Jewish immigration and Oswald Pirow, Minister of Justice (1929-33), assured the Jewish voters of Bethal during a by-election campaign that the National Party would oppose immigration legislation.[156]

The Immigration Quota Act

In the 1929 General Election, the Pact was re-elected with an increased majority. Without any prior notice, in the speech of the Governor General at the opening of Parliament, on 29 January 1930 Malan, despite his prior undertaking, proposed a bill to place certain restrictions on immigration. It was a bolt out of the blue, particularly for the Jewish community.[157]

In introducing the second reading of the Quota Act, Malan emphasised the consensus across party lines for the need and terms of the Bill:

> *The party newspapers have, with very few exceptions, greeted this Bill as one which is long overdue, and not only in principle but also as far as particular provisions are concerned, they have, to a very large extent, given their support. I have, in the short time this Bill has become known to the country, had proof positive that it meets the desire of a very large majority of the people of this country and that in some quarters, in most, at least, it has been hailed with a sigh of relief.*[158]
>
> *The Immigration Quota Act (no. 8 of 1930) came into effect on 1 May 1930. Its main provisions were:*
>
> 1. *Creating a two-tier system for immigrants:*
>   - 1.1 *Unrestricted immigration for persons from countries listed in the Schedule, and*
>   - 1.2 *Restricted immigration for persons from countries not on the Schedule to 50 persons per year*
> 2. *Creating an Immigrants' Selection Board that had the right to permit immigration from Non Scheduled countries subject to certain criteria set out in the Act and Regulations thereto and subject to the maximum of such immigrants in any one year to 1,000.*

The countries specified in the Schedule to the Act were the territories within the British Commonwealth of Nations, USA and countries of Western Europe.

The entire Bill was aimed at severely curtailing Jewish immigration from Eastern Europe, primarily from Lithuania. Malan admitted this in Parliament in 1937 when he said:

> *The Quota Act placed certain countries under restrictions ... We definitely had the tremendous influx of Jews in mind at the time.*

He called on the Opposition to leave party politics aside and consider the Bill as in the national interest, setting out three principles that he believed underpinned the legislation. These were merely a restating of the rhetoric against Jewish immigration from Eastern Europe: maintaining the character of the whites as 'Nordic', assimilability and maintaining Western civilisation, which was said to be different from Eastern European civilisation.[159]

The press, both Afrikaans and English, greeted the Quota Act with approval and continued to call for a halt to Jewish immigration. The Opposition in Parliament, in the main, supported the principle of the Act and the only real opposition to it came from four Jewish MPs (M. Kentridge, C.P. Robinson, E. Buirski and E. Nathan) and a handful of their colleagues.[160]

In light of the statements made by both Malan and Pirow that there would be no change in immigration policy, the Jewish establishment and community at large were shocked and surprised by the introduction and passing of the Quota Act, the consequences of which for the Jewish community of South Africa were deep and considerable. The main source of Jewish immigration to South Africa was blocked. The overwhelmingly Lithuanian Jewish community was cut off from its source, from its family and people. As the Jewish MP C.P. Robinson said in Parliament on 10 February 1930 with great prescience:

> *Do not tell me this is merely a Bill for the exclusion of Lithuanian Jews. It sounds the death knell of any more Jews coming to South Africa. At present it is the poor Lithuanian, tomorrow it may be the Jew from Germany or France that will not be allowed in.*[161]

The sentiment expressed by General Manie Maritz in a speech in Makwassie that the 'arch-enemy' of the Afrikaner was the Jew and that the Jew was to blame for poverty among Afrikaners was echoed in the viciously anti-Jewish cartoons by Boonzaaier's character Hochenheimer in *Die Burger*.

Giliomee states, 'Anti-Semitic sentiments were fuelled by Afrikaner frustration over their lack of economic progress in the city.'[162] In fact the reason lay much deeper: in Afrikaners' view of themselves as white Christians against the black heathen and slaves, which engendered an acute consciousness of race, religion and cultural difference. Hence they needed always to ask '*Wat is jy*' (What are you)?

This anti-Jewish invective and rhetoric from politicians and the majority of the press occurred well before the advent of Hitler and the Nazi Party as a dominant force in Germany. Unfortunately, as we shall see, attitudes only got worse through the 1930s and 1940s.

The manner and timing of the passing of the Quota Act resulted in a deep schism between the Jewish and Afrikaans populations in particular. Jews were now suspicious of and distrusted the National Party of Hertzog and Malan. This in turn resulted in the party adopting an increasingly menacing and threatening attitude towards the Jewish community. In an interview with *Die Burger* on 2 November 1931, Malan stated, 'There is a section of the Jews seeking revenge on the Nationalist Party for the Quota Act, but they are, of course, afraid to come out in the open.' He went on to add that it was 'very easy to rouse a feeling of hate towards the Jews in the country ... if they want to hit us they may be assured that we will hit back.'[163]

A number of Afrikaners who became prominent in politics in South Africa did postgraduate studies at universities in Germany in the late 1920s and 1930s. It was with this background that Louis T. Weichardt, in October 1933, formed the South African Christian National Socialist Movement (SANP), whose activists were uniformed Greyshirts, a paramilitary group that at its peak numbered 2000. Weichardt's offices were in Cape Town and in May 1934 the organisation was registered as a political party, which he took great care to emphasise was an Afrikaner party. This was just the first of many Nazi-type movements that came and went over this period.

The Realignment of Party Politics

During this time, Hertzog became disillusioned with the current state of politics and also felt that the two white groups had to work together to form a South African nation, each recognising the other as equal and respecting each other's cultural heritage. Smuts was also ready to compromise, as he had been languishing on the opposition benches. In the 1933 election, the SAP of Smuts and the National Party of Hertzog stood as a coalition. They won a handsome victory of 136 Parliamentary seats out of 150. They agreed a merger of their parties into the United South Africa Party (United Party) and Hertzog became Prime Minister.

The fusion that Hertzog sought was strongly resisted and eventually rejected by the Cape National Party, led by Malan. With the support of a number of MPs, he founded the Gesuiwerde Nasionale Party (Purified National Party). The names of those who supported Malan read like a 'Who's Who' of South African National Party politics: Paul Sauer (later a cabinet minister), Nico Diedrichs (Minister of Finance and State President), Piet Meyer (Head of SABC), Hendrik Verwoerd (Prime Minister), J.G. Strijdom (Prime Minister) and Albert Hertzog (son of J.M.B. and later a cabinet minister).

From 1933 to 1936, a total of 6,132 Germans fleeing Hitler arrived in South Africa, of whom 3,615 were Jewish. The hysteria over Jewish immigration did not abate. With the impending arrival of the *Stuttgart* carrying 570 German Jews bound for the Cape, a meeting of professors at Stellenbosch University led by Verwoerd protested, supposedly on the grounds that these Jews would cause it to be even more difficult for Afrikaners to make headway in professions and business. Malan, in a speech at the University of Stellenbosch, asserted that Jewish immigration was being organised by '*Joodse geldmag*' (Jewish money power), although Germany was a scheduled country in the Quota Act that he proposed.[164]

The weight of anti-Jewish vitriol in the Afrikaans press, led by Verwoerd in the *Transvaler* and Boonzaaier in *Die Burger*, as well as the support for Weichardt, resulted in Malan's party moving ever more to the right and embracing an open anti-Jewish platform; by November 1936, Malan was calling for the unequal treatment of Jews. The Purified National Party was now adopting an openly anti-Jewish policy.[165]

The census of 1936 recorded the Jewish population of South Africa as 90,645, most of whom or the parents of whom hailed from Lithuania (including Latvia) and other parts of the Pale of Settlement. There was hardly a Jewish family in South Africa that did not have direct family still living in the now independent Baltic States. By now, most were familiar with what was happening to their fellow Jews in Germany and they feared for what may happen to their family and friends still in Europe, particularly in Lithuania.

The Aliens Act of 1937

With all this anti-Jewish fervour, it was not long before another blow against Jewish immigration was to be felt, at the very time that Western European

Jewry was under threat from Hitler. The ruling party introduced the Aliens Act in 1937. Although the Act does not mention any race, creed or religion and makes selection of immigrants the prerogative of an Immigrants Selection Board, which had specific criteria to consider, in his address to Parliament Prime Minister Hertzog made it abundantly clear that 'the influx of the Jews is ... one of the immediate causes for the introduction of this Bill.'[166]

The Quota Act together with the Aliens Act succeeded in virtually stopping any further meaningful immigration of Jews to South Africa from Lithuania at the very time they needed access to a safe haven where they had family and communal support. We now know that the Final Solution, the genocide of the Jews in Lithuania, was more efficient and remorseless than in any other country occupied by the Nazis. It resulted in 95% of all Jews living in Lithuania in 1941 being murdered: 200,000 out of a Jewish population of 220,000. They were not killed in concentration camps, but murdered largely by their fellow Lithuanians within kilometres of their homes.[167] There was hardly a Jewish family in South Africa that had not suffered a loss in this unimaginable tragedy.

The Ossewabrandwag

The National Party (Gesuiwerde) and its elite support group, Die Broederbond, together with its cultural wing, the Afrikaans Taal en Kultuurvereneging (Afrikaans Language and Cultural Society), conceived the idea of celebrating *Die Groot Trek* (Great Trek) by building a monument to the *Voortrekkers* on a hill outside of Pretoria. The foundation stone was to be laid on the hundredth anniversary of the Battle of Blood River (the defeat of the Zulus under Dingane by the *Voortrekkers*) on 16 December 1938. The build-up to this gathering at the monument was a symbolic trek by an ox wagon from Cape Town to Pretoria. This symbolism released a wave of Afrikaner emotion and almost every region named an ox wagon after an Afrikaans hero, sending it on the long journey to Pretoria with outriders sporting beards and the womenfolk dressed in *Voortrekker* costumes. At each town along the way these wagons were met by enthusiastic crowds.

War was looming in Europe and when Britain declared war on Germany in September 1939, the Afrikaners were diametrically opposed to South Africa entering the fray. Hertzog called for South Africa to remain neutral. However, General Jan Smuts, his deputy, saw the coming conflict as a fight for the preservation of democracy and Western civilisation and advocated joining the Allies against Hitler. Hertzog's motion in Parliament on neutrality was defeated by 80 votes to 60. The Prime Minister called for the dissolution of Parliament and the calling of a general election, but the Governor General refused and called on Smuts to form a government.

South Africa's entry into the war resulted in Hertzog's resignation from the United Party, in January 1940, Hertzog and Malan's followers merged into the Herenigde Nasionale Party (Reunited National Party; later just NP), with Malan as leader. It also led to a polarisation of Afrikaans- and English-speaking groups and led to the conclusion that the only way forward for Afrikaners was an 'uncompromising spiritual Afrikanerdom'. There was, it seems, no longer room for a middle way in South African politics on race and colour.

On the back of the Great Trek celebrations and Afrikaners' opposition to South Africa entering the war, the Ossewabrandwag (OB) was formed, with its own paramilitary organisation known as *Die Stormjaers*. The OB was to the forefront of sabotage of the war effort and it adopted an avowedly anti-Jewish policy, attacking the 'British- Jewish democracy', 'Jewish money power' and 'Jewish disloyalty'. It became an Afrikaner populist organisation with a membership variously estimated at between 100,000 (Giliomee) and 300,000 (Shain & Shimoni).[168]

The NP was committed to a parliamentary democracy and would soon be in conflict with the OB and Oswald Pirow's *Nuwe Orde* (New Order), who were dismissive of the parliamentary system. By 1941, the two sides were in open conflict and the NP was suggesting that its members resign from the OB. By 1942, the Broederbond and the NP under Malan were in control and the NP was accepted as the political vehicle of the Afrikaner. This did not mean that the NP was giving up its anti-Jewish rhetoric, however. On the contrary: the Transvaal Provincial Congress of the NP, in December 1940, confirmed its decision of 1937 not to allow Jews to be members. It called on the Federal Council to encourage the NP in other provinces to follow suit, but this did not happen.[169]

By 1943, South Africa and the world were becoming aware of the increasingly barbaric and horrendous treatment of European Jewry. This made the denial of access to South Africa by Jews from Europe all the more difficult to accept. Tens of thousands of Jewish lives had been lost and the blame for this was laid squarely on the Afrikaners and their organisations, with the substantial assistance they had received from the South African press. The United Party won the 1943 General Election with help from the Dominion and Labour Parties, demonstrating that the Jews did not vote for the NP.

In a bizarre effort to change the party's image among the Jewish population, a series of functions were held in Bloemfontein on 8 December 1943 to pay homage to the Jewish citizens of South Africa. To publicise this event, *Die Volk* (The People), an Afrikaans weekly paper, ran a special edition on Friday 26 November 1943 with the headline 'HULLE HET VIR VRYHEID EN REG GEVEG (They Fought for Freedom and Justice)'. Morris Alexander KC MP attended the function on behalf of South African Jewry. In the lead article the paper noted:

> *Net soos Nederlanders en die Grieke, het die Jode dwarsdeur die wereld gely as gevolg van die Nazi wreedheid en onderdrukking. Hulle stryd aan die kant van Vryheid-liewende mensheid van die wereld is gekenmerk deur moed, selfopoffering en vasberaadheid.*
>
> *Dit is om hierdie rede dat die Afrikaners, wat Vryheid bo alles lief het en geloofsvervolging verafsku, hulde wil bring aan hulle mede Suid-Afrikaanse Joodse burgers.*
>
> *(Just like the Dutch and the Greeks, the Jews throughout the world have suffered as a result of Nazi cruelty and suppression. Their struggle on the side of freedom-loving humanity is characterised by courage, self-sacrifice and determination.*
>
> *It is for this reason that the Afrikaners, who love freedom above all and abhor religious persecution, wish to pay homage to our fellow Jewish South African citizens.)*

As is evident above, this was a far cry from the pronouncements of their leaders, D.F. Malan, Hendrik Verwoerd, then editor of *Die Vaderland*, Eric Louw, Foreign Minister, and Boonzaaier of *Die Burger*.

A closer look at the heroes to whom they were paying homage gives the lie to their intentions. Every one either supported or fought with the Boer Republics in the Anglo-Boer War. Nothing was said about the contribution that Jews had made and were making in every field of endeavour in the country.

The Effect on the Jewish Community

How did this anti-Jewish attitude affect the Jewish community and the Kapelus and Hotz teenagers in particular?

Their Litvak background led to a strong ethnic identity as Jews, rather than one based on religiosity, and Zionism was the most important Jewish political movement in Lithuania, so they, like so many of their age group, seemed to eschew South African politics in favour of strong support for Zionism. So much so that, between 1921 and 1939, the funds raised in South Africa for the Keren Hayesod (Foundation Fund), the main fundraising platform for Zionism, were second only to those provided by the USA. In fact, the per capita contribution from this tiny Jewish community was greater than anywhere else in the world.[170] Furthermore, the naked hostility to Jews from Afrikaners and their organisations resulted in the Jewish community aligning and identifying with the English-speaking whites.

With the anti-Jewish attitude of the Afrikaners at home and taking into account what was happening in Europe, the Jewish community fully supported the government of Jan Smuts when it entered the war against Germany on 6 September 1939. This support was expressed in a resolution adopted at the Board of Deputies Congress in 1940:

> *At this critical hour, when the Nazis are destroying the liberties of nations and of individuals and challenging the fundamental ideals of civilisation, this congress of South African Jewry solemnly affirms the obligations that rest upon every citizen and resident of the Union to rally to the defence of the country, and further that the Jewish community will do all its power to assist the Union and its allies in their fight for victory.*[171]

Indeed they did! The records show that some 10,000 South African Jewish men and women served in the Union and Allied forces. This is more than 10% of the Jewish population of the country at that time.[172]

In most Jewish families at least one of the sons would join the forces; the philosophy seems to have been that one son would join up and one would remain at home to look after the family. In the Kapelus family of four boys, two joined the forces, Harry and Natie; in the Hotz family, also of four boys, Cecil and Ellie served in the army.

Many Jewish boys volunteered as teenagers just out of school. Ellie Hotz was one of these and he and Cecil saw service in North Africa and Italy, with both of them rising to the rank of corporal. As we shall see, two of the Kapelus boys, Harry and Natie also enlisted and were in the forces throughout the war.

The interest and dedication to the Zionist cause by young Jews in these years resulted in Young Zionist Societies being formed wherever there was a Jewish

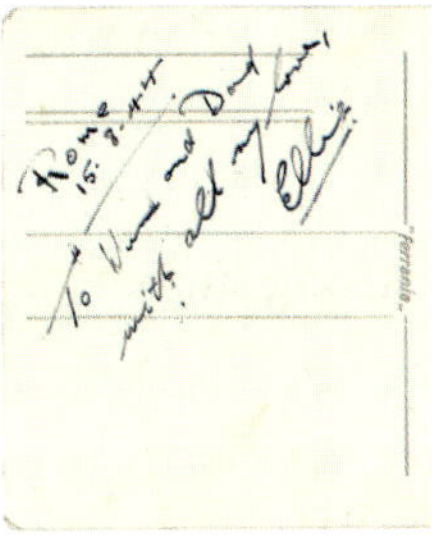

Ellie Hotz (top) and Cecil (left) saw service in North Africa and Italy, with both of them rising to the rank of corporal

community. All of these young people worked for and associated with the Zionist Movement rather than becoming involved in the politics of the day, local or national. In South Africa, 'politics is dominated by race', as Harry Schwartz so accurately points out, and this made many Jews eschew national politics.[173] Instead, the Jews of Calvinia and Van Rhynsdorp, as in many of the country towns and villages, were very involved in local politics. Many served as town councillors and even mayors of their home towns.

The Woodstock Young Zionist Society, early 1930s
Front L to R: Harry Kapelus, ?, Percy Yutar, ?, Natie Kapelus
Back L to R: ?, ?, Kalmanowitz, Mokey Kapelus, ?
Inset: Stone

Lithuanian Jewry's Contribution

In a second wave of Litvak immigration between 1911 and 1930, some 30,000 souls arrived from 'Russia' and, according to the 1936 census, increased the Jewish population of South Africa to 90,645 (now 4.5% of the white population of 2,003,857). This grew to 104,156 Jews out of a white population of 2,372,857 (4.4%) by 1946.[174]

It is thus safe to say that the Jewish population was a substantially homogenous group of Litvaks, the majority of whom came from one province, Kovno (Kaunas). Substantial numbers also came from Vilna (Vilnius) and Grodno provinces as well as Courland. It is remarkable that probably half of the Litvaks hailed from the towns of Ponevezh (Panevezys), Riteve (Rietevas), Plungyan (Plunge), Shavli/Shavl (Siauliai) and Yanishik (Joniskis), all in the Kovno gubernia.[175]

As we have seen, the Litvaks came into an existing Jewish infrastructure that was created by the Anglo-German Jews. Understandably, the first Jewish institutions, such as synagogues and burial societies, were modelled on the English Orthodox tradition. They were the leaders of the Jewish community. However, from 1882 onwards the Litvaks arrived in such numbers and in such a relatively short period that by 1902 the majority of Jews in South Africa had been born in Eastern Europe. It was not long before they took up the leadership role within the Jewish community.[176]

In common with all the Jews of the Pale of Settlement, they were Yiddish speakers. However, their traditional religious education was rooted in the Mitnagdim philosophy, which eschewed and strongly opposed the mystic teachings, emotionalism and sectarianism of the Hasidim, resulting in Hasidism making little inroads in Lithuania and the Reform Movement being unknown.[177]

The other important characteristic of the Litvaks was their view of themselves as Jews. They considered themselves Jews and never Lithuanian. Their self-segregation, the use of their own language, Yiddish, and their rigid observance of their ancient customs, as well as their rejection of integration into their surroundings, meant that they maintained a strong sense of their ethnic identity. So much so, that Yehuda Leib Gordon in his poem '*Haqitsa 'ami*' (Arise my people), encouraged his fellow Jews to 'be a Jew in your house and a man in the street'.[178]

A consequence of not integrating into Lithuanian society was that their political and social activities were mainly focused on Jewish affairs. Although there were the liberal *Folkspartey* (People's Party) and the *Yiddisher Arbeiter Bund* (Jewish Workers Organisation), a socialist movement known as the Bund, the primary Jewish political movement was Zionism.[179] (This attitude changed after Lithuania gained its independence in 1918, however. Jews were to the forefront of the independence movement and were as committed to its success as their non-Jewish compatriots.[180])

The racial and ethnic divisions in South African society were well established by the time the Litvaks arrived in the country. Whites were the dominant race, but even they were divided into English and Afrikaans speakers. The Litvaks as whites were part of the dominant class, with all the privileges that entailed.

In a society riven with ethnicity, there was a weak concept of being South African, even among whites. This reinforced the Litvaks' view of themselves as Jews. Even so, they compromised their religiosity. Some of the Litvaks were artisans such as tailors, shoemakers, builders and cabinetmakers, but by far the majority were traders. Saturday was a work day, so they could not keep their Shabbat. The result was that they created a new tradition: the Friday night service became well attended and families would celebrate the Shabbat by having a festive meal together after attending synagogue. In this way they created a new, different and more relaxed form of orthodoxy that accommodated their new lifestyle while accepting the existing Anglo-Jewish form of worship. As a result, Reform Jewry made little headway in South Africa.

Just as in Lithuania, their strong commitment to and absolute support of Zionism were equally expressions of their ethnic identity as Jews. So much so that South African Jews per capita were the largest group entitled to vote at the World Zionist Congress in 1946, some 39,945, of whom 28,876 cast their votes. In 1950, just two years after the creation of Israel, 50,000 South African Jews were eligible to vote out of a population of 110,000. Every home had a 'Blue Box' in which money for the JNF (Jewish National Fund) was collected.

With this strong sense of ethnic identity came a commitment to charity. There was a deep-rooted tradition of caring for the less fortunate throughout Lithuania. Dov Levin gives a detailed description of the charitable institutions in the Kovno province during the 1890s. In a single year, 1898, they supported 8,662 families in Kovno province, some 23% of Jewish families there.[181] In every city of South Africa the Jews created charitable institutions for their community; orphanages, Jewish Day Schools, *chedorim*, homes for the disabled and Helping Hand Societies/*Chevra Kaddisha* to assist those in need. These were inclusive organisations and every Jew in the community was given help without reference to their religious affiliation.

This is what the Litvaks brought to and bequeathed to the Jews of South Africa. What contribution did the Litvaks and their children, the first South Africa-born generation, make to their new homeland?

The Litvak migration coincided with the flourishing of the diamond mines in Kimberley, the discovery of and development of gold mining in the Transvaal and the industrialisation of South Africa. The cities and towns around the mines provided the trading and financial opportunities. No wonder that the Litvaks were predominantly urban dwellers; some 90% of the Jewish population lived in urban areas from the start.

What is also clear is that the Litvak immigrants did not take long to settle and be economically viable, enabling them to be reunited with their families by bringing them to South Africa.[182] They were predominantly involved in trade, finance, catering and services such as hotelkeeping and the liquor trade. This accounted for some two-thirds of Jewish males and 72% of Jewish females then gainfully employed. In comparison, 20% of white males and no more than 36% of white females of the general population were so employed. It was from these traders that the Ackerman Group, OK Bazaars, Greatermans Stores and many other retail giants came into being.

Manufacturing was the next most important activity; some 16% of Jewish males and 10% of Jewish females were thus engaged, compared with 21% and 13% for the general population. These Jews were some of the pioneers in establishing and growing the South African furniture and clothing industry, as well as food processing and milling.

Those living in the rural areas, some 10% of the Jewish population, were mainly traders, with only about 4% of the total being engaged full time in agriculture. Many traders in the rural areas also had farming interests, but this was not their main economic activity.

In 1926, only 3% of Jewish men were employed in the professions, about the same as the rest of the population. However, given the Litvak obsession with education and unfettered access to tertiary education, the Universities of Witwatersrand (Johannesburg) and Cape Town soon had large Jewish student bodies. By the end of the 1920s, almost 40% of graduates and diplomates at Wits were Jews, as were over 20% of graduates in law, medicine, arts and commerce at Cape Town.[183]

These were the very people who the Commission of Enquiry into Labour in the Cape Colony had said in 1893 were 'a most undesirable people, ... [who] have pushed out many poor shopkeepers and have obtained property intensively'. The 'Russian Jews' were considered to be 'not what the country needed economically', and were variously described as 'undesirable', 'unassimilable' and 'the scum of Europe'.

These 'undesirable scum' and their descendants continued to make a contribution to their chosen fields out of all proportion to their numbers. This is particularly apparent in the professions of law, medicine, accountancy, dentistry and academia. By 1960, 20% of the Jewish population economically active were in the professions compared to 9.7% in 1936. An example of their dominance in the medical profession can be gauged from the fact that nearly 23% of practising doctors in 1960 were Jewish and the percentage among medical specialists was nearly one in three. (Those involved in the 'sales' category declined just as spectacularly, from 48% to 29.1% during the same period.)

Jews were employers rather than employees – they created employment for others. Of the Jews economically active in 1970, some 28% were employers as compared to 12% of the white population.[184] This was the reality rather than the rhetoric.

From Scotland to South Africa – The Dorfman Family Arrive

Louis and Rachel

By the mid-1930s, Louis Dorfman was financially comfortable and quite well known and respected within the small Jewish community of Edinburgh, as well as by the many antique dealers who plied their trade in Scotland.

In the Dorfman family folklore, two reasons are given for why Louis and Rachel left Edinburgh for South Africa. The first is that Louis, who suffered very badly from asthma, collapsed one day while walking home from his shop. He was rushed to hospital and after recovering was advised to seek a different climate in the colonies. We are told that he was warned that his life would be compromised if he did not move to a more suitable climate.

The other reason given by some of the family was that Louis, having been involved in a motor accident that resulted in the other party suffering severe injuries, left to avoid the suit brought against him, using his asthma as an excuse. I have no doubt that both are probably valid!

In any event, in January 1936, Louis and Rachel sold their assets in Edinburgh and sailed from Southampton on the *Kenilworth Castle,* arriving in Cape Town in February 1936. Louis was by then 57 years old and Rachel 53. They gave their address in the Cape as Kalabaskraal. This is where Rachel's brother Simon (Sam) Rieff owned the Railway Hotel. It seems that Louis and Rachel worked with Simon and his wife Malie in the hotel from February 1936 until the end of May 1937, learning the business of running a country hotel.

Mary Dorfman

Mary (Mae) Dorfman sailed from Southampton on the *Dunnottar Castle,* tourist class to Cape Town, departing on 12 February 1937 and arriving in Cape Town on 1 March 1937 to join her parents. She gave her proposed place of abode as Railway Hotel, Kalabaskraal, her occupation as 'Saleslady' and her age next birthday as 32 (in fact she would have turned 33 on 5 July 1937). She gave her marital status as divorced, and she had £100 of her own money deposited with Thomas Cook, as letters dated 11 February and 1 March 1937 clearly show. For the next three months she too learnt as much as she could about the hotel business.

The Move to Calvinia

Louis and Rachel did not stay with Simon for very long. In June 1937, they bought a property in Calvinia for £3,500. On the property was the National Hotel. Louis and Rachel borrowed the sum of £4,500, secured by a mortgage against the property. It seems that the funds were required to carry out substantial renovations to the hotel, bars and off-licences (one for whites and one for Coloureds).

Louis and Rachel Dorfman with Mae and an unknown man standing in front of the National Hotel, *circa* 1937/38

So, by mid-1937, Louis and Rachel Dorfman and their divorced daughter Mae had settled in Calvinia, where there was a thriving Jewish community with a number of other Litvaks who had also lived in the UK before moving to South Africa, more particularly the Helfets.

Calvinia had no direct rail link to Cape Town. Road transport was in its infancy and was used primarily to link towns not directly served by the railway to the railheads. There was a branch line on which goods could be sent by rail via Hutchinson, a station on the main railway line from Cape Town/Johannesburg/Kimberley that ran through De Aar. The distance between Hutchinson and Calvinia is some 400 kilometres. Rail passengers departing from Cape Town/Calvinia would have to take a train to/from Klawer, some 140 kilometres to the southwest of Calvinia. To and from Klawer, passengers would travel by bus through Van Rhynsdorp and Nieuwoudtville, via the Van Rhyns Pass. The journey from Cape Town to Klawer took some 12 hours and the bus journey to/from Klawer/Calvinia about 3 to 4 hours.

Why exactly my grandparents chose Calvinia I have not been able to establish. The town is situated on an escarpment and has a dry, hot climate that would have suited my Zeida, who suffered from asthma. There was also a thriving Jewish community (119 souls in 1936). Many of them were from Neustadt-Sugind, as was Benjamin Klein, whose grandchildren Max, Shirley and Elaine attended school in Cape Town. (In fact, Max was at SACS one year ahead of me. Shirley and Elaine attended the girls' school, Good Hope Seminary in Cape Town. We travelled home by train together as far as Klawer. Amazingly, one of my oldest friends, Brian Kantor, is married to Shirley and we are all still close friends.)

In the coastal resort of Hermanus: Brian Kantor, Max and Elaine Klein, and Ivan

In 1936, Calvinia had a total population of 17,731, of whom 7,482 were white. The Coloured population was in the majority, at 10,249, yet they were by now, in law, being treated as second-class citizens. (There would have been very few black people.) It is important to note that the members of the Calvinia Hebrew Congregation were not all resident in the town itself. The distances between the neighbouring villages are large and many of them had very few Jewish residents and so had no community of their own. Middelpos, Loeriesfontein, Nieuwoudtville and Brandvlei looked to Calvinia as their centre for Jewish life.

Reverend Solomon Berelowitz served as the minister of the Calvinia Jewish Community from 1919 to 1942 and taught all the Kapelus boys Hebrew and their portions (*parshas*) for their barmitzvah. As we shall see, he also officiated at Mae's wedding.

By the mid-1930s most of the children remained in Calvinia to finish their schooling. With a thriving Jewish community, a *shul* and a *cheder* to prepare them for their barmitzvahs (the girls did not have batmitzvahs then), there was no need to send them to boarding school for a Jewish education. The school in Calvinia at that time was dual medium, with subjects being taught in both English and Afrikaans, so most white children were able to complete their schooling in the town. Some inevitably did go to Cape Town for the latter part of their schooling and many went on to study at the University of Cape Town. Most of them maintained their links and relationships with the village and returned to visit their parents and friends. A number of the second generation began their working lives in their family's businesses in Calvinia, so there was quite a thriving young Jewish set with whom Mae could socialise.

Mae lived with a secret, though: she was a divorcee with a son in Scotland. She was also by this time 33 years old and somewhat older than the other young single Jewish people in Calvinia. No one would have thought her to be almost 10 years older than most of her peers in the village, however. She was a petite, attractive blonde with bright blue eyes that sparkled with mischievous fun. Her lively personality and delightful sense of humour hid her age and made her a welcome addition to the Jewish community. She soon attracted the attention of the young Jewish men in the village and neighbouring towns. Although Mae had lived in Glasgow and Edinburgh, big, bustling, sophisticated cities, she seemingly settled into her life in a small town without a trace of bitterness or longing for the bright lights.

Nevertheless, even in a close-knit and helpful Jewish business fraternity, all three of the Dorfmans needed time to come to terms with a very different society to that to which they were accustomed in Scotland. Here there was not only the divide between Jew and non-Jew but also that between English- and Afrikaans-speaking whites and between white and Coloured people, with a further distinction being made in the case of black people.

Louis came face to face with this problem in December 1938 when he was prosecuted for two crimes:

> *Count 1: in that he did wrongfully and unlawfully keep his licensed premises, the Coloured Bar, open for the sale of liquor during a time that he was not authorised by his license to do so, namely at 12.05 pm (Closing time 12.00 pm), and*
>
> *Count 2: The accused did wrongfully and unlawfully give, sell supply or deliver to, or place in possession or control of a native liquor (one glass of wine). The native, under Section 94 of Act 30 of 1928, being prohibited from acquiring or obtaining or being in possession of same.*

The National Hotel had four liquor outlets: a bar for white people (men only); a bar for Coloured men where they could buy wine, beer and spirits by the glass; an off-licence for whites that was licensed to sell wine, beer and spirits by the bottle; and an off-licence for Coloured people, who were restricted as to the amount of wine and spirits they were entitled to buy by the bottle. The licensee was obliged to keep an accurate record of all sales made to Coloureds. In addition, the opening hours that applied to each of these were different. Selling liquor to black people was forbidden.

Louis's evidence was that he was closing the Coloured bar at 12 noon when the police walked in. This was corroborated by a customer he had served in the white bar. On the second count a Coloured customer, Tom Sauls, gave the following evidence:

> *Ek ken Abram Makapan omtrent al 'n jaar. Ek het hom altyd geken as 'n bruin man, net soos ek. Ek het hom nie gesien met kaffers omgaan nie. Ek het hom nooit gehoor Kaffer-taal praat nie.*
>
> *(I know Abram Makapan for about a year. I have always seen him as a brown man, just like me. I have not seen him going around with Kaffers. I have never heard him speak Kaffer language.)*

The nature of the charges, as well as the language used by Tom Sauls, were perfectly acceptable then and illustrate vividly the divide between the races, as well as the prevailing attitude towards people of colour.

The accused was found guilty of the charges against him, and magistrate S.C. Brown gave him a reprimand on the first count and a fine of £3 on the second. However, Louis successfully appealed against the judgment and was found not guilty on both counts by Judge President Van Zijl of the Supreme Court in Cape Town.[185]

Relationship between Jews and Afrikaners

The relationship between the Jews in Calvinia and the largely Afrikaans community during the period 1875-1939 is described as 'cordial and co-operative'.[186] As we saw earlier, the authorities of the DRC in 1878 agreed to change the date of Nachtmaal (communion) when it clashed with the Jewish New Year (Rosh Hashanah). A similar clash occurred in 1932 and once more the local DRC dominee (minister) and authorities agreed to change the celebration of Nachtmaal so that both the Afrikaans and Jewish communities could celebrate their religious Holydays without prejudicing either in their joint commercial relationship.

Arnold Helfet, who was raised in Calvinia, confirms the good relationship between the Afrikaans and Jewish communities.[187] However, he also correctly points out that this relationship in Calvinia and in many country towns and villages changed and was cruelly ruined during the Second World War by the rise of anti-Semitism among Afrikaners.

There appears to be no written record of the relationship between the Jews in Calvinia and the majority of the town's population, who were Coloured. With the formation of the Union of South Africa in 1910 the 'silo society' was in the making and the Jews would by and large have had only a master/servant or arm's-length client/customer relationship with the Coloured people.

The hotels and general dealers' stores played an important role in the life of the town. The general dealers provided the townsfolk with all their needs: household goods, groceries and clothes. The wholesalers in the city sent out commercial travellers who visited the town on a regular basis to offer the general dealers the latest wares, as well as to take orders from the shopkeepers for their supplies. They would provide the hotels with a steady stream of occupants for their rooms and dining facilities.

The hotels were the only establishments licenced to sell alcohol by the glass or bottle. There were no restaurants, so the dining rooms of the hotels provided meals for special occasions and celebrations. The local sports clubs for rugby, tennis, golf and badminton did not have club houses with liquor licences, so the hotels also served as the place where the players would gather after practice or matches against neighbouring villages to enjoy refreshments and drinks. Each club would have its favourite hotel. The bars were for men only, so the womenfolk would join their men in the lounge, where snacks and drinks would be served. Each club would host an annual dance, a formal affair where it was normal to wear 'black tie'. These would either be in the hotel favoured by the club or in the town hall and catered for by the hotel.

Many of the commercial travellers were Jewish working for Jewish wholesalers. They were rarely in town over the weekend, but during the week they would gather in the hotels. Inevitably they would make friends with their local co-religionists and would often pass the time playing cards, more often than not poker or *klawerjas*.

In 1937 there were three hotels in Calvinia, the National, the Royal and the Commercial, all family run. Louis, Rachel and Mae were each responsible for a specific department. Louis was responsible for the bars and off-licences, Mae and Rachel shared the management of the housekeeping and catering/kitchen, while all three dealt with reservations. The hotel served three meals a day, so the kitchen was an important hub. This was very much Mae's forte and she had to plan the menus with the chef and, together with Rachel, order the supplies.

Louis and his barman not only served customers but also had to ensure that the bars and off-licences were stocked. It was a demanding and time-consuming undertaking, particularly for a man of 58 and a woman of 54. This placed a heavy burden on Mae.

Mae and Arnold

When exactly Arnold Kapelus and Mae met we do not know, but we must assume that in such a small Jewish community he would have met her very soon after returning to the farm.

In any event, Arnold started his career as a lawyer with Le Roux & Van der Westhuizen in Calvinia during 1938. Arnold could not live on the farm, and be expected to travel to the Calvinia and back every day as it was some 60 kilometres from the village. His mother, Sarah, still lived in Calvinia. She was on her own, as Fay, now 20, was already in Cape Town. Arnold chose not to live with her, however. We do not know why. Instead, he decided to rent accommodation at the National Hotel. Could it be that Mae and Arnold had by then started a relationship?

Whether they had or not, they now saw each other every day. They also enjoyed the company of a close circle of other young Jewish adults living in Calvinia (Joseph Greengowt, the Klein brothers, Arnold Helfet and the Berelowitz family) and those from the surrounding towns of Nieuwoudtville (Barney, Esther and Julius Fisher) as well as the Sher and Reiff families from Calvinia and Middelpost.

We have no reliable information on how long it took for romance to blossom, but by mid-1940 the couple were engaged to be married. We know this from the date of the ante-nuptial contract they entered into in Cape Town on 1 July 1940. The notary public before whom Arnold and Mae appeared was Nathan Miller,

Arnold's cousin (I still do not know how they are related). The parties are described as follows:

Arnold Kapelus, a bachelor of Calvinia born on 16 January 1915

and

Miriam Dorfman, a spinster of Calvinia born on 21 June 1914

An official stamp on the front of the document states 'Date of birth of both parties ... Other Identification ... Proof filed with counterpart hereof'. I have not been able to find this proof of age. What document Mae could have produced to prove that her date of birth was 21 June 1914 is a mystery. Furthermore, she was a divorcee. Both her birth date (the correct one of 5 July 1904) and marital status as a divorcee were clearly on record with the immigration authorities. What is more, we know that Mae had a son by her previous marriage.

This was the secret with which Mae began her married life to Arnold. Why was all this pretence necessary? In 1940, it would have been unthinkable for a young man to marry a woman ten and a half years his senior. Divorce, particularly in Jewish communities, was considered a disgrace and a divorced woman with a child of whom she no longer had custody would have been considered bad, even decadent. Knowledge of the true facts would have been a severe embarrassment to Mae and her parents and would almost certainly have made it very difficult, if not impossible, for Mae to marry again.

In the event, the couple were married on Boxing Day, 26 December 1940, in the Calvinia *shul* by Reverend Berelowitz. In attendance were Mae's parents, Louis and Rachel, Leib and probably Sarah (behind Louis and Leib in the photograph on the next page). All the Kapelus grandchildren, my generation, remember Sarah (Ouma to us) as a very thin person. Comparing this image to the one of her with Leib just after their marriage, it seems that she was at the wedding. Indeed, it would have been virtually impossible for her not to have attended her son's wedding in a village where the Jewish population was no more than 119 people.

Arnold and Mae's Wedding in Calvinia on 26 December 1940

Mr and Mrs Mae and Arnold Kapelus

From L to R: Arnold, Rachel D, Mae, Louis D, Sarah and Leib

Their retinue from L to R: Esther Fisher, Lionel Marcus, Mae, Arnold, Louis D, Fay K, Natie K and Rachel D

Mae Kapelus

This photograph was taken in a corner of the yard of the National Hotel, Calvinia. Note the corrugated iron tank in the background. This was a common sight in the area and was used to capture rainwater, a precious commodity used for washing woollen garments and by the ladies to wash their hair. The water supply was mainly from boreholes, supplying 'brack' water, high in calcium.

From L to R: Esther Fisher, Fay K (later Farber), Mae and Arnold Kapelus

From L to R: Barney Fisher, his sister Esther, Theresa (Kooksie) K, Nathan K, Mae, Harry K and his wife Rose. Nathan and Harry were both serving in the army

Nathan K, Theresa K (Mokey and Polly's eldest child) and Harry K

The Decline in the Jewish community

By the 1940s, the Jewish population of Calvinia and its environs was beginning to shrink as parents followed their children to the cities. They had garnered some capital and business experience and wished to live near their children and grandchildren in a flourishing Jewish environment.

The effect of this on Calvinia was that when Reverend Berelowitz resigned in 1942, the congregation could not afford to appoint a minister. By the end of the Second World War, the number of Jews in Calvinia itself had become so depleted that services could only be held on the High Holydays, when those from the surrounding towns attended services led by ministers engaged specifically for that task.

The Minute Book of the committee meetings of the *shul* reflected what was happening in the community. The list of members for 1938-40 showed 33 members, including L. Dorfman as well as Leib and Arnold Kapelus. By 1941 the list showed 26 members; by 1954/55 the members totalled some 12 persons. In fact, the minutes show that from 1934 the financial position of the community was under pressure, so much so that a mortgage of £750 was provided by the local bank, secured against the synagogue buildings. The funds were used to repay the smaller mortgage of £350 and the balance to repay the overdraft owed to the bank as well as provide some cash.

The last wedding at the Calvinia *shul* was held on 23 March 1943 between Benjamin Berelowitz and Pauline Edna Sack, who later lived in Oranjezicht, Cape Town, where their daughters, Doreen and Valerie, attended Good Hope Seminary School during the 1950s.

The families who remained in Calvinia no longer had a Jewish education available for their children. As a result, children of school-going age were sent to boarding school in Cape Town, where they could have a good secular as well as Jewish education. Boys went to boarding school by the age of 9 or 10 so that they could prepare for their barmitzvahs. Allan Rieff – son of L. Rieff, the last President of the Calvinia Hebrew Congregation, who died in 1955 – together with his cousins, Ralph and Jack Sher from Middelpost, attended SACS as boarders. Max Klein also attended SACS, but boarded at the Herzlia Hostel in Hope Street, Cape Town. His sisters Shirley and Elaine were boarders at Good Hope Seminary, also in Hope Street. The Rieff, Klein and Dansky families remained in the village until the early 1970s. When Mrs Dansky left Calvinia in 1973 and Mr Jack Sack shortly thereafter, it had not a single Jewish resident.

By and large the relationship between the Jewish and Afrikaans communities in Calvinia remained cordial. So much so that a Mrs Florence Malan wrote as follows in the *Cape Argus* of Cape Town in 1975:

> *The Jews brought joy to Calvinia. No village should be without a Jewish Community. Their homes with lovely linen, silver and glassware that they had brought with them from Europe was a source of inspiration for the pioneers who had been largely cut off from their European roots and immersed in their struggle to exist. Their residence here was a golden period in the history of the village where they helped and supported each other.*

The Family Disperses

Arnold was the only one of the Kapelus family of his generation who lived in their home town of Calvinia. Mokey and Polly were by now the proud parents of a pidgin pair, Theresa (known to all as Kooksie) and Arthur, and lived in Cape Town, where Mokey was helping to build a furniture retail business. Harry and Rose were also living in Cape Town, although Harry was a serviceman in the South African army, as was Natie, the bachelor of the family. When the war broke out, Natie had given up his studies at University of Cape Town to join the army. Fay was also in Cape Town, a 21-year-old single woman working in the city.

The family had always spoken English in the home and primarily Afrikaans outside of it. Arnold was the only one who continued in this way. His siblings had by now moved sharply away from their country beginnings and their acculturation was now very much Jewish, English and city oriented.

In February 1941, Arnold and Mae moved from Calvinia to Van Rhynsdorp, about which there will be much more in the next part of the book. They were then some 118 kilometres from Calvinia, leaving Sarah, Arnold's mother, alone. Furthermore, with Mae's departure, Louis (61) and Rachel Dorfman (56) were obliged to run the National Hotel without her help.

The world was at war and even in the deep rural areas of South Africa the effect of the conflict could be felt. There were petrol restrictions and permits were required for long journeys by car. Permits were not easily given for leisure travel. It was a time to knuckle down and this is what the Dorfmans and Leib effectively did.

By 1944, Leib was ailing and he was no longer able to run the farm effectively as a result of his heart condition, so, as we saw earlier, he engaged a farm manager. Four of his five children were married and he was the proud Oupa of four grandchildren. Leib had the pleasure of being at the weddings of Mokey and Polly (April 1934), Harry and Rose (April 1938), Arnold and Mae (December 1940) and Fay and Harold (August 1942). Mokey, Harry and Fay had made their home in Cape Town and Natie was in Somerset East in the Eastern Cape, from whence he moved to Port Elizabeth.

The young Polly Mandelblat

Mokey and Polly on their wedding day (April 1934)

Rose and Harry (April 1938)

Natie and Jean

Molly, Fay, Harold, Lilly and Kooksie in the front

Back: Mrs Farber, Moly and Lilly (Rachel Kapelus's daughters)
Front: Kooksie, Fay and Leib; August 1942

Leib's Passing

By 1945, Leib was visiting Cape Town for medical attention and had been in hospital, although he returned to Rooi Puts after spending a week or so in Van Rhynsdorp with Arnold and Mae (and the toddler me!). In December 1945, Leib once more needed to be hospitalised and he went to Cape Town, where he was admitted to the Hoff Street Nursing home. Sadly, he died of heart failure on 29 January 1946.

Leib's will, a simple, one-page document, was signed on 28 May 1927. Clause 2 states:

> *I hereby appoint my sons, namely Morris, Harry, Natie and Arnold, and my daughter Fanny as the sole heirs in equal shares of all my estate and effects, movable and immovable, and wherever situate and whether in possession, reversion, expectancy or contingency.*

Morris (Mokey) was appointed to be executor and administrator of the estate.

The will is entirely silent on the maintenance to be paid to Sarah, despite Clause 8 of the Deed of Separation executed on 2 June 1926, which clearly states:

> *Louis Kapelus further binds himself, his heirs and Executors, to make provision either by Will or otherwise, and if he fails to do so, then he hereby burdens his estate to the extent that in the case of he predeceasing Sarah Kapelus, his executors ... shall be bound to pay Sarah Kapelus the monthly payment of £8:0:0 as mentioned in paragraph 7 above, so long as she shall remain his widow, but on her re-marriage this maintenance shall cease.*

The final estate account reflected assets of £3,824.16.2 and the liabilities show that Arnold paid his mother's maintenance for the period April to October 1946, for which he was reimbursed £27. How this sum was calculated is a mystery, as seven months' maintenance should have been £56.

The balance available for distribution to the five children was £2,990.15.11. As Leib still owned Rooi Puts, the farm, valued at £3,000, was transferred to the children in equal shares on 7 February 1949. Neither Mokey, Harry nor Fanny had any interest in the farm, so it was decided that the property should be sold. Arnold and Natie agreed to buy it for £2,700 and the farm was duly transferred to them on 8 February 1949. The cash for the purchase was raised by a mortgage bond on the farm equal to the purchase price. Leib's estate now had cash to distribute equally to each of the five children.

What happened to Sarah? At the time of Leib's death she was still living in rented accommodation in Calvinia. There is no obvious provision for the payment of her maintenance. She had married children living in Cape Town, Port Elizabeth and Van Rhynsdorp and a brother, Jaenkel Marcus, who also lived in Cape Town. Yet none of them appeared to have taken responsibility for her, either before or after Leib's passing. Whatever discussions took place between the children are no longer available to us.

In January 1946, I was a toddler of just over 3 years old. I have no recollection of Leib's demise, but I do remember that Arnold, Mae and I travelled to Calvinia and stayed at the National Hotel. I vaguely remember the hotel and the fact that my parents and grandparents were very busy. I now know the reason.

What happened in the next year or so turned my world upside down.

Farewell to Calvinia

By March 1946, Louis was 67 years old and Rachel some four years his junior at 63. They found that the burden and responsibility of running the National Hotel had become too much for them, and they sold it to Adam Johannes Wahl. Our visit coincided with the sale of the hotel and my parents were helping Louis and Rachel in their move to 54 Fairview Avenue, Woodstock, Cape Town.

The Dorfmans were not rich, but having sold the hotel for £4,500 they had made a profit of £1,000 on the original purchase price; they would also have accumulated some additional capital out of the business over the period of nine years (1937-46). It seems that the original mortgage had been repaid.

Coincidentally, during 1946 Arnold and Mae moved from the semi-detached house opposite the Central Hotel in Van Rhuynsdorp to a larger house in Voortrekker Street near Sunnyside, the home of the Roodt family, where General Smuts delivered his famous address in 1902 after the Peace Conference in Vereeneging.

During and after the move to this larger rented house, I remember that Mae often talked about Sarah and that she was extremely concerned about her. Even as a little boy, I was conscious of the tension surrounding any talk about Ouma. My mother kept on insisting that Sarah be fetched from Calvinia and that she should live with us in Van Rhynsdorp. I do not remember my father's reaction, but there must have been some resistance, hence the tension.

Some time in November or December 1946, we again travelled to Calvinia and this time I do remember seeing Sarah. She was living in what could be described as the servants' quarters in the garden of a house. She was pitifully thin, badly kept and she spoke indistinctly. My mother cried and this upset me and made me tearful. Mae comforted me and told me that we were fetching Ouma to take her with us to Van Rhynsdorp and that she would now be living with us.

For how long had Ouma been living in these conditions? Why had she not been advised by any of her children to apply for an increase in her maintenance payments, which had been fixed at £8 per month in June 1926? After the Depression of the 1930s, inflation had caused a severe increase in the cost of living, and this became even worse during and immediately after the war. Had any of her children helped her financially over all these years? My father had been in Calvinia as an adult and employed as an attorney in the town since January 1938. What had been his relationship with his mother and had he helped her financially? Had he visited her regularly?

We will now never know the answers, but the more I have learnt about my family's history, the more these questions upset and bother me. I have found many photographs of Leib with his children, but not a single photograph of Sarah with any of them, not even in their infancy. It is quite clear that Leib dominated the family scene. There is no evidence or suggestion that Ouma had been a bad mother, as in the deed of judicial separation she is given custody of the three younger children and equal access to the elder boys. Yet it is as if she had been erased from the family psyche. Why?

PART III

The Van Rhynsdorp Years 1941-1960

A Short History of Van Rhynsdorp

The area now known as Van Rhynsdorp was in earlier times known by the name of the river that runs through it, Troe-Troe or Trutro. The original inhabitants of the area were the San (Sonqua), hunter-gatherers, and the Namaqua (Khoikhoi), nomadic herders of sheep, cattle and goats.

As early as 1661, Pieter van Meerhof, on the instructions of Jan van Riebeeck, travelled as far as Trutro in search of the legendary Monomotapa. The district became better known in the early 1680s as a result of the journeys of Captain Olof Bergh and Sergeant Christoffel Henningh in their search for copper, prompted by samples of the metal having been shown to the Governor, Simon van der Stel, at the castle in Cape Town by a number of Namaquas in 1681.

The San and Namaquas remained in the area until they were gradually displaced by the *trekboers*, who moved there in 1700 when they started to establish outposts for grazing their sheep and cattle. By 1732, they had created permanent settlements and farms and more and more *trekboere* started to settle in the area of Trutro. During 1817, Hendrik Nicolaas van Rijn arrived at the outpost and married the daughter of one of the early settlers, Aletta Johanna Wiese. The Opstal, built in 1751 (now 17 Van Zyl Street), became their family home.

The name Van Rhynsdorp derives from a family who have been prominent in the area since 1836, when Sir Benjamin D'Urban, Governor of the Cape, signed the document of the settlement of Troe-Troe, with H.N. van Rijn, D. van Rijn, H.J. Laubscher, J.B. Wiese and T. Wiese among the owners. These families farmed and lived in Troe-Troe and it became known as their family village.

Hendrik Nicholaas and Pieter Benjamin van Rijn played leading roles in public life and in the development of the town and district. Pieter Benjamin's grandson, Dr A.J.R. van Rhijn, a son of the village, later became a Member of Parliament and Cabinet Minister (Mines 1953-58 and Economic Affairs 1954-58) and later the High Commissioner for South Africa in London (1958-60).

By 1868, there were more than 200 permanent residents of Troe-Troe. The settlement had a Justice of the Peace, three shops, a school facility and a post office, as well as a permanent place of worship, known as Het Gesticht. Inevitably, *smouse* (peddlers) started to do business in the area on a regular basis.

When in 1880 the Dutch Reform Church of Troe-Troe became a community in its own right, the 13 families who had been granted the original ownership made a gift of 272 *morgen* (233 hectares) to the community, which was divided into

44 plots. To honour the Van Rijn family for the contribution they had made to the settlement and the district, the Church Board of Troe-Troe applied to change the name of the settlement developed on the gifted land to Van Rhynsdorp. For the time being, the balance of the village continued to be named Troe-Troe.

Van Rhynsdorp was itself declared a magisterial district in 1890, although the seat of the court was within the boundary of Troe-Troe, some 100 metres from the boundary of Van Rhynsdorp. Matters became even more muddled as by law each magisterial district had to be the seat of a Divisional Council. The new Van Rhynsdorp Divisional Council included Troe-Troe. It seemed bizarre to have two towns side by side with different names, so it was decided that name of the whole would be Van Rhynsdorp.

Logically, the town would have achieved Village Management Board status in the 1890s, as it had all the local institutions needed to qualify, but the Anglo-Boer War intervened. The village was administered by the local magistrate and the police.

Van Rhynsdorp During the Anglo-Boer War

Boer forces commanded by Hertzog and Charles Nieuwoudt took Calvinia on 7 January 1901. Hertzog and Nieuwoudt themselves entered the town on 12 January, but left as suddenly to escape the oncoming British forces. They made for Nieuwoudtville, where, as I have related earlier, they confronted Leib. From there they moved stealthily and quickly down the Van Rhyns Pass to Van Rhynsdorp, which they took on 19 January 1901 without a shot being fired.

With his men massed in front of the Magistrates Court, Hertzog read a proclamation declaring martial law; took down the Union Jack and raised the *Vierkleur* of the Orange Free State. The Commandos sang their National Anthem.

The Boer Commandos in front of the Magistrates Court at Van Rhynsdorp on 19 January 1901 [Photograph by courtesy of the National Archives, Cape Town]

The officers of the Hertzog and Nieuwoudt Commandos, shown in front of the Magistrates Court in Van Rhynsdorp on 19 January 1901 [Photograph by courtesy of the National Archives, Cape Town]

There are conflicting reports of how the Van Rhynsdorpers reacted, although a large crowd of residents gathered to witness the flag-raising ceremony. One view is that they watched with sympathetic resignation, a reaction by some in the crowd, ascribed to *Joodse handelaars,* Jewish traders and Coloured constables. The other opinion is that some residents cheered enthusiastically and also sang the Boer national anthem.

It is further reported that many horses and a great deal of fodder and food were commandeered, particularly from the Jewish shopkeepers and merchants, who appeared to have been discriminated against and treated very harshly. On 27 January 1901, a patrol of eight Boers commandeered substantial goods from the *Jodewinkels,* or Jewish shops, in the village of Nuwerus, some 35 miles to the north. This is further evidence of Jewish settlement not only in Van Rhynsdorp but also in Nuwerus as well as in Vredendal.[188]

The British were quick to respond to the taking of Van Rhynsdorp and a large force converged on the village. Early on the morning of 3 February 1901, the Hertzog/Nieuwoudt Commandos left and shortly thereafter the British forces entered Van Rhynsdorp and paraded in front of the Magistrates Court, exactly where the Boers had just 15 days earlier. They did not stay long. After reinstating the resident magistrate and his staff, they left the village the very next day.

The British forces parading in front of the Van Rhynsdorp Magistrates Court in February 1901 [Photograph by courtesy of the National Archives, Cape Town]

Martial law had been declared throughout the Cape and during February 1901 it was enforced in Van Rhynsdorp. According to Scholtz, a special prosecutor, Advocate Harsant, began a witch-hunt against those in the village who had supported the Boers, relying on the evidence of *Jode en Kleurlinge,* Jews and Coloureds, people who were decidedly strongly pro-British.

From February to September 1901, neither the British nor the Boer Commandos remained permanently in Van Rhynsdorp. British convoys would move through the village on their long journey between Clanwilliam and Calvinia, stay for a day or two and then move on to their ultimate destination. In the interim, the Boer forces would use the village for replenishing their supplies. Scholtz reports that during this time a substantial amount of clothing and foodstuff was commandeered from Jewish shopkeepers.

In mid-September 1901, the British withdrew their civil personnel from the village to Clanwilliam, some 50 miles to the south, and from 26 September 1901 until the end of March 1902, Van Rhynsdorp served as the headquarters of the Boer forces in the North Western Cape.

This photograph of Boer officers was taken in Van Rhynsdorp in 1902. It is of particular interest to me as a Van Rhynsdorper as well as an old boy of Stellenbosch University Law School, because Hilgard Bodenstein obtained his doctorate in Law and lectured at Stellenbosch Law School [Photograph by courtesy of the Law Faculty of the University of Stellenbosch]

Towards the end of November 1901, General J.C. Smuts (later Prime Minister of South Africa) arrived in Van Rhynsdorp. He bivouacked in the village and used it as his base while he was harassing small British columns, as well as organising support among the local Cape Afrikaners, who it was hoped would rebel against British rule.

In early February 1902, a large convoy of British troops, some 1,500 men under Kavanagh, Wyndham and Haig (of First World War fame/notoriety) passed through Van Rhynsdorp on their way to Calvinia. The balance of power was changing and the Boer forces were under severe pressure. At the end of March, all the Boer forces withdrew deep into Namaqualand to Garies. It was now relatively quiet in Van Rhynsdorp and the district.

It was shortly after this that a Lem Colyn, a 'rebel' but actually a British spy, joined the Boer forces of Bouwer, one of Smut's officers, in the Van Rhynsdorp area. He was with them only a short time and disappeared as suddenly as he had appeared. Early on 13/14 February 1902, a column of the 10th Hussars, under the command of Lt Col Kavanagh and De Lisle with Colyn, attacked the Boer forces near Van Rhynsdorp at Krans. The Boers retreated to Atties, a farm just south of Van Rhynsdorp. The British forces made Windhoek, on the road between Van Rhynsdorp and Klawer, their stronghold. General Smuts commanded a Commando led by Jaap van de Venter to attack the British in the early hours of 25 February. The Boers suffered severe losses, but managed to take some prisoners, one of them being Colyn.

A court was assembled to hear a charge of high treason against Colyn, with General Smuts serving as the chairman. Colyn was found guilty as charged and was sentenced to death. After receiving the last rites from two DRC ministers, Colyn was executed by firing squad a few hundred yards from the farmhouse at Atties.

The tide was now turning against the Boers and it was agreed to call a Peace Conference in Vereeniging, Transvaal in early May 1902. The attendance of General Smuts was crucial, but in late April he was in Springbok, Namaqualand, some 220 kilometres north of Van Rhynsdorp. To get Smuts to the conference Major Chadwick, showing a white flag, rode through Van Rhynsdorp on 21 April 1902 on his way to Springbok and escorted him to the peace talks.

The British now took command of the area by building forts on Atties farm and along the Olifants River.

By 17 June 1902, Smuts was back in Van Rhynsdorp, where he addressed a very large crowd from the veranda of Sunnyside, the home of the Rood family, advising them of the conditions of surrender by the Boer forces. The conditions included special provisions for the surrender of Cape 'rebels'. In all, 115 men from Van Rhynsdorp surrendered to the British forces at Atties.[189]

The home of the Kapelus family in Van Rhynsdorp between 1946 and 1953 was one house away from Sunnyside. By then this splendid Victorian house had been divided in two, with the headmaster of the school occupying one side and Mrs Rood, the widow of one of the Roods, living in the other.

The Jewish Community of Van Rhynsdorp

The first evidence of a Jewish presence in Van Rhynsdorp is in the records of the Liquor Licensing Board, which was appointed as early as February 1891 and had its first sitting on 4 March 1891 to hear the applications for liquor licences from P.B. van Rijn and S. Zackon.

An entry in *The South African Jewish Year Book* of 1929 by Matz, Isaia Hirsch, Shochet, Mohel, states that he was in Van Rhynsdorp from 1899 to 1901. The number of Jews there and in surrounding villages must have been sufficient to warrant Isaia Matz working there for two years.

By all accounts, there were a number of Jewish traders and shopkeepers in Van Rhynsdorp and environs at that time. Scholtz mentions the presence of Jews several times, but there appears to be no record of their identity or for how long they had been there.

During 1905, the storekeepers of Van Rhynsdorp, in order to comply with the Half Holiday Act 1905, were obliged to select a day during the week on which they would close in the afternoon. This was done by letter, the original of which is attached to the minutes of the Village Management Board and reads as follows:

TO THE CHAIRMAN OF THE VILLAGE MANAGEMENT BOARD, VAN RHYNSDORP

Half Holiday Act 1905

We the undersigned storekeepers in the village of Van Rhynsdorp do hereby respectfully bind ourselves in accordance with Section 2 of Act 34 of 1905 compelling all shopkeepers to close up one afternoon in each week after having selected

Wednesdays
One and all to abide thereby
Dated at Van Rhynsdorp the 19th June 1905

1. *B. Graushyer*
2. *Cohen Brothers*
3. *Sklaar, Slessing*
4. *Joffe Brothers*
5. *S. Fein*
6. *A. Gordon*

So by June 1905, five out of the six shops in Van Rhynsdorp were owned by Jews. This is just three years after the end of the Anglo-Boer war. It is more than likely that some, if not all of them, were already living in the village in 1901/02.

The standing of one, Morris Cohen, was such that he was elected a member of the Village Management Board in April 1906, a position he held until February 1909; in the next round of elections for the Village Management Board in 1909, Solomon Zackon was elected, who as we know was living in Van Rhynsdorp in 1891.

In February 1908, Solomon Rom successfully applied for the transfer of Solomon Fein's business. The Rom family were in the area for generations. They originally lived in Nieuwoudtville and were still living there in May 1937 when Aaron Rom and Joyce Smeiman, also of Nieuwoudtville, posted their marriage banns at the magistrate's court in Calvinia. They married in the Calvinia *shul*. Aaron later owned the hotel in Klawer, built by Philip Press in 1910. His son Selwyn also worked in the family business for a while in the 1960s.

In 1909, G. Silberstein and then Louis Minde successfully applied for general dealer's licences.[190]

The status of Van Rhynsdorp changed to that of a municipality on 23 April 1914 and H. Joffe was elected a town councillor at the first elections held that year. It was a position he was to hold unbroken until 1931 and for a further two years, 1937 and 1938. Joffe was joined on the council by G. Silberstein for the two years 1919-20 as well as by Isaac Frank, who served the village as a councillor from

1919 to 1941 and as mayor for three consecutive terms until he resigned on 14 October 1941.

By 1914, the Jewish community was sufficiently large and organised to appoint Reverend Moshe Altshuler as *chazzan* (although there was not yet a *shul*), *schochet* and *mohel*. In 1918, the community wanted to build a *shul* and Solomon Zackon, now resident in Cape Town, offered them a piece of land, although the efforts came to nought.

The Van Rhynsdorp Zionist Society was started at a meeting in 1918 held at the home of M. Joffe and organised by H. Joffe and Reverend M. Altshuler. A committee was organised and Isaac Frank became its first president.[191]

No minister seems to have been appointed on the departure of Reverend Altshuler (around 1918). By the 1920s, regular functions were being held to collect funds for the building of a *shul*. At what point the community formed a congregation is uncertain, but by 1925 it was known as Van Rhynsdorp Hebrew Congregation. Under the aegis of the congregation, a grand ball was held at the Commercial Hotel on 20 September 1925 to raise funds for the building of a synagogue; or, as the ticket states, 'In aid of Erection of New Synagogue'. A double ticket cost 10/6.

Van Rhynsdorp Hebrew Congregatio

A GRAND BALL

WILL BE GIVEN

ON WEDNESDAY, 20th SEPTEMBER, 1925.

AT THE

COMMERCIAL HOTEL, VAN RYNSDORP.

AT 8 P.M.

In aid of Erection of New Synagogue.

Refreshments will be Provided. DOUBLE TICKET - 10/6

This copy of the ticket to 'A Grand Ball' was kindly provided by Mr Christo Paulsen, Tourism Information Officer at the Tourist Office Museum at Van Rhynsdorp

The fundraising for the building of a *shul* was successful, so a piece of land was purchased from the local DRC and building commenced in early 1928, when the foundation stone was laid by Isaac Frank. The congregation already had a Sefer Torah and a second Torah was purchased in the 1930s. N. Noviosky had served the congregation for a short time from 1924-27, but it now needed a permanent minister. Reverend B. Wulf (later of Upington) took up the appointment and served the community from 1928-37.

I found these photographs of the Van Rhynsdorp *shul*, and those on the next few pages in an envelope in a file recently delivered to the Kaplan Centre for Jewish Studies at the University of Cape Town. They were in the form of slides and were converted to digital images by the university

It is difficult to know how many Jews lived in Van Rhynsdorp at any one time, as the *shul* served the Jews living in the district rather than merely those living in the village itself. Furthermore, census figures for the earlier years included a number of neighbouring villages that fell within the magisterial district of Van Rhynsdorp, including Urionskraal, Klawer, Vredendal (in the very early years), Grootdrift, Nuwerus, Kliprand and Bitterfontein. However, it seems that there were 23 Jews in Van Rhynsdorp and environs as early as 1904 and by 1936 this number had grown to 135, when the community was at its zenith.[192]

Many of the congregants lived in the neighbouring villages of Vredendal, Klawer, Nuwerus and as far away as Kliprand. The boys of families living in these villages would have had to come to Van Rhynsdorp for their Hebrew lessons and tuition for their barmitzvah. It was not possible to do this on a weekly basis, so many of them boarded with Jewish families in Van Rhynsdorp and attended the local school while they were learning for their big day. Barry Cohen, grandson of Morris Cohen and son of Joseph (Uncle Joe to us), who lived in Vredendal, told me that he had boarded with the Galombick family for a year (from 12 to 13 years of age) while he was studying for his barmitzvah.

The first public school was established shortly after the DRC became independent of Clanwilliam in 1877. A new school building was erected in 1892, but by 1913 it was too small to accommodate all the children and it moved to a new and larger building, which was extended further in 1923 and 1925.

We know that N. Gordon was in the first matric class of 1927, and subsequently a number of Jewish children attended the local school. Solomon (Solly) Galombick, who came to the village with his sister Bella, his younger brother Arnold and his widowed mother from Kamieskroon near Springbok, attended the local school. Arnold completed his schooling at SACS, as many of the children of the area did. Solly, however, matriculated from Van Rhynsdorp Hoerskool and jointly held the highest grades ever achieved by a pupil of the school in these examinations. Others to have attended the local school in the years between the wars for some of their schooling were the Joffe brothers, Gelbs and Willie Minde.

In Van Rhynsdorp itself the *shul* was still functioning. Reverend Wulf was succeeded by Reverend M.O. Helman for only a short period until 1940. After his departure there was no permanent minister and Shabbat services were led by members of the community. Dr Berril, the Mayor, Isaac Frank, with the Gelbs, Willie Minde, Kaufman, Righthouse, Rosenthal and Sacks families and the young Kapelus couple, were still in the village to make a *minyan*.

In January 1941, there was still a reasonable Jewish presence in Van Rhynsdorp and the neighbouring villages of Klawer (Rom, Katz and Kelman), Vredendal (Baer, Friedberg, Cohen and Smith), Bitterfontein/Kliprand (Lazarus and Gaffen) and Nieuwoudtville (Fisher). They would attend services on the High Holydays

By now, Joseph Cohen, son of Morris, and his family had moved to Vredendal, where he had established a general dealer's store near the railway station. His son Barry became one of the most successful raisin producers in the area and was in turn succeeded by his son Manuel.

However, in a letter to the South African Board of Deputies dated 8 September 1947, Mr Righthouse advised the board that there were only three Jewish families still living in Van Rhynsdorp. The Jews in the neighbouring towns of Vredendal, Klawer and Bitterfontein had also dwindled or become assimilated, by young men marrying out of the faith. Many of the Jewish traders and shopkeepers kept an interest in their business and homes in the villages, but moved their families to the cities, mainly Cape Town, where they attended services and were members of their local synagogues.

Inevitably, the cost of the upkeep of the Van Rhynsdorp *shul* was becoming a burden to the three families still in the village. It was deconsecrated and the Sefrei Torah were donated to the Schoonder Street *shul*. The building was sold to the local School Board on 30 July 1951. The proceeds were donated to fund a scholarship for postgraduate research at the Hebrew University, Jerusalem worth IL2,000 per year. The donation was given to honour the first executive and committee of the synagogue.

The village flourished under the mayoralty of Isaac Frank. The Town Hall was built in 1938, and in the following year an electricity scheme was inaugurated, two generators having been acquired that were housed in a specially built power station near the Town Hall. Sadly, the power station was demolished in 1974 when Van Rhynsdorp joined the national Eskom grid.

The Town Hall was used for a myriad of activities. The badminton club practised and played its matches against neighbouring villages there, folk dancing took place once a week, and it was often the venue for the annual formal dances of the various sports clubs, such as tennis, rugby and later golf. Until 1994, it was for whites only. There was no cinema and during the late 1940s and early 1950s films were shown in the Town Hall by itinerant cinemas. Initially the public library was at the back of the Town Hall, where it had its own entrance.

Van Rhynsdorp Town Hall in October 2011

Hoërskool Van Rhynsdorp in October 2011

Invitation to Visit Van Rhynsdorp

Our relocation was occasioned by the fact that during 1940, Arnold received an invitation from a firm of attorneys, Minde & Hoffmann, to visit them in Van Rhynsdorp. David Minde's sister, Gertrude, was married to Barnet (Barney) Hoffmann, his partner in the law practice. Willie Minde, his younger brother, also lived and worked in the village at the family business.

David was the son of Louis Minde, the owner of L.H. Minde, a long-established general dealer and produce merchant in Van Rhynsdorp since 10 July 1909. The office of the law firm, Minde and Hoffmann, was directly opposite the store.

Barney Hoffmann had decided to leave Van Rhynsdorp for Cape Town where he joined Fritz Sonnenberg, practising as Sonnenberg & Hoffmann. David Minde remained in the village as a sole practitioner, but in 1940 also decided to leave for Cape Town. Arnold was the only young Jewish attorney in the area and they offered him the opportunity to purchase their practice. However, having only started his career as a qualified attorney in 1938, Arnold was not sufficiently experienced to be a sole practitioner, nor did he have the funds to make such a purchase.

The general dealer's store L.H. Minde, with Uncle Percy and Aunt Lottie Rosenthal standing proudly in front. Note the delivery bicycles parked and ready for use. The building looks exactly as it did in the 1940s except for the burglar bars, although this photograph was taken in the early 1960s. Percy Rosenthal was a cousin of the Minde family who hailed from Latvia, whereas the Minde family came from Plungyan

The offices of Le Roux & Van Der Westhuizen, taken in 1994 with Michael Sarembock (a partner of Sonnenberg, Hoffmann & Galombick) on the veranda and Salim Sheik of London, an interested onlooker

Izak van der Westhuizen had become somewhat of a mentor to Arnold. In the circumstances, it was decided that Le Roux & Van der Westhuizen would buy the practice in Van Rhynsdorp and Arnold would run it under the supervision of his principal. In a letter from Arnold to the Law Society of the Cape of Good Hope dated 18 October 1941, he stated that he had left Calvinia on 15 February 1941 for Van Rhynsdorp, where he was still in the employ of Le Roux & Van der Westhuizen, acting as manager of the Van Rhynsdorp office. The law firm in Van Rhynsdorp would henceforth practise under the name of Le Roux & Van der Westhuizen.

Van Rhynsdorp Becomes Home

Arnold and Mae Kapelus started married life as newcomers to the village of Van Rhynsdorp, living in the Central Hotel owned by Mr and Mrs Righthouse. At that time there were two hotels in the village, both on Voortrekker Street, the North Western Hotel being owned by a Jewish family, the Binders. The Central Hotel was the only double-storied building in the town. There had been a third hotel, the Commercial Hotel, but it had closed by 1940.

Mr and Mrs Righthouse had one son, Wally, who had volunteered to join the South African Army at the outbreak of the Second World War. He was taken prisoner by German forces during the Italian campaign and spent the rest of the war in a prisoner of war camp. At the end of the war he was released and returned to Van Rhynsdorp. However, shortly after his return he had severe appendicitis, which led to a rupture. Sadly, he died, leaving his parents heartbroken and suddenly very old. It was not long after his death that they sold the hotel to the School Board and it became a hostel for girls.

The building housing the Central Hotel, a structure that has not changed since the 1940s

Le Roux & Van der Westhuizen was not the only law firm in the village. There was a rival firm, also a sole practitioner. Van Rhynsdorp was the seat of the Magistrates Court, which sat as a Periodical Court in Vredendal in the 1940s. Twice a year the Circuit Court, consisting of a judge of the Supreme Court of the Cape of Good Hope Provincial Division, sat in Van Rhynsdorp to try criminal cases. A number of young advocates from the Cape Bar travelled with the judge and took turns to act as prosecutor and defence counsel. In the 1940s, South Africa still had a jury system like that of the UK and juries would be selected from the white population of the district. Coloured and black people were excluded from jury service.

The practice bought by Le Roux & Van der Westhuizen had existing clients and Arnold's first task was to retain them and cement his relationship with them while trying to increase the client base. This he achieved with some ease, as his legal acumen and integrity were soon recognised, not only in the town but in the district. When reminiscing about this period, Arnold related an incident that shook his confidence for quite some while.

After he had been practising in Van Rhynsdorp for about six months, he was asked to appear at the Periodical Court on behalf of a woman who was accused of assaulting her husband. He needed to consult with his client and thus had to travel to Vredendal. To do so he needed a permit, as petrol was then rationed. He duly prepared his case and on the day of the hearing he again set off for Vredendal to defend the woman, who was known to all as 'Belinda Blue Eyes'. He arrived in court and when the case was called he addressed the magistrate, informing him that he was appearing for the accused. As he sat down, an established attorney from Vredendal also addressed the court, stating that he was appearing for the accused. The magistrate addressed the accused and asked her who was appearing on her behalf. She promptly replied Mr Van Wyk. Sheepishly, Arnold had to withdraw from court and make his way back to Van Rhynsdorp, having expended time and money on travelling to Vredendal without any recompense. It was a salutary lesson, as he never again agreed to appear in a matter without taking a deposit for expenses and fees.

By 1942, Arnold had expanded the legal practice by opening offices in Klawer and Vredendal, referred to as agencies. He would staff each of these offices on alternate weeks, driving the relatively short distance of approximately 15 miles each morning and returning to the Van Rhynsdorp office mid-afternoon.

By the end of 1941, Mae was pregnant and the couple moved from the Central Hotel to a large, semi-detached house diagonally across the road from the hotel in Voortrekker Street, about 200 metres from his office. They decided that the baby should be born in Cape Town, as there was no hospital in the district and the available facilities might not be able to cope with any emergency. So in the middle of July, Mae went to Cape Town and stayed with her brother and sister-in-law Mokey and Polly in Woodstock.

She was admitted to the Leeuwendal Nursing Home on the evening of 4 August and after a difficult time, Ivan Percival Kapelus, yours truly, was born on 5 August 1942. At my *brith* I was named Yitzchak Peshke ben A'aron. As far as I know, I am not named after or for anybody. As soon as mother and child were able to travel, we set off by train for overnight journey to Klawer and then the short trip by car home to Van Rhynsdorp.

By July 1944, Arnold had made substantial strides in building the practice and had also garnered a little capital. In a Memorandum of Partnership entered into between Izak Petrus van der Westhuizen of Calvinia and Arnold Kapelus of Van Rhynsdorp, for the sum of £150 Arnold acquired a half share of the 'Attorneys business carried on at Van Rhynsdorp under the style or firm of Le Roux & Van der Westhuizen'. The partnership was for a period of three years and, at the option of the partners, could be renewed for a further three.

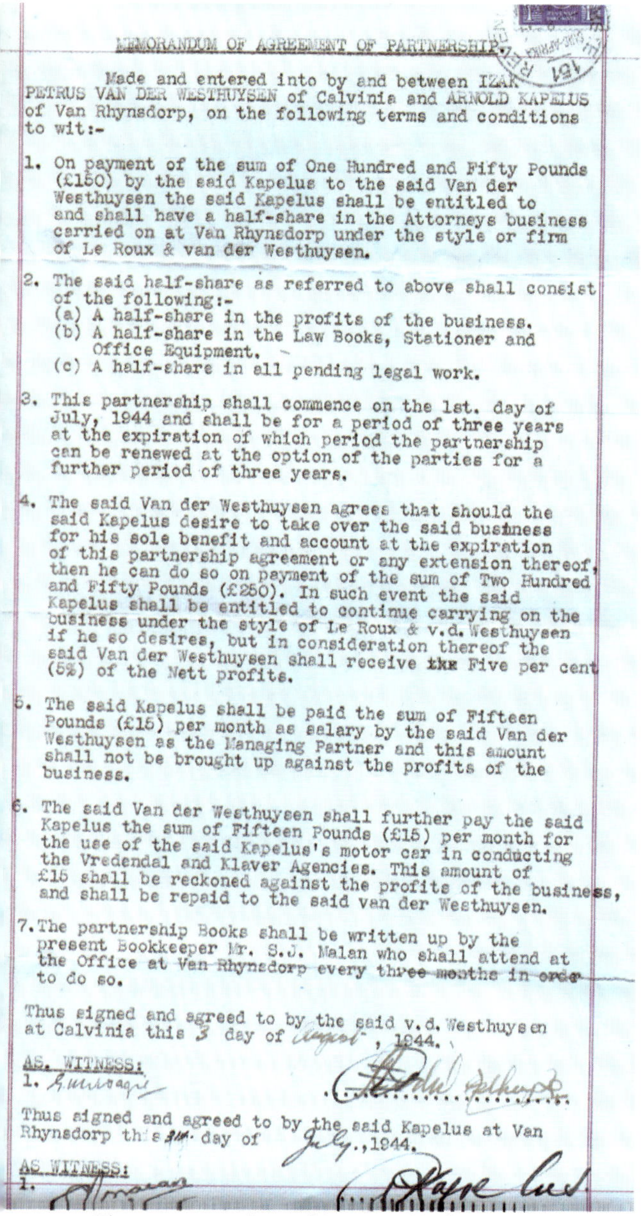

MEMORANDUM OF AGREEMENT OF PARTNERSHIP.

Made and entered into by and between IZAK PETRUS VAN DER WESTHUYSEN of Calvinia and ARNOLD KAPELUS of Van Rhynsdorp, on the following terms and conditions to wit:-

1. On payment of the sum of One Hundred and Fifty Pounds (£150) by the said Kapelus to the said Van der Westhuysen the said Kapelus shall be entitled to and shall have a half-share in the Attorneys business carried on at Van Rhynsdorp under the style or firm of Le Roux & van der Westhuysen.

2. The said half-share as referred to above shall consist of the following:-
   (a) A half-share in the profits of the business.
   (b) A half-share in the Law Books, Stationer and Office Equipment.
   (c) A half-share in all pending legal work.

3. This partnership shall commence on the 1st. day of July, 1944 and shall be for a period of three years at the expiration of which period the partnership can be renewed at the option of the parties for a further period of three years.

4. The said Van der Westhuysen agrees that should the said Kapelus desire to take over the said business for his sole benefit and account at the expiration of this partnership agreement or any extension thereof, then he can do so on payment of the sum of Two Hundred and Fifty Pounds (£250). In such event the said Kapelus shall be entitled to continue carrying on the business under the style of Le Roux & v.d. Westhuysen if he so desires, but in consideration thereof the said Van der Westhuysen shall receive ~~the~~ Five per cent (5%) of the Nett profits.

5. The said Kapelus shall be paid the sum of Fifteen Pounds (£15) per month as salary by the said Van der Westhuysen as the Managing Partner and this amount shall not be brought up against the profits of the business.

6. The said Van der Westhuysen shall further pay the said Kapelus the sum of Fifteen Pounds (£15) per month for the use of the said Kapelus's motor car in conducting the Vredendal and Klaver Agencies. This amount of £15 shall be reckoned against the profits of the business, and shall be repaid to the said van der Westhuysen.

7. The partnership Books shall be written up by the present Bookkeeper Mr. S.J. Malan who shall attend at the Office at Van Rhynsdorp every three months in order to do so.

Thus signed and agreed to by the said v.d. Westhuysen at Calvinia this 3 day of August, 1944.

AS. WITNESS:
1.

Thus signed and agreed to by the said Kapelus at Van Rhynsdorp this 31st. day of July.,1944.

AS WITNESS:
1.

The memorandum of Partnership between Izak van der Westhuizen and Arnold Kapelus

The partnership lasted for the initial three years and in August 1947 Arnold exercised his option to buy the balance of the practice from Izak van der Westhuizen, thus becoming a sole practitioner, although still practising under the name of Le Roux & Van der Westhuizen.

By this time, much had changed in the Kapelus household. We had moved from the house opposite the Central Hotel to a larger one, also in Voortekker Street but further west in the direction of Vredendal. It was one of a pair of similar houses next to each other, situated opposite the old *pastorie* where the DRC minister used to live and, as mentioned previously, one house away from Sunnyside, where General Smuts delivered his speech in 1902.

The next major change in our lives was that grandmother Sarah (Ouma) came to live with us. The mothers of my friends were all known to me as 'Antie' (aunt) and their fathers as 'Oom' (uncle), although they were not related to me in any way. They were involved with all of us children and it was as if we had family wherever we went. In contrast, Ouma seemed to take no notice of me. My mother would insist on her coming to the dinner table to join us for our family meals, but she preferred to eat on her own in the kitchen. All this was very confusing.

Another surprise awaited me. In early 1947, I was told that my mother was going to have a baby. I was to have a sibling. Everyone, even Ouma, seemed to be very excited about the prospect. My sister, Yvonne, was born in Van Rhynsdorp on 21 October 1947. She was five years younger than me. I have no independent recollection of our early years together.

There was no cinema in Van Rhynsdorp, nor did we have television. The radio was on all the time and my father listened to every news bulletin and in particular to all the weather forecasts. Rain was very important. He was not only running his legal practice but also supervising the manager of Rooi Puts farm, some 178 kilometres away. Good rainfall was of paramount importance to everyone in the district, as the financial well-being of all of us was dependent on farmers having good harvests.

Arnold paid regular visits to Rooi Puts and often drove home at night. This was dangerous, as the roads were not tarred and he had to traverse two mountain passes, the Van Rhyns Pass between Van Rhynsdorp and Nieuwoudtville as well as the Bloukransberge between Calvinia and the farm. An additional danger was the 'motor-gates', which consisted of a grille situated between two brick gateposts over which the cars drove. On the side of the grille was a gate, which was closed and only opened by farmers when moving sheep from one pasture to another.

One night in 1948, my mother and I were waiting anxiously for Arnold to return from a visit to the farm. It was late, but I refused to go to bed until he was home and my mother indulged me, as she was all alone. There was a knock on the door and to our surprise it was not Arnold but a neighbour. He told us that Arnold had had an accident between Calvinia and Nieuwoudtville, at one of the motor-gates. His car had overturned but he, thankfully, was unhurt. He was brought home by a passing motorist some hours later.

Brother and Sister Reunited

When the Dorfmans moved to Cape Town, they had to make an investment that would produce sufficient income for them to live on. So during 1947/48, they purchased a block of flats in Rondebosch, near the Liesbeeck River. They could not manage the block of flats themselves, however.

Their eldest son Abraham, Alex to his family, had moved to Canada with his wife Ida in the mid-1920s, where their eldest daughter, Brenda, was born on 22 January 1930. By now Alex was an electric welder and centre lather turner and prospects seemed better in Scotland. They returned to live in Glasgow in early 1933. Ida was soon pregnant with their second child, Evelyn, born in Glasgow on 4 October 1933. During the war Alex worked in the shipyards, but there was a cloud hanging over the family. Ida had been diagnosed with cancer. She suffered great pain and distress and succumbed to her illness on 27 September 1945, leaving Alex a young widower with two daughters aged 12 and 15.

Ida, Alex and Evelyn walking in Glasgow, circa 1942

Three years later, Zeida encouraged Alex to migrate to South Africa with Brenda and Evelyn. He guaranteed to support Alex and Evelyn, who was then 15, with the sum of £300. Brenda, then 18, received a letter from Natie Miller, a cousin of Arnold through the Kirsch family, offering her a position as a secretary in his law practice in Cape Town. The family duly boarded the *Stirling Castle* in Southampton, travelling tourist class and arriving in Cape Town on 3 June 1948.

Evelyn, Alex and Brenda at Ida's grave

Alex had not seen his parents or his sister Mae for over 10 years. There was much catching up to do. Mae travelled to Cape Town with Yvonne by train and welcomed her eldest brother and two nieces to South Africa. She insisted that they spend a few weeks with us in Van Rhynsdorp before they started life in Cape Town. I was then nearly 7 years old and remember their visit with fondness, as Brenda and I formed a special bond that we still have.

Alex and Ida with his younger brother Morris, his wife Polly and their children

Early 1949; Standing from L to R: Brenda, Cecil, Jessie Witkin, Alex and Evelyn; seated, Bobba and Zeida

The reunion of family members went further, as by now my half-brother Cecil (Carl) was also in Cape Town. He was some three and a bit years older than Brenda and they had been close cousins in Scotland.

Zeida and Bobba's idea was that Alex would live in one of the flats and be the caretaker-cum-manager of the block. A ground-floor flat was available and for a short time Alex did live there and manage the building. The free accommodation was welcome, but the income was not commensurate with what he could earn working from a commercial enterprise, so he decided to make his own way. The block of flats was sold, as Zeida could no longer manage it.

Alex quickly settled into life in Cape Town and soon found that his training as an electric welder and centre lathe turner was in demand. In a letter from Zeida to the Immigration Department dated 4 June 1949, in which he reclaims the guarantee of £300, he states that Alex 'is now established in a business – namely Progressive Industries Pty Ltd, Kabrun Building, Main Road, Diep River ... of which he is a partner and a director.'

By now his marital status had also changed. Alex had met and fallen in love with Jessie Witkin and they were married on 7 May 1949.

The wedding party of Alex Dorfman and Jessie Witkin on 7 May 1949
From L to R: Cecil Linkerman, Zeida, Bobba, Jessie's brother, Alex, Jessie, Mrs Witkin (Jessie's mother), Miss Witkin (Jessie's cousin)

Brenda was also living life in the fast lane! She met Ellie Madeisky, a bachelor from Wynberg, and they too were soon married. Ellie and Brenda made their home in Wynberg, Ellie's mother living with them too. I was a frequent visitor to their home once I was at boarding school in Cape Town.

The bride and groom on 30 October 1949 outside the Wynberg synagogue
From L to R: Mrs Madeisky (aunt by marriage and mother of Philip), Ellie's paternal grandmother, Ellie, Brenda, Ellie's mother and Bobba (Brenda's grandmother)

Visits to Cape Town

We paid regular visits to Cape Town to see Bobba and Zeida as well as the Kapelus clan, staying with the Dorfmans at 54 Fairview Avenue in Woodstock. At that time Woodstock had a thriving Jewish population, many of whom were first-generation immigrants. The Washkansky family lived in the house next door to Bobba and Zeida. Many years later, Louis Washkansky was to be the first heart-transplant patient, operated on by Dr Christian Barnard.

The journey to Cape Town was long and tedious, particularly for young children. The road from Van Rhynsdorp to just before Moorreesburg was not tarred. The route from Klawer to Citrusdal, through Clanwilliam, ran along the eastern bank of the Olifants River. It was a narrow, twisting and winding gravel road along the river bank that at times suddenly turned inland to run along the mountain cliffs, high above the river.

It was usual for us to leave Van Rhynsdorp early in the morning, between 5 and 6 o'clock. Mae would pack a hamper of hard-boiled eggs, sandwiches and cake with flasks of tea. We would travel along the river and cross the Piekenierskloof (Grey's) Pass between Citrusdal and Piketberg, stopping in a little forest at the foot of the pass on the Piketberg side. Inevitably, both Yvonne and I would have been car sick on the twisting, turning road and it would have been an immense relief for Arnold and Mae to stop and clean us up, as well as to enjoy a well-deserved breakfast. By then we would have been on the road for about three to four hours.

After the break, we all knew that it was about an hour to an hour and a half before we reached the tarred road about 10 miles after Moorreesburg. Everyone seemed to relax the moment we got onto the tarred surface and there was an element of anticipation and excitement as we all looked out for the first glimpse of Table Mountain in the distance. Now we could sense that the journey of between five and six hours was almost behind us, even though we had not yet reached Malmesbury, the last town that we drove through.

The same journey now is very different. The road is tarred all the way, but of greater significance is that the road from the foot of Piekenierskloof Pass on the Citrusdal side now runs on the western bank of the Olifants River, giving one a splendid view of the Ceder- and Sneeuberge as well as the orange groves and vineyards that lie between the canal and the river.

The approach to the bridge crossing the Olifants River between Klawer and Traval on the way to Clanwilliam, with vineyards as far as the eye can see and the mountains in the background

The view from the road between Clanwilliam and Citrusdal, with the Ceder- and Sneeuberge in the distance and orange groves in the foreground

The Passing of Rachel Leah Dorfman

By June 1951, Yvonne was almost 4 years old and I remember my mother and her spending more and more time in Cape Town, while I was at school in Van Rhynsdorp, being looked after by Ouma and Arnold, although I did not know why. Suddenly in late July, my father, mother and Yvonne travelled to Cape Town. When they left, my mother was in tears. I was told that my Bobba was very sick.

Even though Ouma was at home, my parents insisted that I went to live with Aunt Lilly and Uncle Koos van Wyk, sharing a room with my friend Johnnie and his elder brother Klein Koos. Their smallholding and family home were diagonally across the road from our house.

My birthday was on 5 August and I remember wanting my mother to be with me then. The birthday came and went, but it did not seem like a celebration to me as my mother was not there.

It appeared to be an age before my parents and little sister returned to Van Rhynsdorp. When they did, my mother was wearing a black dress, and was tearful and sad. My Bobba, Rachel Dorfman, had died of leukaemia in the Groote Schuur hospital on 11 August 1951, after a very short illness. Zeida was now living alone in the house in Fairview Avenue. Alex and his family were at hand, though, as was Zeida's brother-in-law Simon Reiff and his daughter Rae Gutman, who also lived in Woodstock.

Mae had been very close to my Bobba and she took her loss very badly. Soon, however, there was a new project to keep her busy. I was told that from January 1952 (I was then 9 years old) I would go to boarding school at SACS in Cape Town. It was time for me to be prepared for my barmitzvah. My mother had a long list of the clothes I needed and she was totally focused on getting me ready for my big adventure.

Triumph and Tragedy

The next two years, 1952 and 1953, proved to be a watershed for the Kapelus family.

In mid-January 1952, we set off for Cape Town and stayed with Zeida at 54 Fairview Avenue for the weekend. My father returned to Van Rhynsdorp on the Sunday morning and in the late afternoon, my mother took me to the SACS boarding school for juniors at Dryfehouse, Orange Street, Cape Town. From now on I only saw my parents and sister during school holidays, four times a year.

It was also the year that Arnold embarked on the most difficult and high-profile legal challenge of his career, the Betty Smith case.

On Saturday night of 11 April 1942, in Nuwerus, a village some 74 kilometres north of Van Rhynsdorp and 16 kilometres south of Bitterfontein, a young schoolgirl, 16-year-old Bettie Smith, died in suspicious circumstances. Her body was found the next day, in a ditch some two and a half miles south of Nuwerus on the road to Van Rhynsdorp.

Bettie was at school in the village. On that Saturday night the teachers staged a play at the village hall. People came from the neighbouring towns and outlying farms to attend the occasion.

During the intermission, Bettie was seen in the company of two men, Louw and Krohn. That was the last time she was seen alive. There had been rumours that she had received a 'parcel' from an acquaintance who worked on the Alexander Bay diamond mine in the very north of Namaqualand. The word parcel had acquired a special meaning in Namaqualand, being a 'parcel of diamonds'.

The Van Rhynsdorp police investigated the incident at the time and a post mortem was carried out by the District Surgeon, Dr Barnett Berril, who was also a general practitioner. Statements from various witnesses were taken, including from the men mentioned as having been seen with Bettie. An inquest was held, but no charges were brought at the time.

Rumours persisted that Bettie Smith had been murdered and in 1952, 10 years after the incident, it was alleged that three men, Andries Brink, Johannes Louw and Bernardus 'Buhler' Krohn, had murdered her for the diamonds and had dumped her body in the ditch. A Preparatory Examination was necessary to decide whether there was sufficient evidence to merit a jury trial in the Supreme Court.

During 1952, amid great interest from locals and the national press, the local magistrate, J.B. Smith, presided over the hearing in the Van Rhynsdorp magistrate's court. Arnold appeared for 'Buhler' Krohn and Arnold Galombick for Johannes Louw. The three accused were sent for trial before a judge and jury in the Supreme Court in Cape Town.

Some of those involved in the Bettie Smith murder case, Van Rhynsdorp, 1952

Amid huge public interest, the trial opened before Mr Justice De Villiers and a jury in Cape Town, on Monday, 9 March 1953. The public was held spellbound by the hearing, so much so that a report was carried on the front page of the evening newspaper, the *Cape Argus*, for seven weeks, from 9 March until 27 April 1953.

The advocates appearing before the Judge President of the Cape read like a 'Who's Who' of the legal profession: Mr A.B. Beyers QC (later Judge President of the Cape) for Brink; H. Snitcher QC for Krohn; and P.J. Wessels (later a Judge of Appeal) for Louw. P.B. Blankenberg QC, the Attorney General of the Cape, was appearing with W.M. van den Berg (also later Attorney General) for the Crown.

Easter of 1953 fell over the weekend of Friday, 3 April to Monday, 6 April. The hearing of the Bettie Smith case was adjourned from 3 April until 9 April for the Easter recess. Arnold had been in Cape Town from early March, only returning to Van Rhynsdorp for the odd weekend, so he dearly wanted to spend the Easter weekend with his family in Van Rhynsdorp. I was at home for the school holidays and my cousin Arthur Kapelus (elder son of Mokey) was with me.

Zeida, who had now been a widower for some 19 months, was lonely and my mother wanted him to move to Van Rhynsdorp to live with her and Arnold. It seemed a good idea for him to come to the village for a few months to see whether it would suit him.

Arnold attended court on Thursday, 2 April and at the close of the hearing travelled to Woodstock to fetch Zeida for the drive to Van Rhynsdorp. My mother, Arthur, Yvonne and I were all excited at the prospect of my father being home. I had not seen him since the start of the hearing.

As it got later and later that night and Zeida and Arnold did not arrive, Arthur, Yvonne and I were sent to bed. We were woken by Mae shrieking, 'Oh my God! Oh my God!' We rushed to the lounge and saw her in tears. Our neighbour, Dr Steenkamp, was there. Slowly, he explained that Arnold had been involved in a motor collision and was in the Malmesbury hospital in a serious and life-threatening condition. Zeida had been killed in the collision. We were not told any other details.

Mae did not drive and the only way we could travel to Malmesbury was to hire a car and driver from Turck's Garage the next morning, Easter Friday. By the early hours the telephone had started ringing and my uncle Mokey was the first to give Mae some details of what had occurred.

Arnold was on the National Road approaching Piketberg. At that point the National Road is bisected by a road that leads from Porterville to Piketberg. Traffic on the National Road has the right of way. It was dark and only the headlights of vehicles could be seen. A car being driven by Abraham Mouton from Porterville to Piketberg failed to stop at the intersection and hit Arnold's vehicle amidships, propelling Zeida into the windscreen, resulting in his death. Arnold was on the side of the collision and suffered multiple injuries, but survived.

Mae was desperate to get to Malmesbury. Luckily, Dr Steenkamp was of great help, as he arranged for transport to take Mae, Yvonne, Arthur and me to Malmesbury. This meant that we had to pass the scene of the collision. As we approached Piketberg we were all in tears. Mae and her brother Alex had to arrange for Zeida's funeral while anxiously waiting for Arnold's condition to stabilise.

In the meantime, the Bettie Smith trial continued to its climax, without Arnold's presence. The seven-week trial ended when the jury, after deliberating for only one hour and thirty-four minutes, returned a verdict of not guilty in respect of all three of the accused.

Arnold was in hospital for over a month. Luckily, the manager of Rooi Puts was able to carry on farming activities without direct supervision. As Arnold was a sole practitioner, the legal practice of Le Roux & Van der Westhuizen had to be manned by another lawyer. Fortunately, Messrs Sonnenberg, Hoffmann & Galombick agreed to second one of their staff, Eliot Osrin, to staff the office in Van Rhynsdorp until Arnold's return.

Ouma's Last Years

Ouma had been living with Arnold and Mae since the end of 1946, when she was 58 years old. She rarely went into the village and spent most of her time in the kitchen. Between 1946 and 1953, the house we occupied had sufficient bedrooms for all of us, but the conditions were quite cramped. There was no meaningful garden.

Once the family moved to the smallholding in Van Riebeeck Street in 1953, Ouma had her own space, an en suite room with its own entrance. She rose early every morning and took to wandering around the grounds, eating the fresh fruit from the trees as they were ripening in season.

She was a very quiet and introverted person. The one family member who made her eyes twinkle and brought a smile to her face was my sister, Yvonne, whom Ouma absolutely adored. She used to keep a secret store of sucking sweets that she shared only with Yvonne, who she called Vonke.

In the kitchen, Ouma and my mother used to bake and cook for the family and staff. Friday, *erev Shabbat*, was a very busy day, as my mother baked her own *challot*, *challah* rolls and bread for the week. A special meal was prepared every Friday for Shabbat dinner. The table was laid with a white cloth and candles were lit, with all the traditional prayers being said. Despite frequent pleas by my mother, Ouma would not join us at the table; she still preferred to stay in the kitchen.

I certainly did not appreciate how old Ouma was and I knew nothing of her background and history. There appeared to be no interest in the past, no stories of how or where Ouma had come from and when and how she and Oupa had met. We simply were not made aware of or encouraged to think about such matters.

I cannot remember a single occasion in all the years Ouma lived with us when my father showed her affection or interacted with her as son and mother. When her other children came to visit us in Van Rhynsdorp, their attention to her was perfunctory. Her brother Jaenkel Marcus, his children, her nephews and nieces did not seem to visit her while she was in Cape Town or ever take her out. My overriding memory is that she was treated kindly but in a condescending manner.

During the summer months of December and January, we would leave the village for a month to six weeks. Ouma could not live at home on her own, so she went to live with one of her children in Cape Town and would return to Van Rhynsdorp with us by car at the end of the holiday. She appeared to enjoy staying with her daughter Fay most of all and in her final years that is where she would go.

By 1960, when I was starting university, Yvonne was at school in Cape Town, so there were only my parents and Ouma at home. In May 1960, my mother went on an overseas odyssey to Scotland and Canada. She had not seen her Scottish family for 23 years. Although her sister, who now lived in Montreal, had visited South Africa in the 1940s, my mother had not seen her brother Danny since 1937, as he too had left Glasgow for Montreal.

While Mae was abroad and Yvonne and I were at school and university respectively, Arnold was alone at home with Ouma. Yvonne had a three-week school holiday from mid-June to the middle of July and I had a month off during that same period.

Yvonne had returned to school by the middle of July and I still had about a week of vacation. Early in the morning of 19 July, Arnold woke me, as he needed help with Ouma. We rushed to her room, where she was lying on the floor. I helped him to lift her onto her bed, since she was not able to move. Arnold explained that he had heard her moaning and on going to her room found her struggling to stay on her feet. We immediately called Dr Steenkamp, who lived next door to us. He was there within minutes and told us that Ouma had suffered a stroke.

Arnold had tears in his eyes, as ever so gently he helped her to be comfortable while we waited for the ambulance that was to take her to the Malmesbury hospital, some 238 kilometres away. He was genuinely shaken and showed emotions I had not seen before.

We both packed our suitcases, me to return to university and Arnold to be in Malmesbury to look after his mother. The Gaffen family, Louis and Julie, who owned the hotel in Bitterfontein, lived in Wellington, a town not far from Malmesbury. Arnold stayed with them while I went on to residence in Stellenbosch.

On the weekend of 22 July 1960, the Kapelus boys, Mokey, Harry and Arnold, with their wives (except Mae) and Fay and Harold Farber, crowded around Ouma's bed. My cousins and I were also there. She was so frail and unable to speak. It was a sad, sombre and yet strange scene. The siblings spoke to each other, but not about Ouma or the times they had shared. They were all concerned with where she should live if she recovered. Ouma had also lost her power of movement and was now totally helpless. Thankfully, she did not survive.

She died on Monday, 25 July 1960, the last of the Kapelus/Dorfman immigrants who had made the journey from Lithuania.

The End of an Era – Leah and David Hotz Pass On

By 1960, when Mike and Jessie Broude were divorced, Leah and David Hotz were the last of the Litvak-born generation whose journey we have followed. David was then the venerable age of 80 and Leah some seven years his junior at 73. They were sprightly for their age and enjoyed the company of Esther and Ann, two teenage girls in the home.

Only one of their children was not living in Cape Town. Cecil, his wife Sally and their three children lived in Windhoek, the capital of Namibia (then SWA).

By 1964, Cecil too had moved in Cape Town and the first South Africa-born generation of Hotzes were all living within close proximity to each other. David and Leah were in quite robust health, enjoying playing *klawerjas* and listening to the radio, with Leah still 'koshering' the meat and cooking some meals. Cecil, Issy and Ellie, their wives and children were regular visitors to 1 Scholtz Road where they lived. Their eldest granddaughter Doreen was recently married and living in Upington. Doreen had given them the joy of two great-grandsons.

In December 1965, Esther, the second oldest granddaughter, became engaged to me. The engagement party was held at the home of their eldest son, Abe and his wife Rae. David and Leah proudly looked on as all celebrated around them.

During 1966, Leah started to complain of pain in her chest and abdomen and by the beginning of April she was very poorly. She was diagnosed with cancer. David was distraught. In the second week of April, Leah underwent surgery at Groote Schuur hospital. Jessie and her brothers as well as Esther were at her bedside every evening. By 16 April 1966 she was desperately ill and the whole family, except for David, were at her bedside. I was with him at 1 Scholtz Road and Esther telephoned me from a call box to ask me to bring him to Leah's bedside, as she was weakening and was not expected to recover.

David and I set off immediately and he kept on asking me whether Leah was still alive. All I could answer was that when Esther telephoned she had been alive. We arrived at the ward moments after Leah had died. We all left David at her bedside. He cried ever so quietly as he said farewell to his beloved Leah, whom he so adored.

David was still living with Jessie, Esther and Ann in Scholtz Road. Soon Esther would be out of the house, as we were married on 18 December 1966.

David Hotz at our wedding
From L to R: Esther, Ivan, Jessie, David H, Mokey and Polly Kapelus
(the first South Africa-born generation of the Kapelus family)

Jessie and Ann now had to cope with David on their own. Esther and I lived only a few blocks away, but we were both working and could not give Jessie all the support she needed. The whole family met in Ellie and Bella's flat to discuss David's future. He had become very frail and Abe and Cecil thought it would be best for him to move to Highlands House, the Jewish Home for the Aged in Highlands Estate.

Esther was vehemently opposed to such a move and became highly emotional and aggressive towards her uncles. Patiently and with rare understanding, Jessie and Ellie brought Esther round and it was decided that David would move to Highlands House, where he had his own little room en suite.

Esther and I with Tina, the dog I had given her on her 20th birthday, visited him regularly. Tina loved David and knew the way to his room. As soon as we opened the car door in the parking area, she would dash off and go directly to his room. Sadly, David simply faded away and on 5 September 1968, aged 88, he died peacefully in his sleep.

The last of the three Litvak families had passed on, marking the end of an era. The children of Leib and Sarah as well as David and Leah, the first South Africa-born generation, were now the elders of their families.

From L to R: Mokey, Harry, Fanny (Fay), Natie and Arnold

The first South Africa-born generation of the Hotz family
From L to R: Issy, Cecil, Jessie, Abe and Ellie

Epilogue

In the Introduction to this book I say:

> *Yet there was another migration: my generation of the family left South Africa for Canada, Australia and the United Kingdom from the 1970s onwards. As we shall see, the reasons and circumstances of our migration in the late twentieth century were very different to those of our grandparents in the late nineteenth and early twentieth centuries.*

The first South Africa-born generation of the Kapelus and Hotz families remained rooted in the country of their birth. They had started from humble beginnings and flourished to become economically comfortable, if not affluent, being able to send their children to good schools and, in most cases, to support their children while they obtained a tertiary education.

They were born into a fast-changing world and were soon to witness and experience the world, and the country of their birth, being engulfed in two major, worldwide conflagrations. They were but toddlers during the First World War that raged in Europe, but it nonetheless caused deep and lasting divisions in the country of their birth that eventually had an impact on their lives.

Their immigrant parents arrived in a country where the society, economically, politically and socially, was based on the colour of one's skin. Whites were the elite and dominant people, their position increasingly underpinned by statute. Whites were treated as if they were the highest caste, with the Coloured people on the next rung with the Asian (Indian) population, and at the bottom of the pile the black people of South Africa.

The white society was also riven by ethnic divisions between Afrikaans and English speakers, with the Jews being seen as a subgroup of the English speakers. However, the Jews were singled out for special treatment in immigration policy from 1902 onwards. Even so, they enjoyed the privileges that being white gave them.

The Litvaks of the Kapelus and Hotz families paid scant attention to these issues as they sought to establish themselves and their families in their new environment. The first South Africa-born generation of these families, our parents, also seemed to be quite passive as far as politics was concerned. Perhaps this was partly because South African politics was dominated by race and, with their background and the history of their people they felt decidedly uneasy and even awkward about this.

As teenagers they lived through the worst economic depression the world had experienced. It was followed by a deep drought that directly affected them, as their parents struggled to keep the assets they had worked so hard to acquire.

The anti-Semitic rhetoric and attitudes that prevailed during the 1920s through the 1940s were followed by the Second World War, in which they were directly involved as young adults. They were witnesses to the horrors of the Holocaust, in which their kith and kin were murdered.

After this darkness came light; they were witness to the birth of a Jewish State, Israel, and lived through an economic boom and a sustained period of peace and prosperity that lasted all of their adult lives.

For them, the year of 1948 brought elation and hope with the creation of Israel, but was also tempered by the election of a National Party government in South Africa that was supported by its cultural organisations, the Broederbond and the Dutch Reformed Church. These organisations had all been avowedly anti-Semitic and racist in their rhetoric, policy statements and political philosophy, particularly so in regard to the black, Asian and Coloured populations of the country.

Amazingly, this National Party government voted in favour of the creation of the State of Israel at the United Nations General Assembly. The Afrikaners' anti-Semitic stance seemed to drift away as they achieved political power and as they, and the rest of the world, finally became aware of the horrors of the Holocaust.

My generation of Kapelus and Hotz/Broude families grew up knowing effectively only one government in South Africa, that of the National Party. We started school in the 1940s and came to adulthood with the world at our feet. As whites, we had every privilege and opportunity to succeed in whatever field we chose. Ours could be described as a golden generation. Largely, we were well educated, professionally qualified and were able to acquire skills and experience beyond our tender years.

By the 1970s it was clear to all that the Jewish population had made a substantial contribution to every field of endeavour in South Africa out of all proportion to their numbers. Yet there was to be a mass exodus by this well-trained Jewish youth.

According to Mendelsohn and Shain, some 38,000 Jews left South Africa between 1970 and 1990. (They state that some 4,000 Israeli Jews entered South Africa.) In 1970, the total Jewish population of South Africa is put at 118,200.[193] The net loss of 34,000 Jews in 20 years is an exodus of some proportions. Tatz, Arnold and Heller report that some 43,600 Jews migrated from South Africa between 1970 and 2007.[194] This is an additional loss of some 9,600 from an already shrinking Jewish population. If the 1970 population of 118,200 represents the highest total of Jews in South Africa, then just over 36% officially emigrated. The total number of Jews who emigrated is probably somewhat greater, as the numbers above do not include the young who left without formally emigrating and therefore without their departure being recorded.

In the period of our education and early adulthood in the 1950s through the 1970s, we flourished in every way. Yet in 1971, the first of my generation of the Kapelus family, my cousin David Kapelus and his young bride Helen, migrated to London and from there to Toronto. They were followed in April 1971 by my sister Yvonne, who went to London to join Ken, whom she married there. Almost 10 years later, in early 1981, Esther and I, with our children Leora and Ilan, also left for England. My cousins Lionel Farber, his sister Vivienne and Carol Myerson and their families migrated to Australia in 1985.

By then, four out of the five of Leib Kapelus's children had one or all of their offspring living abroad. Natie's children remained in South Africa. Leib arrived in South Africa in 1897 and within 74 years of his arrival, the family was on the move again. This time there were no anti-Semitic laws or hatred of Jews driving them from the country of their birth? The very opposite was true: they were the privileged class, successful in their professional and business lives, living in luxury. They were not threatened in any way.

Why did they, like so many of their generation, choose to leave the country of their birth, their families and friends for foreign lands?

There is no one answer, but there are common themes: the push came from not wanting to live in and bring up their families in the 'Apartheid' society, which was fast becoming a police state. The pull factor was a desire to live in a 'normal' society, free from the strains and guilt of racist South Africa, and to enjoy the freedom of a real democracy.

Perhaps the Jewish values and the Jewish history in which they were steeped, and which I have described in this book, played a role in their decision-making.

Notes

1 Shimoni (1980): 5, (2003): 2.

2 Kriwaczek (2005/06): 12-13.

3 Katz (2004/2010): 19.

4 Greenbaum (1995): 5

5 Greenbaum (1995): 2.

6 Greenbaum (1995): 4-6, 8; Prof Dov Levin, Introduction to Rosin (2005/07); Newman (2005): 14; Levin (2000): 43; Wikipedia, 'Lithuanian Jews': 3.

7 Greenbaum (1995): 8.

8 For terms of the Charter see Greenbaum (1995): 8-9; Levin (2000): 43-45.

9 Levin (2000): 43.

10 Greenbaum (1995): 10; Levin (2000): 44.

11 Johnson (1987/1995): 230-231, 233 et seq.; 'The Jewish Diaspora AD 70 to 1497', in Barraclough (1979): 102-103.

12 Johnson (1987/1995): 230 et seq.

13 Johnson (1987/1995): 233 et seq.

14 Johnson (1987/1995): 242.

15 Johnson (1987/1995): 241-245.

16 Newman (2005): 14; Wikipedia, 'Lithuanian Jews': 4; Greenbaum (1995): 13; Levin (2000): 45.

17 Levin (2000): 45; Greenbaum (1995): 14-15.

18 Levin (2000): 45. Alexander imposed a condition on their return. The Jewish Community had to maintain 1,000 armed horsemen; a heavy burden that the leaders of the community made every effort to get rescinded.

19 Levin (2000): 48; Greenbaum (1995): 18.

20 Greenbaum (1995): 51-53.

Householders, the affluent and learned persons who had earned the tittles of 'teacher' (morenu) or 'fellow' (haver) by having satisfied certain specified criteria voted for the members of the Synod. The poor and the lower classes did not have the vote. In any event, most Jews in Lite were leaseholders so they did not have the vote. The more representative body was the kehilla as all householders could vote.

21 Levin (2000): 62.

22 Rosin (2005/2007), Vol. II: 110.

23 Map by courtesy of Dovid Katz, from Katz (2004/2010): 75.

24 Greenbaum (1995): 161.

25 Levin (2000): 64, 65, 77 (Table 4); Ruppin (1940): 27; Johnson (1987/1995): 304.

26 Greenbaum (1995): 166; Levin (2000): 66.

27 Katz (2004/2010): 130.

28 Greenbaum (1995): 174 et seq.; Levin (2000): 67-68.

29 Greenbaum (1995): 180.

30 Greenbaum (1995): 115-127; Bakonis (2001/2007): 73, 74; Levin (2000): 95-99; Katz (2004/2010): 203-11.

31 Leiserowitz (2007).

32 Quoted in Abrahams (1955): 142, fn 11.

33 Greenbaum (1995): 187.

34 Rosin (2005/2007), Vol. II: 108, 111.

35 Rosin (2005/2007), Vol. II: 111.

36 Rosin (2005/2007), Vol. II: 111.

37 Translation of 'Shkud' in Levin & Rosin (1996).

38 'Shkud' in Levin & Rosin (1996).

39 'Traces of Jewish Life in Lithuania', R Paknio Leidykla, in Kairiene & Katz (2009): 120; 'Shkud' in Levin & Rosin (1996).

40 Maynard (n.d.); Wikipedia, 'Siauliai', p. 3.

41 'Traces of Jewish Life in Lithuania', R. Paknio Leidykla, in Kairiene & Katz (2009): 130; Maynard (n.d.): 1 – Vital Statistics and Chapter Two – Description of the Community.

42 Maynard (n.d.).

43 Maynard (n.d.); Rosin (2005/2007), Vol II: 310 et seq.

44 Ruppin (1940): 29 et seq.; Levin (2000): 77 et seq.

45 Vol. 1 of Newman et al. (2006): 43.

46 However, the growth and then sudden fall of the Jewish population of Lithuania is much more revealing. It had grown from 248,100 in 1847 to 755,000 (including Suwalki) by 1897, falling to 260,000 in 1923, a mere 26 years later. A mass exodus by any standards and among those was the Kapelus family. By 1940, it was down to 220,000. (See Levin (2000): 77, Table 4.)

47 Saron & Hotz (1995): 73-76.

48 Newman (2000).

49 Issroff (2008).

50 Rosin (2005/2007), Vol. II: 110, 114-115.

51 Herrman (1935): 11-27; Wilson & Thompson (1969), Vol. I: 187; Giliomee & Mbenga (2007): 40; Wikipedia, 'Portuguese Explorers, Age of Discovery 1415-1542'; 'European Exploration of Africa, Chapter 4, Portuguese Expeditions' in Barraclough (1979): 156, 157.

52 The VOC was the first company to issue stock to the public. Capital was raised in six cities: Amsterdam, Zeeland (Middleburg), Enkhuizen, Delft, Hoorn and Rotterdam. The total share capital raised was Guilders (f) 6,424,588. Of the original subscribers in 1602, there appear to have been two known Jews, Stephanus Cardozo with an investment of f1,800 and Elizabeth Pinto, who invested f3,000. In 1604 Emanuel Carvalho and Diego Diaz Querido bought shares to the value of f1,900 and Belchior Mendes, a pioneer of Haarlem Jewry, f13,500. By the 1650s the Jewish shareholding had become a substantial portion of the VOC's working capital. Despite the number of Jewish investors, the VOC did not employ Jews as it had a policy of only employing Calvinists. Strangely, the Dutch West Indies Company, which also had a substantial number of Jewish shareholders, not only employed Jews but encouraged Jewish immigration to the territories that it controlled and administered. The headquarters of the VOC and the seat of the Governor-General and Council of India was Batavia, Java, from where it regulated Dutch trade and government in Asia subject only to the control of the Here XVII. Governors were appointed to rule '*buiten comptoiren*' or branch offices in Amboyna, Banda, the Moluccas, Malacca, Ceylon, Macassar and northeast Java (some time later also at the Cape of Good Hope), reporting to the Governor-General in Batavia.

53 Schrire (1910).

54 By the time he left the Cape in 1662, he had built a mud fort and round it a hospital, a stable for horses, enclosed grazing for cattle and sheep as well as a vegetable and fruit garden close by, and so was able to provision the company's ships as well as any others that might call at the Cape.

55 Wikipedia, 'Dutch East India Company: The VOC': 1-9; Wilson & Thompson (1969), Vol. I: 187 et seq.; Hermann Giliomee (2003): Chapter 2, 22 et seq.; Thompson (2001): 33-51.

56 Giliomee (2003): 56-57.

57 Scholtz (1964): 30-31.

58 Giliomee (2003): 202.

59 Thompson (2001): 88. The original is to be found in a work of John Bird, *The Annals of Natal 1495 to 1845*, Vol. 1: 459.

60 Herrman (1935): 55.

61 Gluck (2010): 22-23.

62 The Sloman family suffered a most painful loss when their son Mark was murdered by Xhosa raiders in August 1823 while he was tending cattle on their farm. After five years, Sloman gave up farming and settled in Cape Town, where he traded as a merchant. He participated in the Jewish communal life of Cape Town until his death in 1849. On her husband's death, Mrs Sloman started a business importing and selling women's finery and was accepted among the merchants of the city. She continued her membership of the congregation and she and her children continued to make a valuable contribution, as is shown by the 'veil for the altar', presumably curtain for the Ark, which she and her daughters had made and had presented to the congregation on the opening of the synagogue with a framed Hebrew inscription. These items were presented to the congregation accompanied by a letter stating: 'Mrs Sloman and family request the honour of presenting to the Jewish community of Cape Town for the use of the synagogue the accompanying veil for the altar as likewise the framed Hebrew sentence ... and humbly pray that the God of Israel will graciously crown with success the efforts made to establish in Africa the ancient faith, and bestow His blessings on the little flocks that will assemble to worship their Creator in the temple consecrated to His service.' John Norton moved to Grahamstown and by 1837 he was in business as a merchant under the name of Norton & Co., in partnership with a Forbes Still and later with one H.B. Kirsch. He played a part in the formation of the first Jewish Congregation in Cape Town and was instrumental in the founding of the Jewish community of Grahamstown. He died on a trip to the UK in 1848. Joshua Norden was still farming in 1840 after his brothers had left the land. Benjamin had become a trader in the interior, but soon settled in Cape Town as a merchant, where he played a leading role in the development of the Jewish community.

63 Herrman (1935): 100.

64 Benjamin Norden, later to play a leading role in the establishment of the first Jewish congregation in Cape Town, was another early trader to visit Natal in 1832 and is said to have been a friend of Piet Retief, the *Voortrekker* leader. On his visit he was the bearer of a letter from Sir Benjamin D'Urban to Dingane. Norden is reported to have done 'good business on his own behalf with the Zulu King. He took away at least two and half tons of ivory with him.'

65 Herrman (1935): 109-111.

66 Simeon Marcus and his two sons Fred and John, Morris Sloman (1820 Settler), Abraham Horn, Nathan Moss (son-in-law of S. Marcus), Adolph Gordon, Benjamin Norden (1820 Settler), Siegfried Fraenkel (first Jewish doctor in South Africa), David Hyman Canstatt, Morris Hart and his young son Edwin, Samuel Rodolf, Nathan Birkenruth, Lewis Marcus, Joseph Mosenthal (founder of the mohair industry in South Africa) and Joseph Charles Hess.

67 Samuel Rodolf opened the service with Kol Nidrei and the next day took the Musaph (additional service) service. David Canstatt led Shachrit (morning service), Simeon Marcus read Mincha (afternoon service).

68 Shain (1983): 1, following the statement by Abrahams (1955): 14 (see Mendelsohn & Shain (2008): 26.

69 The first marriage solemnised in a synagogue wholly according to Jewish ritual was that of Isaac Saul Solomon and Frances Amelia Sloman in 1851, performed by Reverend Isaac Pulver, the first Jewish Minister in South Africa. In fact he had already resigned from this post, but was still the official marriage officer and no one else was empowered to conduct the ceremony. Abrahams (1955): notes to Chapter 1.

70 Wilson & Thompson (1969), Vol. II: 11, note 3.

71 Feinstein (2005), on pass laws, pp. 57, 58; on job reservation legislation providing what work could be done by whites and blacks, pp. 74-82.

72 Marks & Rathbone (1982/1987), on Kimberley, labour and compounds 1871-1888, pp. 51-68; Wilson & Thompson (1969), Vol. II: 12, 31; Thompson (2001): 118-122.

73 Scholtz (1964): 7 et seq.

74 Thompson (2001): 115.

75 Giliomee (2003): 237; Thompson (2001): 120; Wilson & Thompson (1969), Vol. II: 14.

76 Giliomee & Mbenga (2007): 196.

77 Kaplan & Robertson (1991): 22; Wilson & Thompson (1969), Vol. I: 114; Giliomee & Mbenga (2007): 200.

78 Van Onselen (1982): 2.

79 Meir David Hersch published in *Hatsefira*, a Hebrew weekly in Lithuania, translated by S. Rappaport (1950) 'Rand Jewry 1893', *Jewish Affairs*.

80 Kaplan & Robertson (1991): 17-18.

81 Giliomee (2003): 201, Table of White South African Population Circa 1860, 282; Giliomee & Mbenga (2007): 189; Thompson (2001): 136 et seq.

82 Giliomee (2003): 238; Wilson & Thompson (1969), Vol. II: 309; Thompson (2001): 137; Nasson (1999) 27.

83 Thompson (2001): 141; Nasson (1999): 24.

84 Wilson & Thompson (1969), Vol. II: 320-324; Thompson (2001): 138-141; Giliomee (2003): 242-243.

85 Smuts & Alberts (1988): 122 et seq.

86 Smuts & Alberts (1988): 122 et seq.

87 Newman et al. (2006).

88 Smuts & Alberts (1988): 122.

89 Storrar (1984): 31.

90 Smuts & Alberts (1988): 102.

91 Work began in 1875. From Wellington the line was built through the Tulbagh Kloof to Worcester and De Doorns and then via two tunnels, where it reached Touws River (then called Montagu Road) by 1877. On it went through Matjiesfontein and on to Laingsburg and Beaufort West in the Karoo and finally to De Aar, the largest railway junction in the Cape Colony. Here the railway line split, and by 1885 it reached Kimberley.

92 Summarised Memoirs of Sir David Harris, *Pioneer, Soldier and Politician*, Chapter II.

93 Wikipedia, 'Barney Barnato'.

94 South African Friends of Beth Hafetutsoth (2004), Vol. II: 23 et seq.

95 Photograph by courtesy of Ceres Togryers Museum.

96 Illiquid Case: *Estate Johannes Marquard vs Lewis Kapelus* 1902. NASA, Cape Town; Source: DOC; Volume 4/1/864.

97 Illiquid Case: *Michaelis Baumann vs Louis Kapelus* in the Supreme Court of the Colony of Cape of Good Hope, 12 January 1907.

98 Giliomee (2003): 257-258.

99 Nasson (1991/2002): 122 et seq., (1999): 107; Giliomee (2003): 258.

100 Smuts & Alberts (1988): 135.

101 Nasson (1991/2002): 122, 138.

102 Nasson (1991/2002): 124.

103 Nasson (1991/2002): 129; Giliomee (2003): 258.

104 NASA Source CSC, Volume No 2/1/1/1021, Ref 203, Illiquid Case; Appeal; Calvinia\ Lewis Kapelus Versus Van Der Byl and De Villiers, 1924.

105 As told to me by my Uncle Natie Kapelus and confirmed by my father, Arnold Kapelus.

106 Mendelsohn & Shain (2008): 25-26; Abrahams (1955): 29.

107 Shain (1983): 3, 4.

108 Shimoni (1980): 5.

109 Shimoni (1980): 5.

110 Shimoni (1980): 5, (2003): 2.

111 Mendelsohn & Shain (2008): 46.

112 Giliomee (2003): 315 et seq.

113 Shain (1983): 127, Appendix 1; Shain (1994): 22-23.

114 Gustav Saron, 'At the Turn of the Century', published in *Who's Who in South African Jewry*, 61 et seq.; Shain (1983): 12.

115 Shain (1983): 18-20, 51 et seq.; see also the scurrilous anti-Semitic cartoons published by *The Owl*, in Shain (1983): 33-44.

116 Saron & Hotz (1955): 91-95, 249-253; Shimoni (1980): 15-17, (1983): 25-31, 58-60; Mendelsohn & Shain (2008): 57-60.

117 Saron & Hotz (1955): 261, 262.

118 Giliomee (2003): 394.

119 Churchill (1958), Vol. 4: 295-298; Wilson & Thompson (1969), Vol. II: 326-327.

120 Giliomee (2003): 255; Nasson (1999): 221.

121 Giliomee (2003): 255-256, 264; Churchill (1958), Vol. 4: 301; Thompson (2001): 143; Nasson (1999): 223-224; Wilkins & Strydom (1978): 37.

122 Giliomee (2003): 260-264; Nasson (1999): 228-231; Wilkins & Strydom (1978): 37-39.

123 Churchill (1958), Vol. 4: 301.

124 Giliomee (2003): 356.

125 Wilkins & Strydom (1978): 36-50, 140-176; Giliomee (2003): Chapter 11.

126 Information booklet, Calvinia Museum; Calvinia information issued by Calvinia Municipality.

127 Information booklet, Calvinia Museum; Calvinia information issued by Calvinia Municipality.

128 *Eufees – 1947*, issued by Dutch Reformed Church.

129 *Eufees – 1947*, issued by Dutch Reformed Church.

130 Saron & Hotz (1955): 14, 21, 30; Herrman (1935): 193; South African Friends of Beth Hafetutsoth (2004), Vol. II: 154 et seq.

131 South African Friends of Beth Hafetutsoth (2004), Vol. II: 128.

132 For a list, see South African Friends of Beth Hafetutsoth (2004), Vol. II: 118.

133 Saron & Hotz (1955): 14, 193, 311-312; Herrman (1935): 13, 208; South African Friends of Beth Hafetutsoth (2004), Vol. II: 117 et seq.

134 South African Friends of Beth Hafetutsoth (2004), Vol. II: 128-129.

135 South African Friends of Beth Hafetutsoth (2004), Vol. II: 128, 'Population Statistics'; Lieba Robinson (1985) 'Looking Back on Calvinia', *Jewish Affairs*, July, 23.

136 NASA Source CSC, Volume 2/1/1/675, Ref 83, Illiquid Case: *F. Kirsch & Co versus Louis Kapelus*. Claim for the recovery of money.

137 According to a note on the Deed of Transfer 7912 of 1924.

138 Wilson & Thompson (1969), Vol. II: 24, 25.

139 Wilson & Thompson (1969), Vol. II: 139.

140 Wilson & Thompson (1969), Vol. II: 139.

141 Wilson & Thompson (1969), Vol. II: 141 et seq.; Mendelsohn & Shain (2008): 117 et seq.; Giliomee & Mbenga (2007): 291-292.

142 *De Rebus*, June 1994, p. 401.

143 See Duplicate Driver's Licence.

144 See Share Certificate No. 198.

145 South African Friends of Beth Hafetutsoth (2004), Vol. II: 311.

146 The above is quoted from the Kaimowitz-Katz-Kaye Family Website.

147 Saron & Hotz (1955): 40, 41; De Saxe (1929): 357.

148 Saron & Hotz (1955): 376.

149 Saron & Hotz (1955): 377; Shain (1994): 114.

150 Giliomee & Mbenga (2007): 279-282.

151 Giliomee (2003): 323.

152 Wilson & Thompson (1969), Vol. II: 176; Feinstein (2005): 85; Giliomee (2003): 346.

153 Shain (1994): 115.

154 Shain (1994): 118.

155 Shain (1994): 118-137; Giliomee & Mbenga (2007): 278; Saron & Hotz (1955): 376-377; Giliomee (2003): 416-418; Shimoni (1980): 86-96.

156 Shimoni (1980): 93; Shain (1994): 137.

157 Shimoni (1980): 86, 97.

158 Shain (1994): 137.

159 Shain (1994): 137-138; Shimoni (1980): 97-98.

160 Shimoni (1980): 99, 100; Shain (1994): 138, 139.

161 Saron & Hotz (1955): 379; Shimoni (1980): 105; Shain (1994): 140.

162 Giliomee (2003): 418.

163 Shimoni (1980): 107.

164 Giliomee (2003: 416-417; Shimoni (1980): 116.

165 Shain (1994): 145-146; Giliomee & Mbenga (2007): 278-279.

166 Shimoni (1980): 143, 144.

167 Sutton (2008); Ivan Kapelus, *Reflections on a Visit to Lithuania*; Bakonis (2001/2007).

168 Shain (1994): 147, 149; Giliomee (2003): 441-442: Shimoni (1980): 128, 130.

169 Giliomee (2003): 440; Shimoni (1980): 133-135; Wilkins & Strydom (1978): 108-111.

170 Shimoni (2003): 2.

171 Herrman (1935): 254, 255.

172 Herrman (1935): 251.

173 Harry Schwartz, in the Introduction to Tzippi & Fischer (1988).

174 Greenbaum (1995): 85-88; Shimoni (2003): 3.

175 Greenbaum (1995): 121.

176 Greenbaum (1995): 127-145.

177 Greenbaum (1995): 220-255.

178 Mendelsohn & Shain (2008): 89-99.

179 Shimoni (1980): 364; Mendelsohn & Shain (2008): 157-159.

180 Shimoni (2003): 5.

181 Levin (2000): 91, 92.

182 An article by Louis Hotz, 'A Survey of the Jewish Population in South Africa', De Saxe (1929): 35-43, analyses the distribution of as well as the economic activities of the Jewish population up to 1926.

183 SA Jewish Board of Deputies: Congress Resolutions 31 May-2 June 1940.

184 Saron (2001): 185-186; Mendelsohn & Shain (2008): 118-120.

185 Saron (2001): 186; Mendelsohn & Shain (2008): 120. Rex versus Dorfman 1939 in NASA, Cape Town Source-CSC; Volume No 1/3/1/43.

186 Robinson, 'Looking Back on Calvinia'.

187 Arnold Helfet, son of Leon Helfet, who was the longest-serving and foremost Jewish member of the Calvinia Municipal Council (1908 to 1918), in his article 'Van "Uitlanders" tot Calvinia se Boere-Jode' ('From Foreigners to Calvinia's Farmer-Jews'), *Buurman*, March 1977.

188 Scholtz (1964): 160.

189 Scholtz (1964): 164-173.

190 Records of the Village Management Board Minutes 1904 to 1914, Volume 3, VRD National Archives, Cape Town compiled by M.S. Meyer 1987.

191 South African Friends of Beth Hafetutsoth (2004), Vol. II: 398-399.

192 South African Friends of Beth Hafetutsoth (2004), Vol. II: 399, Population Statistics.

193 Mendelsohn & Shain (2008): 183.

194 According to Tatz et al. (2007): 251.

Bibliography

Aaron, Sam (2005) *A Guide to Jewish Genealogy in Lithuania*, London.

Abrahams, Israel (1955) *The Birth of a Community*, Cape Town.

Agranovski, Genrich & Guzenberg, Irina (2008) *Vilnius – 100 Memorable Sites of Jewish History & Culture*, 3rd edn, Vilnius.

Aubrey, Newman (2005) 'The Jews of Lithuania – Timeline', *Jewish Renaissance*, 4(4, July): 14.

Bakonis, Evaldas (ed.) (2001/2007) *Jewish Life in Lithuania,* Exhibition Catalogue, Vilnius.

Barraclough, Geoffrey (ed.) (1979) *The Times Atlas of World History*, London.

Belling, Veronica (1997) *Bibliography of South African Jewry*, Cape Town.

Botma, François (1997) *Ceres van Gister en Eergister*, Pretoria.

Bubnys, Arunas (2008) *The Holocaust in Lithuania between 1941 and 1944*, Vilnius.

Churchill, Winston (1958) *A History of the English Speaking Peoples – Volume 4: The Great Democracies*, London.

De Saxe, Morris (ed.) (1929) *The South African Jewish Year Book 1929*, Johannesburg.

Feinstein, Charles H. (2005) *An Economic History of South Africa – Conquest, Discrimination and Development*, Cambridge.

Giliomee, Hermann (2003) *The Afrikaners – Biography of a People*, Charlotteville, VA and Cape Town.

Giliomee, Hermann & Mbenga, Bernard (2007) *New History of South Africa*, Cape Town.

Gluck, Janus (2010) 'Jews with van Riebeeck', *Jewish Affairs,* 65(3).

Goldberg, David J. & Rayner, John D. (1987) *The Jewish People, Their History and Their Religion*, London.

Greenbaum, Masha (1995) *The Jews of Lithuania – A History of a Remarkable Community 1316-1945*, Jerusalem.

Herrman, Louis (1935) *A History of the Jews in South Africa*, Johannesburg/Cape Town.

Herrman, Louis (1941) *A Centenary History – The Cape Town Hebrew Congregation 1841 to 1941*, Cape Town.

Hoffmann, N.D. (1996) *Book of Memoirs – Reminiscences of South African Jewry*, Cape Town.

Issroff, Saul (2008) *Jewish Migration to South Africa – Passenger Lists from UK 1890 to 1905 Volume I & 1906 to 1930 Volume II*, Cape Town.

Jewish Renaissance (2005) 4(July).

Johnson, Paul (1987/1995) *A History of the Jews*, London.

Kairiene, Audra & Katz, Dovid (2009) *Sounds of Silence*, Vilnius.

Kaplan, Mendel & Robertson, Marian (1991) *Founders and Followers – Johannesburg Jewry 1887-1915,* Cape Town.

Katz, Dovid (2004/2010) *Lithuania Jewish Culture*, Vilnius.

Kaye, Simone (1990) 'The Enterprising Benjamin Norden', *Cape Jewish Chronicle*, December.

Kriwaczek, Paul (2005/2006) *Yiddish Civilisation – The Rise and Fall of a Forgotten Nation*, London.

Leiserowitz, Ruth (2007) 'Litvak Migratory Decisions in the Second Half of the 19th Century and Their Consequences', Presented at the Third Annual Seminar of the Israel Genealogical Society, 17 November.

Lerer Cohen, Rose & Issroff, Saul (2002) *The Holocaust in Lithuania 1941-1945*, Jerusalem.

Levin, Dov (2000) *The Litvaks – A Short History of the Jews in Lithuania*, Jerusalem.

Levin, Dov & Rosin, Josef (eds) (1996) 'Plunge', *Encyclopaedia of Jewish Communities of Lithuania*; Translation of the Plunge chapter from *Pinkas Hakehillot Lita (Encyclopaedia of Jewish Communities of Lithuania)*, Jerusalem.

Marks, Shula & Atmore, Anthony (1980) *Economy and Society in Pre-Industrial South Africa*, London.

Marks, Shula & Rathbone, Richard (1982/1987) *Industrialisation and Social Change in South Africa – African Class Formation, Culture and Consciousness 1870 to 1930*, New York.

Maynard, Jeffrey (n.d.) *The Jewish Community of Siauliai*, ShtetLinks, JewishGen.

Mendelsohn, Richard & Shain, Milton (2008) *The Jews in South Africa, an Illustrated History*, Jeppestown.

Nasson, Bill (1991/2002) *Abraham Esau's War – a Black South African War in the Cape 1899-1902*, Cambridge.

Nasson, Bill (1999) *The South African War 1899-1902*, London.

Newman, Aubrey (2000) 'Trains and Shelters and Ships', Paper presented at a seminar under the auspices of the Jewish Genealogical Society of Great Britain, April.

Newman, Aubrey (n.d.) 'The Union Castle Line and Emigration from Eastern Europe to South Africa', Teaching paper.

Newman, Aubrey N., Evans, Nicholas J., Smith, J. Graham & Issroff, Saul (2006) *Jewish Migration to South Africa, The Records of the Poor Jews' Temporary Shelter, 1885-1914*, Cape Town.

Rhind, David & Walker, Michael (1996/1997/2003) *Historical Railway Postcard Journeys in Southern Africa*, St James, Cape.

Rosin, Josef (2005/2007) *Preserving Our Litvak Heritage Volumes I & II*, League City, TX.

Ruppin, Arthur (1940) *The Jewish Fate and Future*, London.

Saron, Gustav (2001) *The Jews of South Africa – An Illustrated History to 1953*, Johannesburg.

Saron, Gustav & Hotz, Louis (eds) (1955) *The Jews in South Africa – A History*, Cape Town.

Scholtz, P.L. (1964) 'Die Historiese Ontwikkeling van die Onder Olifants Rivier 1660-1902', Doctoral thesis, Pretoria.

Schrire, Gwynne (1994) 'In the Belly of the Whale – The Journey to South Africa 1880-1910', *Jewish Affairs*, Winter.

Shain, Milton (1983) *Jewry and Cape Society*, Cape Town.

Shain, Milton (1994) *The Roots of Anti-Semitism in South Africa*, Charlotteville, VA.

Shain, Milton (1998) *Anti-Semitism*, London.

Shain, Milton & Mendelsohn, Richard (eds) (2000) *Memories, Realities and Dreams – Aspects of the South African Jewish Experience*, Jeppestown, South Africa.

Shimoni, Gideon (1980) *Jews and Zionism – The South African Experience 1910-1967*, Cape Town.

Shimoni, Gideon (2003) *Community and Conscience – The Jews in Apartheid South Africa*, Lebanon, NH.

Smoliakov, Hirsch-Tsvi (1996) 'Memories of Plunge – Reminiscences of Ya'akov Bunka', *Jerusalem of Lithuania*, 1996.

Smuts, Dene & Alberts, Paul (1988) *Die Vergete Grootpad deur Ceres en die Bokkeveld*, Cape Town.

South African Friends of Beth Hafetutsoth (2004) *Jewish Life in the Country Communities*, Johannesburg.

Storrar, Patricia (1984) *A Colossus of Roads – Thomas Bain*, Cape Town.

Sutton, Karen (2008) *The Massacre of the Jews of Lithuania*, Jerusalem.

Tatz, Colin, Arnold, Peter & Heller, Gillian (2007) *Worlds Apart – The Re-migration of South African Jews*, New South Wales, Australia.

Thompson, Leonard (2001) *A History of South Africa*, 3rd edn, New Haven, CT.

Tzippi, Hoffman & Fischer, Alan (1988) *The Jews of South Africa – What Future?* Johannesburg.

Van Onselen, Charles (1982) *Studies in the Social and Economic History of the Witwatersrand 1886-1914 – 1 New Babylon, & 2 New Nineveh*, Johannesburg.

Wilkins, Ivor & Strydom, Hans (1978) *The Super Afrikaners – Inside the Afrikaner Broederbond*, Johannesburg.

Wilson, Monica & Thompson, Leonard (eds) (1969/1970/1973) *The Oxford History of South Africa Volume I, South Africa to 1870 & Volume II South Africa 1870- 1966*, Oxford.

Index